D0775503

Advance praise for *Destructive Leaders and Dysfunctional Organizations*

"*Destructive Leaders and Dysfunctional Organizations* is unique in its approach, with examples of leadership we can all relate to. It is enlightening to understand abusive and uncivil leader behavior from a psychological perspective. This is a must-read for employees and managers alike. Thank you Dr. Goldman for your multi-disciplinary insights."

LEANNE ATWATER, Professor and Department Chair, C.T. Bauer College of Business, University of Houston

"Unlike many accounts of organizational dysfunction in the OD literature, Alan Goldman is direct and unapologetic when it comes to identifying and acknowledging psychopathology in contemporary organizations. His book promotes a clinical model and dialogue about human behavior in organizations that some scholars in the field would prefer not to have. If, as I have come to observe, addressing psychopathology in the workplace is about listening deeply and containing individual pain and anxiety, then Goldman's book is required reading in the field."

MICHAEL A. DIAMOND, Professor and Director, Center for the Study of Organizational Change, University of Missouri

"A razor-thin line, Alan Goldman tells us, separates the genius from the dark, tormented souls of many powerful and influential leaders. Goldman is not afraid to tackle this paradox head on, thus uncovering the Jekyll and Hyde personalities of many leaders and the toxicity that can suffuse an organization when narcissism, obsessiveness and other leadership dysfunctions go unchecked. This is a hugely illuminating book on the nature of leaders and leadership. It will be of great value to educators, researchers and those leaders who are wise enough to acknowledge their potential for error, delusion and folly."

YIANNIS GABRIEL, Professor of Organizational Theory, University of Bath

"*Destructive Leaders and Dysfunctional Organizations* is the first book to detail critical psychological issues in leadership and their organizational impacts in an accessible manner with diagnostic insights and practical solutions. A must-read for serious scholar-practitioners of the management sciences and anyone who works with changing organizational behavior."

DAVID W. JAMIESON, President of the Jamieson Consulting Group, Inc. and Practicum Director of the American University/NTL MSOD Program, Washington, DC

"Anyone who has to deal with toxic leaders will find this book enlightening as it shows the way to diagnosing their underlying psychopathology. You will also enjoy Alan Goldman's skillful handling of some very tough customers."

MICHAEL MACCOBY, author of *The Leaders We Need and What Makes Us Follow* and *Narcissistic Leaders: Who Succeeds and Who Fails*

"It's out of the closet! In their times, revelations about spousal abuse and then about clerical abuse shocked people – but they also led to remedial action. Goldman's cases illustrate leadership abuses and the disturbing consequences when senior, powerful people suffer from mental aberrations. Every senior manager needs to understand the issues raised in this book in order to see how destructive leaders cause their associates and their businesses to suffer. Goldman's book can contribute to widespread recognition and solutions to the dark side of corporate life – so that executives can be on their toes and ready to act."

ROBERT H. SCHAFFER, consultant and author of *Rapid Results! How 100-Day Projects Build the Capacity for Large-Scale Change*

"In this absolutely fascinating book, Alan Goldman presents us with important cases of toxicity in leaders, but more importantly, he shows how individual pathology infects the entire organization and how coaching, consulting and therapy have to work together for some period of time to help both the individual and the infected organization. The

book also shows the importance of using diagnostic tools to identify both the pathology and the necessary remedy."

EDGAR H. SCHEIN, Professor Emeritus, MIT Sloan School of Management, and author of *Process Consultation* and *Organizational Culture and Leadership*

"In response to corporate and leadership crises, Goldman's consulting and coaching narratives deliver deep insights into the pathological mechanisms of dysfunctional organizations and their leaders. His analysis of denial and resistance, greed and hubris, anger and narcissism is stimulating and thought-provoking. CEOs, scholars and students of leadership and organizational behavior will find powerful material in Goldman's unveiling of toxic leadership in areas as different as education, government, medicine, fashion, engineering and construction. *Destructive Leaders and Dysfunctional Organizations* is a very timely, helpful, action-oriented book and an extraordinary 'must-read' for corporate and business leaders, politicians, media leaders, management consultants and coaches alike."

GINKA TOEGEL, Professor of Leadership, IMD, Lausanne, Switzerland

"Evidence of errant and dysfunctional behavior by senior executives – and the misuse of their position and power – has increased in recent years and has justifiably become a matter of profound public concern. In this interesting book, Alan Goldman examines cases from his consulting work with top executives of counterproductive workplace behavior and illuminates some of the underlying psychological factors which have resulted in the pathological scenarios described."

MICHAEL WALTON, CLS Fellow, Centre for Leadership Studies, University of Exeter

Destructive Leaders and Dysfunctional Organizations: A Therapeutic Approach

Organizational behavior and leadership research has traditionally been deeply influenced by positive psychology and appreciative inquiry. Yet, in recent times, a wave of corporate scandals and spectacular organizational failures has forced management and organizational theorists to rethink this approach. Unethical CEO behavior, white-collar crime, property deviance, employee grievances and lawsuits, organizational terrorism and workplace violence have all provided the impetus for an examination of the darker side of leadership. In *Destructive Leaders and Dysfunctional Organizations*, Alan Goldman draws on his extensive experience as a management consultant and executive coach to provide a fascinating behind-closed-doors account of troubled leaders and the effect they have on their organizations. Featuring clinical case studies, ranging from the fashion industry to an aeronautical engineering corporation, the book explores the damaging effects of destructive leadership on organizations and provides the tools necessary for early recognition, assessment and treatment.

ALAN GOLDMAN is Professor of Management at Arizona State University. He has many years' experience as a management consultant and executive coach to a range of corporations in the USA and Japan.

Destructive Leaders and Dysfunctional Organizations

A Therapeutic Approach

ALAN GOLDMAN

CAMBRIDGE
UNIVERSITY PRESS

CAMBRIDGE
UNIVERSITY PRESS

University Printing House, Cambridge CB2 8BS, United Kingdom

Published in the United States of America by Cambridge University Press, New York

Cambridge University Press is part of the University of Cambridge.

It furthers the University's mission by disseminating knowledge in the pursuit of education, learning and research at the highest international levels of excellence.

www.cambridge.org
Information on this title: www.cambridge.org/9780521717342

© Alan Goldman 2009

First published 2009
Reprinted 2010

A catalogue record for this publication is available from the British Library

ISBN 978-0-521-88880-6 Hardback
ISBN 978-0-521-71734-2 Paperback

Contents

Extended Table of Contents

Preface

Destructive Leaders and Dysfunctional Organizations: A Therapeutic Approach is the result of a journey that has led me to graduate school, research, writing, and the life of a professor and consultant. As a professor I have always been fascinated by the stories of movers and shakers. In this book I bring the narratives and human dramas of leaders and companies front and center stage. From behind closed doors I have heard swearing and cussing, prayers, confessionals, and self-disclosures that serve up the intricacies and complexities of leadership. As an external coach who is immersed with the client I strive to fully enter the organizational culture. I am committed to first and foremost understanding how a leader lives in her world. From the vantage point of the consultant-as-an-anthropologist I strive to hear what they hear, see what they see, think what they think and feel what they feel. Much like Sigourney Weaver in *Gorillas in the Mist*, I must enter the lived world and community en route to partaking in genuine conversations and observing real phenomena. Each chapter represents engagement in another professional and corporate culture ranging from engineering, heart surgery, and real estate development, to high couture fashion and sports and athletic wear.

ACKNOWLEDGMENTS
I trust that the narratives and dramas that unfold in these pages will sufficiently usher you into the trials, struggles and toxicity of extraordinary leaders and their companies. Central is the discovery that all of the leaders presented in this book are both superb and exemplary as well as troubled and toxic. All leaders described harbor psychological hurdles and even psychopathologies. As a management consultant and leadership coach I heavily rely upon my training in counseling and

clinical psychology to adequately assess, work with and provide interventions for the high toxicity levels of individuals and companies.

A razor-thin line emerges at times in my work with leaders as their complex personalities and behavior encompass both the superfunctional and the dysfunctional, the superlative and the toxic. In some cases the assessment trail leads directly to the cognitive and emotional makeup of an individual leader and in other scenarios much of the nexus can be found in ill and abruptly conceived company policies, downsizings and restructurings.

During the course of writing *Destructive Leaders* I have reached deep into my personal array of human resources. First and foremost I want to offer a heartfelt "thank you" to my exceptionally supportive colleague, Professor David Van Fleet, Department of Management, Arizona State University. David has always been there for me. Whenever I have been excited or doubtful about ideas for this project I naturally walked down the hallways and around the corridors to David's office. Sparks frequently flew during our conversations. In David's presence I connected many dots and always walked away clear and strong.

On a very personal note, my mom has entered into numerous conversations with me over some of the key ideas in this book. As a business woman she has a keen sense of leadership and human capital and has been an advisor, source of wisdom, and motivator. I also want to call attention to my wonderful children, Ben and Olivia. Many of the narratives and concepts in this book have been brought up during our commuting hours in the car and during the course of the last couple of years. I have always listened extremely carefully to their reactions to what I pitched their way as they have provided a perspective that is uniquely honest and perceptive.

I also want to thank Paula Parish and Cambridge University Press for their belief in this book and in the author. Paula has been extremely patient, supportive and insightful throughout the reviewing, writing, rewriting and editing process. She has been integral in this book becoming a reality.

BRIDGES, NOT WALLS

Finally, I am hopeful that the focus on toxicity and dysfunction calls attention to the need to continue to build bridges between research streams spanning neighboring disciplines of management, psychology and communication. As a communicator I trust that the revealing of the subtext and darker side of companies and leaders serves the higher visions of positive leadership and extraordinary performance. The most prolific heads of organizations provide testimony that leadership can be a baffling and subtle blend of brilliance, turbulence and pathology.

Introduction: leaders and organizations in search of treatment

The paranoid top executive will seek out and promote others who share his obsessions. The histrionic leader will recruit only dependent, passive and second tier managers so that he himself can make all the key decisions. All of these selection biases maximize the impact of the neurotic styles of the top executives and allow them to endure.

(Kets de Vries & Miller, 1984a, p. 38)

CONSULTING WITH COMPANIES ON THE EDGE

Management consulting and executive coaching necessarily involves dimensions of psychotherapy and psychiatry. When leaders and organizations seek out external experts it is never an exercise in pure pragmatic problem solving. The enigmas and explosive nature of the mind and emotions of leadership are typically under question. Seemingly brilliant and successful leaders may secretly harbor excessive and debilitating fears, obsessions and histrionics. Besieged by grievances and pending litigation the executive board of a heart institute desperately searches for explanations of the erratic and abusive behavior of their renowned heart surgeon (see chapter 3).

In *Destructive Leaders and Dysfunctional Organizations: A Therapeutic Approach* I unveil both the external consultants' and the clients' narratives and interpretations of organizations and leaders on the edge. Who knocks on the consultant's door? Why do seven-figure leaders and CEOs send emails, call on their personal cells at 1 a.m., and request a candid meeting in the middle of the night? At stake is more than a behind-the-scenes look at the underbelly of business. What I disclose is a detailed view into what perplexes, ails and haunts movers and shakers. It is certainly not a case of revealing the dirt and scandals of politics or big business. This book is rather an opportunity to explore and examine cross-sections and prototypes of the darker, destructive side of outwardly successful companies and leaders.

In *Destructive Leaders* I present and interpret my cases in order to conjure up discussion and debate over the complexity of leaders and their companies. Excellent organizations and strong leaders are not particularly tolerant of their shortcomings and frailties. As experts themselves, they are not immune from seeking out specialists who can provide assessments and interventions for that which they cannot penetrate on their own. Oftentimes fully cognizant of the limits of logic and the rational mind, clients hope to unravel and find keys to better controlling intellect, emotions and the subconscious.

Why is it that a finely honed and chiseled approach to emotional intelligence unleashes extraordinary motivation and productivity while an inability to control frustration, hyperactivity, anger and fear destroys human capital? Acutely intelligent leaders seek out the key to what I sometimes term "internal operations management." Leaders seek antidotes to what undermines themselves and their companies. When a senior vice president sends an unanticipated email to an external expert it may signify the first step en route to a unique and privileged communication. Lurking beneath the surface issues and wedged in between the problems I have found a full range of existential drama and Shakespearean dilemmas. What is submerged under the carefully tailored suits and between the finely tuned PowerPoint slides of corporate clients can never quite be predicted.

OPENING PRIVILEGED DOORS OF LEADERSHIP

Destructive Leaders and Dysfunctional Organizations invites my readers into the chambers of decision makers who seek counsel. I open the doors to companies who have been unable to find solace or satisfaction from internal agents ranging from colleagues and human resource professionals to employee assistance counselors. Through referrals, default or otherwise, companies seek out the assessment of external consultants from diverse domains such as management science, leadership behavior and organizational therapy (e.g., see Schein,

2005). Client companies present dysfunctional scenarios that submerge their best minds in complex human capital problems. Trained in organizational behavior and systems analysis, I have reached a point where I am no longer sucked into nebulous complexity. Despite the multiple plots, counterplots and subconscious dramas presented by a troubled client, there is always a need to simplify whenever possible. Is there a nexus? How can I locate the most pressing and urgent issue at the center of the questioning and organizational storm? Is there a leader going through family and emotional upheaval? Without a nexus there can be no deliverables.

Through this book you will see a movement toward singling out a smaller subset within the context of larger systems problems. In other words, I may scan, probe, question and assess the entire organization, but I will almost always settle down to a shorter-range, high-impact focus on a toxic individual leader or dysfunctional process. In some cases this entails a skill set that eludes internal consultants and human resource professionals in the form of detailed psychological evaluation and treatment. A DSM-IV-TR diagnosis (*Diagnostic and Statistical Manual of Mental Illness*) can be necessitated due to the fact that a leader may be going through a recurrence of life-long battles with depression, attention deficit hyperactivity disorder or recently discovered upheaval attributable to a separation anxiety or a borderline personality disorder (American Psychiatric Association, 2000). In other cases there is no semblance of a highly toxic, full-blown individual psychological disorder, but rather the recurrence of company-wide interpersonal and team stressors or workplace conflict stemming from ill-conceived formal policies, traumatic downsizings or other semblances of upheaval.

DISCLOSING CONFIDENTIAL CONSULTING NARRATIVES

Destructive Leaders and Dysfunctional Organizations places you in the middle of the action. Hopefully lessons will be learned from the consultation narratives with prototypes to be derived. The stories emerge from many walks of business and corporate life.

- An international fashion couture group employs a leadership coach to attempt to penetrate the ongoing incivility and depression of their masterful head designer (see chapter 6).
- A Fortune 500 senior manager of an athletic wear company contracts with a consultant as part of his response to allegations against him alleging verbal and physical abuse (see chapter 7).
- Distraught and devastated by the destructive and bizarre behavior of the head of the research and development division, an aeronautical engineering corporation requests an evaluation and treatment for their billion dollar innovator, Dr. Josh Julia (see chapter 9).

Worth noting is the fact that in the above consultations no immediate assessment instruments or empirical data were sought by the consultants. Conditioned by their past experiences with metrics-driven, hit-and-run consultants, the client companies and executives were resistant, if not somewhat distressed. As a consultant and coach I was inundated with basic philosophy of science questions:

- How can you deal with our destructive leadership and the threat of litigation if you do not immediately administer assessment instruments to provide us with the hard data?
- Can we identify the good guys and the bad guys?
- Who is guilty of what?
- Have we erred in some of our company policies?
- How in the world can you determine whether we are dealing with a toxic leader or a dysfunctional system if you do not generate data on the front end?

The responses offered are inseparable from the philosophical axioms underlying the approach of *Destructive Leaders and Dysfunctional Organizations* to coaching, consulting and organizational therapy. To be too quick to engage in a quantitative approach can represent an attempt at shortchanging, rushing and providing metrics where there is no fundamental, rooted understanding of the organization and individuals in question. In other words, in the consultations presented in this book there was a need for observation, interviews, and immersion prior to, or in concert with, the administering of standardized assessment tools. If 360 degree feedback is deemed appropriate, that will most likely come at a later stage in the consultation.

"GORILLAS IN THE MIST" — ON-SITE ANTHROPOLOGIST

It is no simple matter to have executives who are pumped up and committed to a fast lane and rapid-fire return on investment (ROI) pseudo-empiricism and instantaneous solutions do a turnaround and buy into an "old world" engagement of consultants. On one occasion a CEO blurted out that "I follow your anthropology approach to doing this consultation but your 'gorillas in the mist' technique is still a little hard for me to take. Goldman, you're a little over the top ... but I still like you." Apparently this executive was equating the participant observer consultant with an old Sigourney Weaver movie where she portrayed an anthropologist who learned about the gorillas by living with them and becoming a part of their family. The corporate client was not that far off the mark and he certainly made his point effectively. Ironically, I expressed my pleasure with his analogy.

> Yes, Mr. Seymour, you get it. You are on target. I am the anthropologist who will swing through the corporate trees with your engineers.
> Once we share bananas I'll be able to better tell you what's what.

Although it was not always possible to move the executive decision makers beyond a state of "healthy skepticism," in all of the *Destructive Leaders* consultations the clients eventually became true believers as soon as they experienced desired outcomes. Once we received the initial green light from the upper echelon the road work began. We always went native and cohabited with the corporate gorillas. Immersed in the everyday organizational culture, the consultants spent long hours as observers in natural, everyday work settings. Numerous interviews and individual leadership coaching and psychotherapy provided further diagnostics and blueprints for interventions.

Following a thorough and customized engagement with the highest-toxicity venues and individuals, there occasionally was a need to proceed with such quantitative measures as: the administering of 360 degree multi-rater feedback for leaders; emotional intelligence instruments; negotiation and conflict resolution measures; communication apprehension assessments; and organizational stress assessments.

In the final analysis I have been able to successfully convey and live by the motto that electronic communications and technology are a fast message and people and cultures are a slow message (Hall & Hall, 1994). Within an initial 100-day assessment and intervention phase, clients learn to be patient and accept that the real data may emerge in an incidental conversation in front of a Coke machine. Although this venue lacks the guise of empiricism, I gather data wherever it raises its head, particularly when the guard is down in naturalistic settings.

One afternoon, I spent a dollar and twenty-five cents on a Diet Coke and in the process learned that a frantic leader first discovered that he had ADHD when he was nine years old. Until the time of this informal confessional the employee assistance counselors were convinced that irrational and inhumane corporate production policies were driving the poor senior manager to the outer limits of stress. It was no such thing. Prior to this confessional at the Coke machine, the senior engineer had consistently and consciously withheld his case history from the employee assistance program (EAP) and corporate colleagues. The ADHD was a pre-existing condition necessitating psychotherapy, leadership coaching and appropriate medication (see chapter 2). Although workplace stressors can serve to aggravate, accelerate and bring out of remission old ADHD symptoms, it would be naïve and insufficient to construe the pressures of company life as sufficient cause for Jason Javaman's maniacal public behavior with subordinates. *Lacking an adequate skill set, previous consultants attempted to bypass the leader's psychological history.* Some twenty-five years after the breakthrough work of Kets de Vries and Miller (1984a,b), companies and consultants are still missing the boat. Rather than chasing your tail and attempting to find the nexus of hyperactive, frantic and inappropriate leader behavior within the organizational system at large, why not secure the assistance of a DSM-trained management specialist who recognizes ADHD when he sees it and runs a structured clinical diagnosis? Suffice to say that ignorance is the mother of toxicity. Moreover, there was little impetus for Javaman to reveal his ADHD until he felt that he was sufficiently involved in a caring dialogue and supportive relationship (e.g., see Buber 1965, 1970). The non-threatening approach of the organizational therapist and consultant working with Javaman in the day-to-day culture of the engineering firm helped to establish a "gorillas in the mist" familiarity (see chapter 2). In this relationship, serious self-disclosure was just another conversation and hardly constituted a confessional.

WILD CARDS

Lord knows that management consulting and executive coaching are imprecise arts and sciences. We are not dealing with strict axioms, clear presuppositions and formal geometric truths. At very best we are immersed in the realm of high and low probability, not unlike court-rooms marked by attorneys who present evidence for four versions of the same death-by-surgery malpractice case. I can assure you, however, that there are consulting firms that live or die based on their ability to render the highly improbable into the semblance of a clear and concise science. Masterful needs assessments and precise, itemized deliverables are the backbone of the "flock of seagulls" styled consulting businesses. The meter always appears to be running. Consulting teams are assigned to the clients. It must appear as if the intangibles are tangible and the tentative is quite precise. Take heed. The world of high-level consulting can be extremely exploitative with the client companies and leaders walking away from the fray with the illusion that they have found treatment from a true team of healers. This is the drama and showman-ship that Pinault candidly revealed in *Consulting Demons: Inside the Unscrupulous World of Global Corporate Consulting* (2000).

Destructive Leaders does not offer a neat sanitized approach to assessing and treating the dysfunctional behavior and woes of either leader or company. The somewhat deceptive appearance of the seemingly floundering anthropologist-styled consultant is a constant. I offer testimony that the diagnostic phase of treating toxic leaders and companies necessarily involves much detective work. The slick corporate consultants are already running the numbers on their 360 degree feedback when the experts in *Destructive Leaders and Dysfunctional Organizations* are still moseying about. In this book, you will find that interviews, case histories and extensive observation take priority over premature attempts at quantification.

The wild cards emerge from consultant engagement. Divorced from the need to be distant and objective the consultants in this book are committed to being non-threatening, emotionally intelligent, trustworthy and entertain many of the communication attributes of the therapist in a helping relationship (e.g., see Maslow, 1971; Rogers, 1989) – or what Martin Buber once termed an "I–Thou" communication (1965, 1970).

Wild cards emerge from company narratives that provide context, texture and causality for dysfunctional behaviors and toxic leadership. Once the prospect of trust and a helping relationship is established with clients (not always possible of course), storytelling and self-disclosure increases. The emergence of thick, rich narratives provides data not usually available through mainstream "objective" assessment tools. Narrative provides much of the database. An initial narrative unfolds as the consultant observes behavior in the workplace. In addition, historical narratives are compiled from interviewees unveiling toxic interpersonal and leadership behavior. This is epitomized in the case addressing three failed mitral valve surgeries and the subsequent pending malpractice litigation (chapter 3). In chapter 4 the consultation depicts two executives who have a habit of hiring attractive senior managers while they are inebriated in their favorite strip club. Wild cards emerge in the confessionals of the CEO and vice president of Black Valley as they provide insight into the company's poor track record with senior managerial hires and a toxic turnover rate.

TEAR DOWN THE WALLS

As a professor of management who moonlights as a consultant, coach and therapist, I do not approach the work as a significant means of added income. I am committed to working with organizations and leaders much as I work with undergraduates and MBA students. I can offer in all sincerity that I have been more on a quest for truth, compelling narratives and extraordinary data than motivated by financial gain. I must admit that I have rather profited academically from my ability to write about my consulting work and won best paper awards from the Academy of Management (2005, 2007) and published a number of articles in academic journals in management, psychology, organizational behavior and leadership. In *Destructive Leaders and Dysfunctional Organizations: A Therapeutic Approach*, I am committed to relaying a few of the more fascinating consulting narratives that I have partaken in to incite dialogue and serve as a wake up call to both companies and corporate leaders as well as to academics and consultants. Toxicity is very much for real as the dark side is forever present in even the most successful leadership. Accurately diagnosing and treating toxic leaders and companies, however, is a troubled arena.

From where I now sit, tearing down the walls conveys an over-riding objective marked by stimulating dialogue over how upper-echelon leaders and companies struggle to deal with the destructive and irrational side of doing business. In *Destructive Leaders* I open up the doors to a few of the more revealing consultations. Hopefully this will help to tear down the walls of corporate denial, resistance, greed, hubris and misinformation.

A WORK IN PROGRESS

Destructive Leaders and Dysfunctional Organizations: A Therapeutic Approach remains a work in progress. After it is published it will still be in the process of being written and rewritten. The enigmatic, mysterious elements of human behavior cannot be removed from company life – only better understood in all of their intricacies and complexity.

I invite you to communicate with me and share your leadership and company narratives.

PRIVILEGED COMMUNICATION

The names of the leaders and companies have been changed due to the privileged communication and confidentiality requirements of my agreements with clients. Moreover, whenever deemed necessary, I have also altered elements of the storyline, facts and scenarios to protect the identities of client companies and leaders.

Hubris and narcissism: the dark underbelly of leadership

A certain degree of narcissism is perfectly natural and even healthy. A moderate measure of self-esteem contributes to positive behaviors such as assertiveness, confidence, and creativity, all desirable qualities for an individual in any walk of life, but particularly so for business leaders. At the other end of the spectrum, however, extreme narcissism is characterized by egotism, self-centeredness, grandiosity, lack of empathy, exploitation, exaggerated self-love, and failure to acknowledge boundaries. In this severe form, narcissism can do serious damage. This is especially true within an organization, where the combination of a leader's overly narcissistic disposition and his or her position of power can have devastating consequences.

(Kets de Vries, 2006)

EXTREME HUBRIS OF TOXIC LEADERS

Hubris and narcissism speaks volumes when unraveling the complex behavior of leaders. Curiously, there is even more than initially meets the eye when attempting to decode the dark and troubled side of leadership. Stories abound as the media has feasted on the upper-echelon conflicts and debacles at Vivendi Universal, Global Crossing, Enron, Tyco, WorldCom, and a "Who's Who" list of Fortune 500 corporations and executives. An infamous circle of corporate leaders have shamelessly exhibited the farther reaches of hubris in the form of greed, excesses, arrogance and unbridled bluster. The toxic leadership of Jean-Marie Messier, Gary Winnick, Kenneth Lay, Jeffrey Skilling, Dennis Kozlowski, and Bernard Ebbers has permanently engraved the darker and destructive side of organizational behavior into the collective conscience of Wall Street, corporate life and business schools around the world.

No longer is it conceivable to limit business discourse to the positive or heroic dimensions of leadership. The daunting spectacle of falsification of documents, manipulation of the stock market, shameless lying and strategized bankruptcies have left thousands of employees ruined. Moreover, conspiracies, grand larceny, corporate looting and massive accounting fraud have shaken the rafters of commonsense, decency and rational explanation. Of even deeper concern is the fact that the toxicity of the leaders in question would not have been possible without supportive corporate cultures and commitment from true believers – in the form of followers.

Woven throughout the daily excesses and exaggerations of tabloid journalism reports of toxic leaders are legitimate, recurring and core issues undermining organizations and their stewards. Corporate decision makers, politicians and academics alike ask a preponderance of questions about those at the top. Why has there been such a seemingly pronounced and recent surge in dysfunctional and unethical behavior in high places? Why is it that experts increasingly point toward hubris, narcissism and pathological attributes when dissecting the fall of individuals from positions of power and influence? How can we explain that we have been repeatedly blindsided by betrayals, scandals and overall toxic behavior in our leaders?

UNVEILING THE DARK SIDE OF LEADER AND COMPANY

In this book I unveil the fears, frailties, conflicts, phobias and pathologies of leaders who have risen to positions of power in their organizations. As an executive coach, management consultant and organizational therapist, I have been in a position to observe the weaknesses of seemingly strong leaders and the threats facing highly successful but fearful organizations. Rather than theorizing and speculating from a distance, I speak as an insider who was hired by CEOs, presidents, human resource departments and troubled leaders to dissect and right their wrongs. Originally trained as a researcher and academic, I had to adjust to a fast-paced corporate world where an external expert is on a strict timeline. I am frequently reminded of "deliverables" and providing a "complete package" by a due date. I must produce rapid results as a consultant when I am contracted to assess and intervene on:

- an upcoming media story on engineers who did not disclose known defects in a commercial aircraft that they designed – resulting in permanent injuries and death;
- a CEO who carries out a clandestine agenda through his vice president and demands that the VP plant false evidence and destroy the careers of his enemies; and
- a brilliant heart surgeon who is world renowned but such a terror to work for that she allegedly drove members of her operating team to botch routine surgical procedures, resulting in the deaths of three patients.

BEYOND THE TRANCE OF METRICS

I do not feature standardized assessment instruments, nor do I prioritize quantification when probing the dark side of leadership. It is not unusual for me to find at the onset of a consultation that there has already been an unscrupulous, toxic deployment of 360 degree feedback, and a myriad of other measurement tools – utilized to manipulative and toxic ends. I typically find the manipulation of data by internal and external experts as a means of validating and perpetuating dysfunctional agendas.

I am not in any hurry to measure or quantify. I have learned that tests and measurements on the front end can be presumptuous, premature and rather upsetting to organizational members. I agree with Schein (2005) that contrary to the modus operandi of the majority of consultants, the administering of formal diagnostics constitutes more of an intervention than an assessment. I rather enter the company culture from an interactionist and helper perspective and gingerly explore, communicate, probe and question. I see myself more as a detective and analyst than as a data collector and quantifier.

In this book I present consulting and coaching narratives that invite you into the rich and textured lives of leaders' imbalanced quests for excellence and their toxic drives for world-class recognition and acclaim. I closely scrutinize the hunger of leaders to be the best despite the detrimental costs in mental and emotional well-being. I attempt to make sense out of the derailment, casualties and company-wide dys-function incurred by sometimes brilliant yet toxic high achievers. For instance, the narcissism and hubris of Dr. Gina Vangella (chapter 3) serves as a prototype of the toxic leader and dysfunctional organiza-tion. Her holier-than-thou attitude is thoroughly destructive. She experiences extreme frustration at being unable to successfully com-municate with her surgical team and the cardiology division of Beach Harbor Heart Institute. Questions abound. How can a heart specialist be among the top three mitral valve surgeons in the world and falter miserably when it comes to relationship management skills? Can poor people skills escalate into conflict and toxicity at the surgical table? How could it be that such technical and medical superiority is inter-twined with the outer extremes of emotional unintelligence? The abbreviated response to the search for a source of this costly toxicity is "hubris and narcissism."

THE NARRATIVES OF TOXIC LEADERSHIP

The narratives in *Destructive Leaders and Dysfunctional Organizations* go into more detail than is typically encountered in cases written up and based on coaching and consulting assignments. I present complex psychological dimensions driving and impinging upon leaders and organizations – challenges sometimes too difficult, intricate or politicized for a company to internally address or over-come. As an external expert I am brought in by companies to solve the unsolvable, to rise above the familiarity and politics hindering organ-izations from resolving their own problems and to offer fresh perspec-tives and solutions. I shy away from tricks and superficial assessment tools geared toward dazzling clients with quantification and mislead-ing metrics. I am more of a detective with the inclinations and instincts of an anthropologist and therapist. I must be patient as I face my patients. When successful I engage clients in extensive dia-logue and privileged self-disclosure. I enter into a zone of long-winded narratives, conflicts, and ongoing people dramas that ultimately pro-vide context and depth for the pressing issues at hand. The drama of each leader and organization unfolds as part of a perplexing and some-times messy search for truth – as I am on the lookout for irregularities, unspoken agendas, fears, undetected patterns of causality, repetition of errors, weak links, blind spots, and an occasional big fish that rots from the head down.

The thick and alluring qualities of the toxic leader are epitomized in the eccentricities and unexpected twists and turns of the leaders portrayed in *Destructive Leaders and Dysfunctional Organizations: A Therapeutic Approach*. A case in point is the innovative leadership of Favio Burnstein portrayed in chapter 6. The fashion guru, designer and leader of the research and design division of Sergio Mondo Fashion House of Miami Beach, Florida must be experienced in all of his contradictions, flamboyancy and extraordinary creativity. These sterling qualities have to be ironically juxtaposed alongside his ongoing "separation anxiety disorder" characterized by desperate responses to turnover and instabil-ity in the workplace. How can a ground-breaking leader in the fashion industry also suffer from depression and recede into a dark and closely guarded life-long struggle with borderline personality disorder (see American Psychiatric Association, 2000). Caught within a dysfunctional web of despair that was largely invisible to outsiders, Favio projected that he was an extrovert, a mover and a shaker, and the life of the party. But in reality Favio existed in a jail of his own making. When Burnstein's pathologies were in remission he was temporarily released from his fears and burdens and was productive beyond the expectations of his Sergio Mondo associates. The intermittent escape from his pathological cell and the taste of freedom from his on-again, off-again fears propelled him to great heights and a quest for achievement not easily rivaled in those who are not driven by the turmoil of pathology. At stake is not only the unraveling of toxic sources in leaders, but the role of pathology in birth-ing and accelerating extraordinary levels of production.

DAMAGED, PATHOLOGICAL, TROUBLED LEADERS

Be prepared. A damaged, pathological and troubled leader is not just a single dysfunctional entity. That is far too simple. The toxic leader must be understood within the context of organizational culture. As we know from corporate debacles at the hands of Messier, Winnick, Lay, Skilling, Fastow, Kozlowski and Ebbers, it only takes one rotten apple to infect the barrel, but the rest of the apples are infected to varying degrees. Although quite troubling, it is nevertheless quite true that one toxic leader can wield unwieldy power – especially once the organizational system is subverted and restructured to promote, protect and advance dysfunctional agendas. In this book I repeatedly attempt to alert the eye and mind of the reader to both find and focus on the eye of the organizational storm. Succinctly, there are those cases where the nexus of dysfunctional policies and behavior can be traced to a nexus in a toxic leader. This will be illustrated and brought to life throughout the book.

For example, in chapter 5, the depiction of the fashion industry gone astray, I unveil Favio Burnstein's depression as a powerful force that necessarily impacted the Sergio Mondo Fashion House and wreaked havoc with productivity, morale and profits. In chapter 3, Dr. Vangella's narcissism at Beach Harbor Heart Institute dramatically influenced the Beach Harbor cardiology division, resulting in questionable patient deaths initially attributed to human conflict at the operating table. In chapter 4, the description of "upper-echelon sabotage," the CEO, Dr. Blackman, and his vice president, Mr. Graystone, provide an *unintended manual* for toxic recruitment and selection for Black Valley Enterprises. By breaking all the rules and hiring two managers over drinks in a smoke-filled bar, a toxic agenda was set. They invalidated normal interviewing and selection procedures. The word leaked out. Selection and hiring became increasingly ad hoc, and improvisational, and it became perfectly okay to set your own personalized or idiosyncratic stage for wining and dining the next vice president of Black Valley Enterprises. Personnel selection and hiring rules were made to be broken regardless of the consequences. The sheer audacity and the extreme measures of hubris driving these two executives propelled them to believe that they could defy the odds and the rules and come up with strong hires while inebriated and doused with carnal motives. Graystone and Blackman were in fact driven by egotism and a failure to acknowledge well-established personnel boundaries. Toxic leaders not only infect and negatively impact an organization – they also set a destructive example and agenda for perpetuating dark side hubris and narcissism.

TOWARD EXPECTING THE UNEXPECTED

Perhaps the most slippery and difficult theme in this book is to fathom that narcissism and extreme hubris is not necessarily born of a leader who is consciously and strategically selfish and full of himself. In returning to the seemingly diabolical strategies of the destructive leaders of Vivendi, Global Crossing, Tyco, Enron and WorldCom, we must ask a fundamental question. Were the leaders in question 100 percent driven by pure hubris and excessive doses of narcissism or was there also a measure of psychopathology in their bad behavior? In the cases of Messier, Winnick, Lay, Skilling and Kozlowski, I was not personally involved in the investigations and I do not have an insider's knowledge. I strongly suspect, however, that at least 10 to 20 percent of toxic leader behavior (at a bare minimum) is driven by mental and emotional disorders. The sheer enormity of the abuses suggests that an intentional, purely strategic and masterminded heist is unlikely. Certainly, pure evil and out-of-this-solar-system degrees of hubris and narcissism may be at the core of the despicable raping of corporations, stakeholders and a bamboozled public. But it is not a stretch to entertain that perhaps one out of the five fallen leaders would have represented a field day for clinical psychology and psychiatry.

Why am I traveling in this direction and asking potentially unsettling topical and rhetorical questions that may displease organizational strategists and decision makers? It directs attention to the dark underbelly of leadership. Sometimes the behavior of our leaders is so preposterous that it begs for "outside-the-box" assessments that fall significantly beyond the capabilities and bags of tricks afforded to business, management and HR experts. This is a recurring theme throughout these pages. Without the unexpected in leadership and lack of preparedness of organizations there would be no book, narratives or consultations to speak of. Additionally, cognizance of the toxicity of leaders cannot be adequately accounted for without some recourse to clinical psychology and the type of diagnostics afforded through use of the *Diagnostic and Statistical Manual of Mental Disorders* alternatively referred to as the DSM-IV-TR (American Psychiatric Association, 2000).

A case in point is Dr. Gina Vangella of the Beach Harbor Heart Institute (chapter 3). The heart surgeon expresses a holier-than-thou and condescending attitude toward subordinates and colleagues. Is she narcissistic? Is she smitten with a voluminous, out-of-control pattern of self-love indulged in by some professors, middle managers and professional violinists? Is Dr. Vangella one of many professionals who ritualistically practice a "love thyself" agenda central to their rise to leadership and prominence? Or might the surgeon be driven by something more serious, far-reaching and potentially toxic in the form of a narcissistic personality disorder? Not to be confused with commonplace narcissistic "traits," a narcissitic personality disorder mandates a list of recurring symptoms over time that essentially undermines and disables the leader in her work and personal life. Such was the case with Dr. Vangella. Although the designation of a psychological disorder does not diminish the responsibility of the perpetrator nor makes the heart surgeon less accountable, it does, however, establish that the toxic behavior is somewhat out of conscious will and control. This is strategic information for organizations that are attempting to provide early detection and coaching for workplace, customer and patient conflicts and disturbances.

The prospect of detecting a personality or psychological disorder is beyond the diagnostic range of executives and human resource professionals and may at best be within the expertise area of an employee assistance counselor. There is a tendency to look the other way and avoid any assessments that may be viewed as presumptuous or acts of insubordination, particularly when dealing with the semblance of extreme hubris or excessive narcissism at the top of the organization.

Typically, the symptoms become so extreme that if not appropriately handled internally there is a growing need for an external coach and consultant. Unfortunately, this call usually arrives fairly late in the day when too much damage has already been done. I can testify to this unfortunate truth.

DIAGNOSING HIGH-TOXICITY LEADERS

This book does in fact assess difficult-to-diagnose leaders within organizations who are largely unintentional in their high toxicity levels. *The most common maladies of hubris and narcissism* are accompanied and extended by a number of pathologies that disable organizations which then become dysfunctional. In *Destructive Leaders and Dysfunctional Organizations: A Therapeutic Approach*, I disclose these pathologies and examine the diffusion of toxic behavior throughout each respective organizational system.

Psychological Disorder	Leader and Chapter	Organization
• Adult attention deficit disorder	Jason Javaman	(2) Cornelius Ltd.
• Intermittent explosive disorder	Jason Javaman	(2) Cornelius Ltd.
• Narcissistic personality disorder	Dr. Vangella	(3) Beach Harbor Heart Institute
• Histrionic personality disorder	Sidney Graystone	(4) Black Valley Inc.
• Passive aggressive personality disorder	Dr. Blackman	(4) Black Valley Inc.
• Obsessive compulsive personality disorder	Dr. Gaston	(5) Johnstone-Mumford International
• Borderline personality disorder	Favio Burnstein	(6) Sergio Mondo
• Separation anxiety disorder	Favio Burnstein	(6) Sergio Mondo

Psychological Disorder	Leader and Chapter	Organization
• Depression	Favio Burnstein	(6) Sergio Mondo
• Antisocial personality disorder	Rick Boulder	(7) WinnerWear Inernational
• Histrionic personality disorder	Markus Renee	(8) Cavendish & Bodark
• Body dysmorphic disorder	Josh Julia	(9) Elija Ltd.

As will be pointed out throughout this book, the assessment of individual disorders in leaders is ultimately inseparable from the toxic behavior and dysfunction experienced by the organization-at-large. *In most organizations, a longstanding disorder in a prominent and active leader clearly diffuses throughout a division and workforce and is eventually interspersed throughout large companies.* In other words, we wind up looking not only at an individual leader such as Jason Javaman (see chapter 2) with an adult attention deficit disorder, but also at the fact that the larger system has been affected and now resembles an organization with attention deficit disorder.

HYPODERMIC NEEDLE AND PARTICIPATORY APPROACHES

So how do we approach the possible diagnosis of a leader with a psychological disorder within the context of an operating organizational system? Moreover, how does the leadership coach or management consultant work with a troubled leader while they are still an intricate, if not critical, part of their institution? The external expert must address how they will enter and work with the individual leader and the organization as a system. Will it be a top-down or a more lateral approach? How does the client conceive of the relationship with the expert? Will the client assume a passive role in response to the more aggressive behavior and interventions of the consultant? Or will the client be an active participant?

As indicated in the title of this book, many organizations are increasingly conscious of the destructive side of leader behavior. Quite specifically, organizations and troubled leaders are looking for the ultimate expert, doctor, surgeon, accountant, coach, therapist and consultant – all rolled into one – to solve their corporate malaise and spreading toxicity. As a coach and consultant I agree with Schein (1987) that how I respond to the client is crucial. In other words, I am hardly just on a fact-finding and data-driven mission, but am rather engaging myself in the client's culture and communication style by virtue of walking through their front door. How I gather information, ask questions, interact with leadership and set up the parameters of the consultation are all paramount. In the most basic and serious sense, as soon as I begin a dialogue with the client I am no longer purely in the assessment or diagnosis mode. *All consultant–client interaction qualifies as intervention.* How I make determinations is of vital importance. Why? I am rarely diagnosing and treating a client as a patient in isolation. When engaged with organizational consultations I am, of necessity, dealing with systems concerns.

The traditional "doctor knows best" approach will always have its place in some consultations, particularly those marked by crisis, urgency or a client organization or culture deeply conditioned to the old-school vertical model. This omnipotent positioning of the consultant-as-doctor was addressed by Gallessich (1983) when she called attention to the "hypodermic needle model approach" to consultation. In this model the expert serving the client is expected to "act upon" the organization by metaphorically injecting it with an elixir or medication to clear up the ills that ail it. As briefly mentioned, in cases of corporate crisis, urgent calamities and the threat of doom, an old-style theory X approach is likely to be perceived as what is most compatible with the need for generating lightning fast, centralized decisions and interventions during the darkest corporate hour. Short of an "SOS" state of emergency, companies and leaders are better off if they consider engaging their external expert in more rather than less dialogue (e.g., see Buber 1965, 1970). The process of engagement is a high priority. Once the organization or leader is actively involved in a partnership with the consultants, this will render the hypodermic needle model into an obsolete, second-best format. Fully engaged and immersed, the client and consultant become partners committed to the unraveling of organizational dysfunction and leadership toxicity.

It should be noted, however, that this theory Y-styled collaboration does not fit all leaders or client organizations – the consultant must patiently listen to the clients' values, predispositions, needs and expectations. Surely more dialogue and collaboration is preferable, but there will be those clients and organizational cultures that only seem to respond to a hypodermic needle approach (e.g., see Bradford & Porras, 2005).

EMPOWERING THE CLIENT

In the case of Dr. Gina Vangella (chapter 3), I was faced with an extraordinary challenge that led to breaking some new ground not only in the assessment and intervention but also in how I was going to develop a unique and customized collaborative relationship with the client. The surgeon undoubtedly brought high levels of hubris and narcissism into play in her Cardiology Division and at the operating table. After hours of observation, interviewing Vangella, her superiors and associates, I was of the opinion that the very act of coming up with a diagnosis might be perceived as a hostile intervention and a threat to the egotistical doctor. Keeping in mind that she was one of the top mitral surgeons in the world – and was worth saving at any cost as far as Beach Harbor was concerned – I proceeded gingerly. Dialogue and participation with the client was of utmost importance. Clearly, if I dared to put a hypodermic needle model of consulting into play I would meet up with major resistance. I rather adopted an extremely lateral, participatory approach that I first encountered during my formal clinical and counseling psychology training en route to my licensure. I can never forget my clinical psychology professor who told us her war story of allowing a reticent and resistant but terribly bright patient to choose her own pathology out of the psychiatric diagnostic manual. I had never directly put this strategy into play but once I was far enough into my second diagnostic session with Dr. Vangella I somehow reached into the back of my mind and came up with the excessively participatory approach to diagnosis. Why? A brilliant surgeon with a seriously toxic streak when it came to human interaction required something other than a typical theory X approach to assessment. Although the strategy was risky, I reasoned that I am quite comfortable partnering with corporate clients in the most radical sense, requesting that they become a direct and engaged partner immersed in their own assessment and intervention. In a similar fashion I was not truly going to get anywhere without a 90 percent + buy-in from the renowned surgeon. Since she was undoubtedly a supreme narcissist oozing with hubris I reasoned that I would temporarily join her side, play into her temperament and stroke her ego and vanity fair. Rather than fight her extraordinary hubris, why not partner with it and empower her to be in the driver's seat and make some sound decisions for a change? I slowly but surely moved toward the ultimate empowerment of the therapeutic and organizational patient. Moreover, I suspected that I could paradoxically feed into the pathology with a lateral, enabling incision and would have a far better chance of addressing and disabling the source of her toxicity at Beach Harbor Heart Institute.

After much solidarity building I introduced Dr. Vangella to the DSM-IV-TR (see American Psychiatric Association, 2000). She of course had some familiarity with the manual via her medical school training and her interaction with psychiatrists prior to, and following, a few of her heart surgeries. As I leafed through the book I startled her by stating,

> Dr. Vangella, I cannot follow the rules of my profession with you. You are the exception not the rule. Your intelligence is several steps beyond any patient I encounter and I can only do business with you if you are willing to enter into this assessment as a partner. Are you willing to look through a section of this book and choose the diagnosis that you find most fitting to what you have been experiencing through these recently troubling times? I assure you that this is a private, protected, secure and privileged communication between

> you and me. In my clinical judgment – I would be quite comfortable in
> proceeding in this manner assuming you are in agreement?

Dr. Vangella was brimming. She was extremely pleased and immediately engaged. She reached for the DSM-IV-TR and noticed that I already had a paper clip secured around approximately twenty pages. Not a word was spoken for some thirty minutes as Dr. Vangella leafed through the manual and carefully read the fine print through reading glasses propped at the very lower edge of her nose. The look on her face coupled with her attitude and demeanor spelled "intrigued, amused and challenged." During the time that she looked through the book I made some notations, shuffled through my file and even walked about the office taking care of a few odds and ends.

> After about thirty minutes of silence, Dr. Vangella, spoke in a
> breathy voice. 'Doctor, I have found the diagnosis that fits me. There
> is only one that fits and I am quite sure you know what I am going to
> point to.'

She very securely and knowingly handed me the manual turned to page 714 and diagnosis number 301.81 (American Psychiatric Association, 2000). She chose the "narcissistic personality disorder." I was quite pleased and comforted by the fact that my judgment was on target.

I do not recommend that therapists or executive coaches readily employ this approach when addressing possible psychopathology in leaders. In fact, I am quite sure that it would be repudiated by a vast majority of my psychology brethren. I will assure you, however, that I have only used this technique once. Happily it was only with Dr. Vangella. Although I was measured and secure in my gamble, it ultimately was a form of personal and professional lottery. This time around I felt an exuberant victory. My judgment was on target!

Perhaps from this example it becomes clear and graphic that a process and partnering approach to working with leaders and corporate clients stands in sharp contrast to the top-down hypodermic needle model. Granted, by playing the traditional analyst and doctor-knows-best role I could have eliminated what might appear like soft tissue non-sense and rapidly cut to the chase with a definitive diagnosis. Under the circumstances how stupid would that have been? By incorporating Dr. Vangella into the process I was also able to secure full partnership with Beach Harbor Heart Institute for the larger systemic issues involved in the positioning of Dr. Vangella, post-diagnosis, within her Cardiology Department. At stake was the arriving at the same diagnosis via two distinctive pathways. If you choose the dialogic and process route you will in most cases create a more active and engaged client who participates in the process and empowers themselves, the experts and the consultation. For the first time in her period with Beach Harbor Institute, Dr. Vangella was ready to become an upstanding corporate citizen.

COACHING PROTOTYPES

Dr. Vangella's assessment with the therapist and executive coach and the subsequent intervention with Beach Harbor Heart Institute are a prototype for this book. Leaders can be worked with, approached and engaged by a leadership coach and subsequently reintegrated into their organization. With a customized assessment an ADHD leader who brings extraordinary energy, motivation and productivity to his organization can be salvaged from excessive, wild and abrupt behaviors by establishing professional and workplace boundaries and excluding himself from potentially frazzling duties (chapter 2).

Occasionally a highly toxic leader must be released from his organization. Not all toxic leaders are salvageable. Elimination and removal befits some organizational cancers. Other disturbed leaders such as Favio Burnstein (chapter 6) can be retooled and reconceptualized to partake in innovative interventions such as dual leadership.

AN INVITATION TO DESTRUCTIVE LEADERS AND
DYSFUNCTIONAL ORGANIZATIONS

In the pages that follow I usher you into the world of eight consultancies and narratives. I did not set out to find leaders and organizational clients who were memorable characters immersed in complex plots and whodunnits. But fate had it that organizational life and leadership cannot be separated from drama. In *Destructive Leaders and Dysfunctional Organizations: A Therapeutic Approach* I reveal toxic leaders and dysfunctional organizations in search of treatment. It is my hope that these cases speak to the leaders and organizations in your professional life – ultimately supplying ideas, strategies and interventions for healing the toxic and making the ordinary, extraordinary.

2　**The enigma of an unintentionally toxic leader: an emotionally turbulent, destructive and impulsive workplace**

> When I am at a business lunch and really need to listen to the conversation, I can only get part of the story because I am trying so hard to shut out the noise of other conversations and distractions in the room. I am aware of meaningless word fragments that come catapulting at me from every direction, of dishes clattering, phones ringing, people moving about. The people with me seem to have a fence around them that protects them from this barrage of noise and activity. I don't have a fence.

(Miller and Blum, 1996, p. 36)

ANTIDOTES TO A DYSFUNCTIONAL AGENDA

Alongside well-established research into positive leadership (e.g., see Luthans, Youssef & Avolio, 2007; Nelson & Cooper, 2007) a darker and dysfunctional side of organizational behavior has recently emerged as a topic of serious concern to management researchers, practitioners and consultants (e.g., see Goldman, 2006a, 2008 a,b; Griffin & O'Leary-Kelly, 2004; Kellerman, 2004; Kets de Vries, 2006; Lipman-Blumen, 2005; and Lubit, 2004). Influenced by the role of toxic leaders in the disturbing corporate practices of Bear Stearns, Enron, Arthur Andersen and Fortune 500s, both public and private sectors seek assessments, downside protection, alternatives and antidotes to the dysfunctional and hurtful agendas undermining organizational life. How can organizations better anticipate destructive leader behaviors that derail corporate covenants?

Of widespread interest are the premeditated, unscrupulous agendas and organizational misbehavior of unethical leaders (e.g., see Ackroyd & Thompson, 1999). Far less scrutinized, however, is the unintentionally toxic behavior of otherwise accomplished and successful leaders acting out of psychological turbulence and driven by obsessions, phobias and narcissism (e.g., see Kets de Vries & Miller, 1984a,b; Maccoby, 2007) and personality disorders (Goldman, 2006a,b). The unsettling phenomenon of an accomplished leader driven by unconscious psychological forces and toxically impacting an organization is the focus of this chapter. This dark side of leadership and organizational behaviour represents a pressing yet difficult-to-assess terrain for management scholars, consultants and practitioners.

Writing from the vantage point of the engaged external consultant, I provide a perspective less visible to the academic and practitioner communities, in part due to the dictates of consultant–client privilege. In the consulting case and narrative that follows I alter both the proper names and identities of the client organization and its members in order to preserve client confidentiality. It is my intention to disclose an organizational text typically not available to outsiders.

A PROBLEM IN LEADERSHIP

The Missile Weaponization Division at Cornelius Ltd. has struggled at its company-wide, quarterly meetings. Jason Javaman, Sr., Manager of the MW Division has emerged at these meetings as an "abrasive, cocky, impulsive, forgetful, interrupting and fidgeting motor mouth who rubs much of the workforce the wrong way." To paraphrase, Dr. Percy Sandoval, CEO of Cornelius, Javaman effectively alienates 90 percent of Cornelius employees. In a word he is "dysfunctional."

Javaman frequently does not allow his subordinates to finish a sentence without interrupting them; he blurts out inappropriate, crude answers to problems and questions generated at company meetings. From the perspective of an outside observer it appears as if Javaman is barely in control of his own behavior at times – as if his emotions have run amok and he is oblivious to the central role of emotional intelligence to leadership (e.g., see Goleman, 1998, 2006). Javaman constantly fidgets, checks for phone messages, scans the internet on his laptop, gets subsumed in text messages and is not always mentally or emotionally available for colleagues and staff. In his personal office space, Javaman is perpetually in disarray with stacks of misplaced papers and files, countless disorganized messages tossed about on scraps of paper, plastic grocery bags full of personal credit card invoices and utility bills, with random notes and five-month-old newspapers thrown about the floor and shoved into filing cabinets and bookshelves. The manager is chronically running late, forgetting about scheduled appointments and meetings, misplacing memos and documents, and forever searching for emails on his PC monitor and Blackberry.

During company meetings Javaman has a very tough time presiding over his employees. In the eyes of his employees he is seemingly disinterested in what subordinates have to say, receiving personal calls and text messages during the proceedings, and typically excuses himself several times during a meeting for the bathroom, allegedly urgent messages and pressing executive matters. At board meetings Javaman appears to be looking around the room and dissecting every air duct and spider's web. He is oddly distracted by the hum of the air conditioner, an array of emotions and thoughts playing on his mind. He pays little attention to the PowerPoint presentation. When called upon, he sometimes stumbles and pretends to be attuned to the proceedings. His simple physical presence at group meetings represents a minefield of interpersonal disasters.

IMPACT OF THE TOXIC LEADER

Based upon reports from the CEO, Dr. Sandoval, upper-echelon leadership has increasingly noticed that at least a dozen or more engineers in Javaman's division seem to be following suit and unwittingly mirroring their boss's bad behavior. They regularly interrupt each other, are impatient and abrasive, fidget like crazy, multitask to the point of absurdity, frequently run late and seem to be climbing the walls as they are unable to adequately focus on pending projects. First it was Javaman and then his engineers who appeared to be in constant disarray, losing their professional demeanor, and increasingly transforming into abrasive, distracting colleagues lacking in rudimentary public decorum and etiquette. Following the prompts of their leader, a single engineer's dysfunctional behavior morphed into a toxic division-wide phenomenon impacting both internal and external customers.

The head of HR, Jean Claude Artaud, attempted to address some of the troubling and mounting complaints surrounding Javaman. Artaud found Javaman to be quite charming at Cornelius luncheons and cocktail gatherings but extremely frustrating and evasive when questioned about the strange, divisive behavior engulfing colleagues and customers. Javaman smilingly assured Artaud that it was just a case of overload and long hours. During their second meeting Artaud directly addressed mishaps and conflict within the Missile Weaponization Division. The HR director became increasingly frustrated with the evasive, shallow, brush-off given him by Javaman. In his nicest available inflection Artaud offered Javaman a referral to speak with a psychotherapist in the employee assistance program (EAP). Javaman laughed out loud and immediately rejected the idea, arguing that ...

> perhaps you need to first find an employee with some psychological problems if you want to bring some business to EAP. I realize they're lonely up there on the 7th floor. Maybe hang out in my division and pluck out an engineer or two for therapy. I won't mind. Have a nice day.

Javaman proceeded to exit the room after announcing that "our meeting is now officially over." Artaud was dumbfounded and reluctantly moved the issue back upstairs to the CEO, Dr. Sandoval.

Curiously, Sandoval was already privy to much of what was happening in the Missile Weaponization Division and he was also aware of Javaman's denial and resistance when confronted with his disruptive behavior and HR's referral to the EAP. Sandoval's conviction that "I have a problem with Javaman that is increasingly metastasizing and becoming a companywide issue" was compounded when he personally received an email from a top-tier corporate customer in Saudi Arabia. Riyadh Petroleum International (RPI) informed

Dr. Sandoval that they were about to shift their business to a competitor if they had to have any further direct dealings with Javaman.

CONSULTANT AND CEO

Faced with the inability of the Cornelius HR and the EAP to treat Javaman, Dr. Sandoval felt even greater pressure and urgency to turn the troubling behavior of his engineers around before it further impacted the Missile Weaponization Division and the entire organization. Dr. Sandoval contacted a management consultant and leadership coach recommended to him by the dean at a major MBA program. After an exploratory and contractual meeting I entered as the external consultant and coach to Cornelius Ltd. At my second meeting with Dr. Sandoval I attempted to obtain some background information on the Javaman situation, reports of Javaman's agitated behavior with HR, his refusal of HR's referral to the EAP, and the overall state of affairs at Cornelius Ltd., specifically within Javaman's Missile Weaponization Division. Dr. Sandoval was quite articulate regarding his concern for both Javaman and the greater good of Cornelius Ltd. Sandoval viewed Javaman's recent issues as part of larger divisional and company-wide concerns. In Dr. Sandoval's way of seeing things...

> Mr. Jason Javaman has been an enigma for all involved at
> Cornelius Ltd. He is loved, he is repelled. He is superior. He is a
> fool. He is the best and the worst. It all started with the frazzled
> Mr. Javaman, the brilliant but absent minded professor and
> discombobulated engineer. The problem is that Javaman's
> frenzied behavior and utter confusion seemed to be spreading
> like a virus. His people skills are abysmal. And people skills are
> going into the dumpers throughout his division! It is sad. Phone
> calls are met with frequent interruptions and failure to wait a
> turn to speak. They somehow manage to have their multiple
> cell phones and pagers ringing whenever I am attempting to
> address them in a quarterly meeting. Although I have struggled
> to understand these toxic behaviors as a divisional or even

companywide epidemic, I nevertheless have to come back to Javaman as the nucleus, the center of the storm. He is genesis! He is an enigma!

For both Sandoval and much of Cornelius, Ltd., the erratic, enigmatic, conflict-provoking behavior centered about Javaman had reached an intolerable point. The stressor that put Dr. Sandoval over the edge was an email he received from a top-tier Saudi corporate client threatening to terminate further business dealings with Cornelius Ltd. if they did not provide a leadership alternative to Javaman. Moreover, it was evident to Sandoval that Javaman was clearly not receptive to any of the attempts at dialogue or assistance offered by the HR director, Jean Claude Artaud, or the EAP head counselor, Dr. Irving Whitman.

The situation was further complicated by the fact that Javaman also had a history as a successful leader who had been instrumental in Cornelius' early global ambitions and international sales over recent years. Percy Sandoval was particularly adamant about pointing out the "complex and enigmatic personality" of Javaman in the workplace. Sandoval made a point of insisting that I not overlook that Javaman's repertoire included a turbo-charged, ultra-motivational upside that provided some impressive "fuel injected" leadership. Sandoval reiterated in many ways that:

> Javaman is both extremely productive and seriously destructive to his colleagues and subordinates. His dysfunctional behavior has spread and he is a toxic leader in our company. We need an antidote, a remedy, a potion and medication that will break the source and reach of Javaman's behavioral virus!

FROM NEEDS ASSESSMENT TO INTERVENTION

Based upon subsequent interviews with Dr. Sandoval, a series of consults with Jason Javaman, extended dialogues with staff and engineers, and three weeks of participant observer involvement, I was ready to utilize 360 degree feedback in the hope of obtaining both a qualitative and a quantitative perspective. I was not surprised to learn from HR that there had been "three ludicrous attempts at 360 degree feedback in the Missile Weaponization Division and in the company at large" that were marked by a total lack of follow-up and support from upper echelon leadership. Quite relevant were numerous reports on Jason Javaman's striking disregard for the data generated by the failed 360 attempts. In the final analysis the metrics generated from the three failures consisted of a pile of 360 degree paperwork designated for "garbage in, garbage out." Not that surprising was the fact that the data wound up in the local garbage dump also known as Javaman's office. The costly 360 degree data collections were wedged in between old newspapers, coupons, bills, and twelve-year-old files chaotically stuffed in Javaman's file cabinet. Rumor had it that you could occasionally find a ten-year-old tuna sandwich and Oreo cookies from before the millennium if you got to the bottom of one of Javaman's file drawers. But that was a dangerous task.

A fresh attempt was made to try 360 degree feedback. After several briefings regarding the power and impact of properly administered and collaborative 360 feedback, I proceeded with the equivalent of "juror instructions" and a tutorial in the hope of soliciting some serious support from Javaman's division and upper-echelon leadership. This (fourth) time around, top leaders, HR and all relevant Cornelius players were brought on board. Attention was given to the positive implications and "truth serum" to be derived for Cornelius Ltd. With appropriate commitment in place, the 360 degree feedback was administered.

Javaman was overwhelmingly rated as a poor listener, displaying abysmal relationship and team building skills with significant interpersonal shortcomings. In addition, there were many superlatives and respect also shown Javaman. In the words of CEO Sandoval, Javaman was an "enigmatic leader." This time around, however, the data was carefully scrutinized and interpreted with full participation from Javaman. Javaman settled down and carefully listened to the overwhelming criticisms as well as the numerous reports on his leadership ability and strengths. He reluctantly began to accept that he was perceived as a brilliant, innovative, and sometimes charming leader who was also abrasive, impatient and disorganized. The overriding concern was one of shedding light on the fact that Dr. Javaman had been engaged in "perpetrating relationship damage."

LEADERSHIP COACHING AND CLINICAL PSYCHOTHERAPY

During my first two sessions with Dr. Javaman I focused primarily on tangibles within the workplace. Part of our coaching contract was the need to secure a "professional organizer." Javaman worked for several weeks on his office with Ms. Marissa Kline in an effort to bring some semblance of order to the area. The process was a bit overwhelming as they generated approximately thirty-five to forty storage boxes full of old papers, newspapers, notes, downloaded materials, bills, etc. The vast majority of the boxes were to be discarded as trash. In addition, Javaman was able to put together many additional boxes of old books to be donated to a local charity. During this time I worked with Javaman on skills such as priorities, emails, delegation, time management, face-to-face contact with the workforce, increasing efficiency with staff, subordinates and customers, and scheduling.

Throughout the coaching, numerous references were made to the 360 degree feedback findings as Javaman struggled to be less defensive and more accepting of the multiple raters. He was not pleased with the behavioral critiques and patterns that emerged from the data collection, but his devastation was somewhat tempered by the strong positives.

As we proceeded deeper into the consultation, the fine line between leadership coaching and clinical psychotherapy became increasingly blurred as many of Javaman's shortcomings as well as positive behaviors appeared to be linked to an extremely hyperactive, impatient, mental, emotional and interpersonal modus operandi. In sessions with Javaman I observed behaviors in our face-to-face dialogues that mirrored or mimicked the "dysfunctional behaviors" reported in his workplace. In routinely obtaining a case history of Javaman's childhood and adult home life I found that his past was characterized by some of the same behaviors reported on the shop floor of Cornelius: disorganization; lateness; interruptions; extreme impatience; losing keys and constantly misplacing documents and essential tools for daily workplace functioning. I sensed that Javaman was indeed "driven by a motor;" for example, he had a frantic, hurried and out-of-proportion pacing to otherwise routine activities. A variety of symptoms clearly signaled that there was a strong chance that Javaman was suffering from *adult attention deficit hyperactivity disorder* (see Hallowell & Ratey, 1994; Hartmann *et al.*, 1996; Wender, 1995). Indications were that he had been in a state of significant mental and emotional disarray since childhood and that his disorder was deeply interwoven in the behavior that was wrecking havoc at Cornelius Ltd. His erratic and difficult-to-control patterns of behavior were not only troubling Javaman himself, but he was also unwittingly "perpetuating ADHD networks of dysfunctional behavior" throughout the ranks of the company's engineers (see American Psychiatric Association, 2000, pp. 85–93).

The ADHD assessment, however, was not limited to Javaman. It also applied to the Missile Weaponization Division. The long-term ADHD toxicity had metastasized and impacted many of the divisional members and overall operations. Suffice to say that much as the pathology of one member of a family inevitably envelops the lives of all members, the toxicity of an organizational leader is similarly diffused throughout a division and entire workforce (e.g., see Goldman 2006a, 2008a; Kets de Vries & Miller, 1984a,b).

The Javaman toxicity had spread and escalated throughout the workplace, with an overall disorganized, frazzled, forgetful, impulsive, driven, "chronically late" blueprint etching itself deeply and profoundly within the behavior of the organization as a whole.

INDIVIDUAL AND ORGANIZATIONAL INTERVENTIONS

The far-reaching, debilitating consequences of Javaman's behavioral disturbance required both individual and organizational interventions to break the patterns of toxicity. Foremost was a collaborative organizational effort consisting of the leadership coach, CEO Sandoval, the HR and EAP directors of Cornelius Ltd. Following Javaman's official ADHD diagnosis it became apparent that the toxicity was in fact largely "unintentional." Curiously, Javaman was largely relieved by the diagnosis. He immediately offered to waive his confidentiality and aggressively communicated his "behavioral issues" throughout the organization – resulting in a mixture of confusion, empathy and much goodwill. In conjunction with the diagnosis, Javaman received prescription drug therapy, coaching for his division and his family, and the extended use of a "clutter consultant" who worked 24/7 with Javaman to establish a filing system and bring order to his office life.

The most significant intervention came from the leadership coach and was reluctantly agreed upon by upper management. Javaman would be provided with an Associate Senior Manager and Assistant Director. Marcus Castrolano was appointed to this new position and it marked a radical shift from a single to a dual leadership format. By assuming the majority of the "left brain" administrative functions, this allowed a new freedom for Javaman to develop his talented "right brain" leadership in areas of R&D, innovation and teamwork.

SALVAGING A TOXIC, YET PRODUCTIVE LEADER

From meetings with CEO Sandoval, members of the executive board and the interpretation of the 360 degree data it became apparent that despite his toxicity and "idiosyncrasies" Mr. Javaman received over 90 percent support from colleagues and subordinates. Coworkers took notice of Javaman's innovativeness, enthusiasm, ground-breaking vision and ability to work with teams – largely overshadowing his annoying and destructive tendencies of chronic lateness, disorder, rude and abrasive behavior, extreme disorganization and other dysfunctional behaviors related to his ADHD disorder (e.g., see American Psychiatric Association, 2000; Weiss, 1996; Wender, 1995). Intent upon salvaging their toxic, yet productive, leader, Cornelius Ltd. subscribed to the approach of:

(a) assessing and treating Javaman as an executive suffering from a behavioral disorder;

(b) adjusting, attuning and modifying organizational operations to accentuate Javaman's primary contributions to the organization (innovative, creative, interpersonal, team, enthusiasm); and

(c) minimizing his deficiencies (lateness; disorganization; distractedness). Fortunately, Cornelius Ltd. had deep enough pockets to create a second leadership position alongside Javaman en route to a successful restructuring of both Javaman's position and the Weaponization Division of the company.

TOXIC BEHAVIOR IN REMISSION

In the two years following the individual and organizational interventions, Cornelius Ltd. has reported a rise in innovation and productivity in the Weaponization Division. Periodic consultation has proceeded on both the organizational and individual level with Javaman receiving both leadership coaching and psychotherapy on a regular (weekly) basis. During this period Javaman has received two awards for outstanding innovations and has also accelerated on interpersonal and team levels with his colleagues and peers. On the deficit side, Javaman was the target of a single internal grievance for "irrational and explosive treatment in the workplace." This grievance was settled amiably through the Cornelius ombudsperson and was a pressing subject for several months during Javaman's leadership coaching and psychotherapy sessions. The gravity and immediacy of the problem has since subsided and Javaman's toxic behavior is, in the words of CEO Sandoval, "in remission."

Working in close proximity and in harmony with Cornelius HR, we gradually relieved Javaman of some of his chronic organization problems by delegating as much of the record keeping, administrative and paperwork as possible to the newly created Associate Senior Manager, Marcus Castrolano, and two new administrative assistants. Two years after the initiation of dual leadership and two years into an ongoing psychotherapy and leadership coaching regime, Javaman and his division are far less divisive, experiencing a newly formulated camaraderie and team success, and breaking innovative and lucrative ground with a growing international clientele. Javaman increasingly illustrates insightful, creative and inspired leadership as the "clutter" is progressively removed from his desk and interpersonal work life. After much debate and huge doubts expressed behind closed doors by HR and upper management, the depth and quality of Javaman's work has overshadowed his battles with ADHD and a related intermittent explosive disorder (see American Psychiatric Association, 2000, pp. 663–667).

Curiously, the alleged spread of ADHD symptoms and behaviors among Javaman's colleagues has quietly subsided throughout the division and the organization – as the leadership coach offered, collective remission was inevitable with the turnaround and recovery of their leader. Upper-echelon management states that Javaman will stay. He is a worthy investment for Cornelius Ltd.

UNINTENTIONAL MISBEHAVIOR OF A LEADER

Are organizations adequately prepared to assess and work with toxic leadership? This chapter raises concerns surrounding unintentional leader toxicity. As an enigmatic leader whose abruptness, impatience and rude behavior is juxtaposed with exemplary, transformational leadership, Jason Javaman is involuntarily expressing his attention deficit hyperactivity disorder (ADHD). Cornelius Ltd. is not unique in its inability to assess unintentionally toxic behavior. Upper-echelon management, HR and internal experts typically lack the expertise to distinguish between intentionally destructive and unethical leader behavior and the unintentional misbehavior of a psychologically troubled leader. In the case of Jason Javaman, he presented his organization with enigmatic leadership combining positive, visionary and resonant qualities with toxic tendencies of chronic lateness, extreme disorganization and an inability to appropriately focus his attention and appropriately respond to subordinates and colleagues. After a concentrated program of one-on-one leadership coaching and psychotherapy for adult ADHD and appropriate medication, Javaman exhibited a capacity for a normative, even superior ability to control his sense perception and emotions.

Based on this consultation case, organizations are alerted to the complexity and enigmas of leadership toxicity – extending beyond the selfish and clandestine and into the neurotic and disordered terrain of psychological disturbances. A driven and successful leader may harbor positive as well as dysfunctional motivations (e.g., see Lowman, 2002). I invite you to entertain this broad terrain and expand your organizational repertoire into the assessment of unintentional leadership toxicity.

3   The narcissistic leader: world-renowned and quite arrogant

> In a position of leadership, people suffering from this kind of disorder become fixated on power, status, prestige, and superiority. They overvalue their personal worth, arguing that, as exceptional people they deserve special privileges and prerogatives. They act in a grandiose, haughty way, expect special favors, flout conventional rules, and feel entitled; they're unempathetic, inconsiderate to others, exploitative, and unconstrained by objective reality.
>
> (Kets de Vries, 2006, p. 22)

THE ALLURE OF THE TOXIC LEADER

Central to an understanding of toxic behavior in dysfunctional organizations is the prevalence and allure of the narcissistic leader. Beginning with the coining of the term "narcissism" by Havelock Ellis (1998), more than a century of ongoing research and speculation over the clinical condition of "self love" has ranged from Freud's description of a narcissistic personality type (1931/1950) to the view that narcissism in its extreme constitutes a personality disorder (Kernberg 1967, 1989a). In recent years organizational behavior researchers have increasingly assessed and described the high incidence of narcissism among noted and successful business leaders including Steve Jobs (Robins & Paulhus, 2001), Michael Eisner (Sandowsky, 1995), and David Geffen and Kenneth Lay (Kramer, 2003). Characterized by long-term agendas marked by extreme hubris, a preoccupation with personal egotistically driven needs for power and admiration (Kets de Vries & Miller, 1997) and grandiose visions and self-centered needs (Glad, 2002), the narcissistic leader can appear oblivious to constituents and display a troubling and dire lack of empathy for followers and organizations (Conger, 1997).

In this chapter I move beyond the mainstream preoccupation with the study of narcissism as a personality trait in leaders. This consultation and narrative focuses on the seldom acknowledged incidence of the leader with a clinical diagnosis of Narcissistic Personality Disorder. This diagnosis is epitomized in a "pervasive pattern of grandiosity" and a "need for admiration and lack of empathy" as described in the American Psychiatric Association's (APA) diagnostic manual, the DSM-IV-TR (American Psychiatric Association, 2000).

The rarefied and specialized expertise of a world-class heart surgeon who heads a Department of Cardiology at a renowned center for excellence sets the stage for the following study of a toxic leader displaying narcissistic personality disorder. Elite and privileged to the core, Dr. Gina Vangella of Beach Harbor Heart Institute qualifies as a first-order narcissist who officially grows into a full fledged diagnosis of a personality disorder. The mitral valve surgeon's technical expertise and credentials are impeccable but her extreme self-absorption and inability to express empathy with patients or members of her surgical team eventually culminated in serious ramifications for the surgeon and her institution.

A WORLD-RENOWNED LEADER WHO IS QUITE ARROGANT

Dr. Gina Vangella is a brilliant, acclaimed heart surgeon and an international patron of the arts. Dr. Vangella is also a toxic leader. She lives a privileged life, considers herself above mortal criticism and is a self-proclaimed elitist. In her leadership role at the Beach Harbor Heart Institute, Dr. Vangella regularly engages in destructive, self-serving behavior. The doctor is allegedly quite difficult to work with and fashions herself as a "superior aesthetic being." Despite her high status in world cardiology circles, Dr. Vangella has been repeatedly accused by colleagues of abusive, demeaning, arrogant and condescending behavior. The human resources department and the Beach Harbor CEO reported to Dr. Vangella that they were inundated with the "threats" of formal grievances by colleagues who individually and collectively reported that "the work environment was growing entirely too dysfunctional."

Deeply disturbed by Dr. Vangella's unspoken yet assumed requirement that she "be worshiped," colleagues, nurses and staff continued to tiptoe around her. Her position of esteem and authority has afforded her white-collar privilege – despite her toxic and disruptive behavior. Colleagues are not exactly sure of how to respond to or approach Dr. Vangella. After all, she is their superior and there is fear of retribution. The situation becomes further compounded at the surgical table as members of the surgical team point fingers at the surgeon. Dr. Vangella's toxic behavior is making the entire cardiology division increasingly dysfunctional. Can Dr. Vangella's toxic behavior be assessed, explained and treated before there are even more serious consequences? Is a highly stressed, increasingly dysfunctional surgical team prone to mistakes at the operating table? Unless this disturbing situation surrounding Dr. Vangella is resolved, her immediate surgical team is fearful of what could go wrong. Malpractice? Who has the authority and qualifications to step in before it's too late? Dr. Vangella's colleagues see the handwriting on the wall. They are fearful that the people conflicts and toxicity levels may be beyond the expertise of Harbor Beach HR or upper management. Will an external consultant be called upon to put out the fire before the toxicity further spreads and irreparable damage is done?

A NARCISSISTIC LEADER

Dr. Gina Vangella is the Chief Surgeon and Director of the Department of Cardiology at the Beach Harbor Heart Institute, a center for excellence known around the world. Dr. Vangella is quick to talk of her "great fortune" and "brilliance" and has many admirers within Beach Harbor. In her flamboyant way, Dr.Vangella always seems to demand attention and respect. The majority of her subordinates believe that Dr. Vangella is "an incredible surgeon, highly intelligent and a capable leader of the department." Some colleagues will go to the ends of the earth for her. Over the past seven years, however, the doctor has increasingly conveyed a sense of "entitlement" to her coworkers and staff. At times, Dr. Vangella seems to be very preoccupied with herself, is sparse in her communication with colleagues and despite wide-spread admiration, there are a few colleagues who privately perceive her as being "arrogant and haughty." According to one fellow surgeon, "Dr. V. expects that all the pieces will fit into place and that she will have an idyllic, flawless scenario when it is surgery time. But that's not the real world and she can't even begin to accept that."

Dr. Vangella has oftentimes boasted of her fluency in the French language, and her passion for French Symbolist and Surrealist literature, poetry and fine art. Dr. V. considers herself a "French Surrealist Artist." Articles appearing in the *Beach Harbor Heart Letter* (the hospital newsletter) have announced exhibits of her paintings and sketches at local art galleries and her membership in the "exclusive and world renowned 'Post-Modernist French Surrealist Society of Artists'" (e.g., see Artaud, 1958; Balakian, 1970; Baudelaire, 1965; Breton, 1972). Shifting from artistic to medical circles, Dr. V. is also extremely well known for having studied in Paris with the master heart surgeon, Dr. Françoise Merleau-Ponty, who perfected the minimal incision mitral valve heart repair. This procedure is performed on individuals who have mitral valve regurgitation, where there is a back flush of blood, with the blood supply not being able to move appropriately through the heart muscle and the body. Without surgery to repair or replace the faulty mitral valve, the patient is at risk of developing an enlarged heart that eventually will fail and result in premature death.

Dr. Vangella is sought out around the globe for her skills as a surgeon. She has been one of the most heralded and productive mitral valve surgeons in the world. As Director of Cardiology, Dr. Vangella oversees a world-class assembly line of mitral valve procedures. Her productivity has been the talk of the town at cardiology conferences across North America, Europe and the Middle East, as she has averaged as many as five successful mitral valve surgeries per day. Her productivity has catapulted Dr. Vangella and the Beach Harbor Heart Institute to the top tier in cardiology. Beach Harbor is held in such high esteem that the fifth floor is referred to as the "Saudi floor" or the "black gold floor." This is due to the large number of Saudi royalty and "oil families" who come to the institute for heart surgeries. The fifth floor is reserved for the ongoing Saudi constituency.

Dr. Vangella is determined to be the best. She speaks of her surgical procedures as "flawless." Dr. V. is looked up to as an extraordinarily high status doctor by her patients and their families. She is what you might even describe as "worshiped." Following successful surgeries she is often showered with expensive gifts by the patient's family. The problem among nurses, fellow surgeons, hospital staff and administrators is that Dr. V. also expects similar adulation from all employees and colleagues.

As Director of the Department of Cardiology, Dr. Vangella calls monthly surgeon, nurse and staff meetings, where she typically shows up twenty minutes to half-an-hour late. On several occasions she has walked in late talking on her cell phone, and continued the conversation while a roomful of colleagues and subordinates overheard her side of the conversation.

Occasionally there were some whispers of Dr. Vangella's "venomous and tragic divorce," a battle that was staged over two years in the local municipal court. One baffled colleague spoke at one of the monthly meetings while they were all waiting for the fashionably late Dr. Vangella. "How can such an elegant, refined and brilliant lady be in so many conflicts and such a nasty divorce? I guess she's just unlucky." It was as if the hospital staff wanted to believe in Dr.V. They were true believers and enabling followers. Suffice to say that Dr. Vangella was quite dependent upon the praise and support of her colleagues. In the light of day there was a careful crusade to avoid any mention of toxicity.

Removed from the adoring public eye, another constituency was developing. There were a number of behind-the-scenes venues buzzing with negative talk about the doctor: at watering holes; hospital parties; and team building weekends in the wilderness. Despite her alleged brilliance and extraordinary medical, surgical and artistic talents, employees began quietly talking among themselves that Dr. Vangella had a "Napoleon complex" and "wants to be worshiped 366 days a year!" Agitated about a pattern of selfish, narcissistic behavior over a period of years, a growing group of hospital nurses and heart surgeons were not signed up to the largely unwritten and unspoken hero worship agenda. The protest first began in the form of a grapevine that insidiously grew over two years. They accused the loyal followers of Dr. V. as "being in denial." The grapevine spoke of Dr. V.'s lack of empathy and coldness toward her colleagues and staff. Colleagues stated that Dr. V. "spent an extraordinary amount of time complimenting herself to colleagues, never stopped acting self-important, was self-absorbed and rude in public, and in many instances even exaggerated her commendable accomplishments far beyond recognition." According to one report, "Dr. V. was never simply satisfied with doing a good job. She had to be ignoring and emotionally abusing her colleagues while she was busy shattering surgical precedent and sending shock waves across the Atlantic." Fellow surgeons, nurses and staff reported that Dr. V. became harder and harder to work with and be around. Complaints levied against Dr. V. were further accelerated when four independent sources stressed that the doctor had been "exploitative of others in order to achieve her personal goals."

To complicate matters, the grapevine talk and organizational gossip increasingly got back to Dr.V. She was privately devastated by the extreme criticism taking place in the hospital trenches. Vangella publicly blamed nearly everyone in sight for her problems. She could be stern, loud and extremely vocal. At times, however, she appeared to vacillate between acting superior and being highly self-critical. Sometimes Vangella withdrew and confessed to Dr. George, a surgeon she occasionally confided in, how badly she felt about the rumor mill. George reported that Vangella stated that "I question myself more than I want to admit to. I feel unworthy and fragile sometimes ... especially when I am being so maliciously maligned." Clearly the dark organizational underbelly was able to throw Dr. V. into states of reflection and defensiveness. Dr. George was concerned that the gossip might eventually impact Dr. V.'s performance. Dr. V. revealed to Dr. George that:

if even a fraction of those ugly indictments were true I would feel as if I do not deserve my international reputation. I might even question my ability to perform surgery at a world-class level.

At another point, Dr. V. stated to Dr. George that:

Dr. Workman doesn't realize how much I admire his surgical technique. He accuses me of being a bitch and acting arrogant, when I feel humbled and envious of his great skill.

But to fellow doctors and staff, Dr. V. was known as the "ice queen." Whenever anyone would even insinuate that there was reason for questioning, doubting or criticizing Dr. V., she responded with what Dr. Workman mockingly described as "an icy stare from the tundra North – worthy of our in-house, self-anointed movie star."

Fellow doctors complained that Dr. V. was "unbelievably sensitive to her own needs" and "incredibly insensitive to her colleagues' and staff's needs and feelings." They reported to HR that Dr. V. was "all about herself" and "that's not the way it should be since surgical teams are always at the edge of the cliff, performing life and death procedures." Criticism reached a crescendo when after three failed mitral valve surgeries, the talk around the hospital cafeteria was that "Dr. V. made the surgical team crazy with her 'type A' and holier-than-thou nastiness. It's obvious that her team was doomed to botch up." Questions lurked whether Dr. V. was also insensitive to the patients' needs?

In response, Dr. V. further withdrew from contact with hospital doctors, staff and administrators and retreated into a world of elite French and European heart surgeons and artists. She immersed herself in her circle of artists: successful painters, ballet stars, classical musicians, actors and actresses. In the words of a fellow surgeon, "Dr. V. walks around with her nose in the air and thinks she's better than everyone else." It was undeniable that Dr. V. was traveling in elite artistic and medical circles. Yet behind closed doors, Dr. George admitted that

I am knocked out that Dr. Vangella doubts herself so deeply and appears to be envious of some of the surgeons and nurses who don't even have half of her talents and expertise. She is an enigma!

A HEART INSTITUTE BESIEGED BY GRIEVANCES

After years of admiration for Dr. Vangella, HR was suddenly besieged by complaints and the threat of internal grievances. But no one dared to file a formal complaint. This was considered too risky. The common thread in the informal grievances was that Dr. V. had an insatiable need for excessive admiration and "ridiculous levels of respect and subservience" and lacked empathy for anything other than her own accomplishments. The consensus was that Dr. V. lived in a fantasy land of otherworldly artistic love and aesthetics, perfect surgeries, exquisite art and superior, gorgeous beings. She was forever admiring and brushing her very long blonde hair in every available mirror and constantly seeking out her reflection in glass windows and doors. Dr. V. besieged her colleagues for attention, always "fishing for compliments" and talking about how she went to "the best medical institutions" and will "only buy Gucci briefcases." She bragged that she went to the "best hair stylist West of Paris," and that some of her colleagues "obviously dressed themselves in Wal-Mart" and "have their hair cut at the Salvation Army or Super Ghetto Cuts." You might say that she was high maintenance.

CONSULTATION WITH DR. VANGELLA

Catapulted by the tragedy of three failed mitral valve surgeries and the accompanying talk on the grapevine about the Napoleonic and grandiose behavior of Dr. V., HR needed to step up talk with the surgeon. The HR director explained that there were three legal cases looming alongside pending informal grievances specifically naming Dr. Vangella. To complicate matters, three of the internal grievances were a direct result of "incidents" that took place during the failed mitral valve procedures – all serving as potential fodder in lawsuits against Beach Harbor. Dr. Vangella was informed that two of the three pending grievances cited that "Dr. V. went ballistic, freaky and frantic when a fellow surgeon asked for clarification on her decision making during one of the failed procedures." An in-house investigation revealed that Vangella screamed out several times during the surgery, "how dare you question my judgment!" According to reports, the screams sent shivers down the spines of several members of the operating team. When the surgeries failed, Vangella spewed out scathing remarks and accusations at her medical associates. It appeared as if her fragile ego could not allow for personal failure and it had to be blamed on her colleagues. Worse still was the possibility that the conflict itself had directly contributed to what could be construed as surgical mishaps.

HR proceeded to spell out their response steps regarding the soon-to-be-filed grievances, carefully informing Dr. V. of the procedures for compliance that needed to be followed. HR also informed Dr. Vangella that it was protocol to request that she schedule an appointment with a therapist in the employee assistance program. Dr. V. declined and stated that:

> I need an executive coach or management consultant who can guide me on how to deal with all of the bottom feeders, vultures, pigeons and sea gulls around this hospital.

The hospital complied and called in a management consultant. HR and the President of Beach Harbor, Dr. Marvin Calding, presented me with their own needs assessment and diagnosis. Dr. Vangella was, in their collective opinion, an:

> outrageously self-centered, egotistical lady who is a fright to work under but is nevertheless quite brilliant and one of the very few surgeons around the world who is trained in the procedures of Dr. Merleau-Ponty.

The President and HR were in fact troubled by the fact that Dr. Vangella was much more than an egomaniac and narcissist. She was also an extremely productive heart surgeon and until the recent failed surgeries and the groundswell of complaints, Dr. Vangella was their superstar. Was she just a difficult genius? Calding himself stated that he was "a bit amused by Vangella's manner with him during several talks." He continued on that:

> unless I was dreaming, I would have thought that Dr. Vangella
> thought that she was the superior and I was the subordinate! I could
> use language to describe her attitude but I will refrain from doing so.

It was decided with HR that no needs assessment or interviews would be held with Dr. V.'s colleagues. It was my mission to initially focus exclusively on Dr. Vangella, in the form of consultation and coaching.

Dr. Vangella was visibly disturbed, indignant, defensive and arrogant at the onset of our first consultation session. Her behavior was consistent with the theory of threatened egotism and aggression (Baumeister, Smart & Boden, 1996; Penney & Spector, 2002), a theory that predicts that "narcissistic individuals would be more likely to engage in counterproductive workplace behavior, especially in response to threat" (Spector & Fox, 2005, p. 165). Dr. V. told me how, when initially informed of employee complaints pending against her, she felt deep hurt and outrage and "scolded the HR manager and ridiculed her as an inferior who had no right to question her better and superior." After a period of indignant ranting and raving, Vangella revealed that she was already taking medication prescribed by her internist for "anger and stress management issues." Up until this point Dr. Vangella's people skills and clashes were construed as classified data.

DSM-IV-TR INSUBORDINATION: SELF-DIAGNOSIS

Once a careful case history was taken, I switched hats from high-impact management consultant (Schaffer, 2002) to rapid-cycle leadership coach, to brief existential psychotherapist (e.g., see Strasser & Strasser, 1997). In the course of the early consultations I informed Dr. Vangella of my broad training, preparing her that "I might have to change hats during our consultation." Equipped with a DSM-IV-TR text, I showed Dr. Vangella several Cluster B personality disorder diagnoses and asked if any of these applied to her. She read through the diagnoses with great interest and was extremely thorough. She stated that she thought she had a few symptoms from all of the disorders and commented that "having a few symptoms is idiotically normal. Is it not, Dr. Consultant?" I replied in the affirmative. I pressed to find out if there was any disorder that she felt fit her better than all the others. My strategy was one of respect, inclusion, collaboration, and an uprooting search for how Vangella construed her world, all basic tenets of existential psychotherapy. In response to my inquiry regarding the disorder in the DSM-IV-TR that best fit, Vangella replied:

> Yes. You know which one. The Narcissistic Personality Disorder. How in the world do I wind up at the knees of the top Parisian heart surgeons and artists and strive for the unreachable? Of course I'm a narcissist. I'm proud of that. And isn't it a question of to what degree, doctor? That's what drives me and makes me successful. It's why I achieve and strive for unusual levels of excellence. I've read that wildly successful leaders are oftentimes narcissists. Deny that if you can, Doctor.

The diagnosis she chose was DSM-IV-TR 301.81, *Narcissistic Personality Disorder* (American Psychiatric Association, 2000). Dr. Vangella was absolutely on target. *Yes, narcissism is the initial driving force behind many leaders*. It can be the driving engine and result in extraordinarily high levels of productivity (see Maccoby, 2003, for an examination of the "productive narcissist"). But it is *a question of degree*. How many of the symptoms do you present? How long have the symptoms been present? Do they significantly impair your personal, social and workplace functions? What is the impact on your organization? I empathetically communicated to Dr. V. that as much as the narcissism propelled her accomplishments, voracious ambition, and drive for excellence, she was not *as* functional when it came to interpersonal relationships in the hospital. Lurking was the very touchy point as to whether interpersonal problems stemming from narcissism had in fact entered into the operating room and diminished her abilities as a heart surgeon during any of the failed procedures. We discussed the narcissistic symptoms at length. We further discussed the role of emotions, emotional intelligence and emotional *unintelligence* (e.g., see Goleman, 1998). We investigated how some of her colleagues felt as if they were "targets" for her disruptive, unreasonable behavior. We explored how and why the narcissistic personality disorder diagnosis fit. It turned out that Dr. V. had a history dating back to when she was about eleven years old illustrating repetitive, deeply rooted personality tendencies toward narcissism.

TREATMENT YIELDS NO MORE FAILED HEART SURGERIES

It was a meeting of two doctors from two different worlds. I was deeply moved and impacted by Dr. V.'s personality disorder. Dr. Vangella is formidable. In my estimation, there was no way to try on a diagnosis and a possible intervention without Dr. Vangella's buy in. Eventually this was achieved in large part by means of establishing a trusting therapeutic relationship. I alternated between psychotherapist and a high-impact leadership coach and consultant who was rapid-cycling an assessment and intervention with a dysfunctional leader. The counseling and consultation was a collaboration with the client. It was the result of an open book dialogue. In my follow-up with Dr. Vangella, I got in the loop with her internist and also continued with our counseling "sessions" that were part executive coaching and part psychotherapy.

Following the diagnosis, Dr. Vangella's internist created a new "cocktail" of medications that more directly addressed the personality disorder. Eventually, Dr. Vangella came around herself and stated that she would accept the label of "narcissistic personality disorder" and "silently wear it as a symbol of why she was a protégée of Dr. Merleau-Ponty and why she got involved in Surrealist art." She went on to state that "Salvador Dali, André Breton and Antonin Artaud would all be proud of my royal pathology" (e.g., see Artaud, 1958; Breton, 1972). If I was interpreting her words accurately it appeared as if *Dr. Vangella was getting a bit narcissistic about her narcissistic personality disorder*. That was a first.

No consultations with other employees were pursued following the Vangella diagnosis. The subtleties of this case initially necessitated that the focus would be on Dr. Vangella and secondly on the Beach Harbor institution and workforce. Dr. Vangella was protected by the Americans with Disabilities Act, although I wondered whether the act encompasses "Surrealist Parisian Artists with Disabilities." Dr. Vangella opted not to be officially accommodated or identified in the workplace despite the fact that her diagnosed personality disorder qualified her for specialized treatment. After four months of consultations and therapy combined with a successful program of medication, Dr. V. began to tone down and temper her arrogance and self-indulgent behavior to the point where she became sufficiently affable and tolerable in the workplace. She deescalated her toxicity from a high to a moderate level. Consultations were continued, one to two times per week, for a period of eleven months.

Dr. Vangella became a bit more self-mocking, playful and humorous about her narcissistic passions. She even made a few friends at Beach Harbor. No colleagues or staff filed formal complaints against her. Following several successful communication sessions between Dr. Vangella and concerned colleagues, the informal grievances were all withdrawn. *There have been no further reports of failed mitral valve surgeries for the past three years*. I wondered whether the undetected narcissistic personality disorder had in fact been the dysfunctional force resulting in the failed surgeries. I never said that. To date, two malpractice suits have been filed against the hospital and Dr. Vangella. Both suits were settled out of court. The word is out that a third suit may be coming shortly.

LEADER AND COMPANY-WIDE NARCISSISM

This case study provides a strategic sampling of a professional suffering from a personality disorder and its implications for coworkers and organizations. I utilized a systemic organizational analysis of dysfunctional behavior and toxic leadership, and proceeded with management consulting, leadership coaching, and psychotherapy. The psychotherapeutic intervention with Dr. Vangella involved structured clinical interviews and usage of the DSM-IV-TR as the primary tools for assessment of the pathology and its impact on the workforce. These tools were critical to the assessment. The seriousness of the toxic leadership condition presented required assessment tools and interventions typically falling outside the expertise of management and HR professionals. Unable to adequately assess the problem internally, Beach Harbor Heart Institute turned to me as the external agent functioning as consultant, coach and therapist.

The Vangella case exemplifies a "pre-existing" pathology that was imported by the surgeon into her organization. The toxic behavior was not a direct result of organizational influences. This does not discount, however, a myriad of stressors or workplace factors that may have accelerated Dr. Vangella's symptoms. Providing treatment for a leader with narcissistic personality disorder does not negate a broader "company on the couch" investigation of possible company-wide narcissism worthy of further assessment and intervention.

The diagnostic manual used in this case, the DSM-IV-TR, is obviously not a manual to be pulled off the shelf by the average supervisor, HR manager, leadership researcher or management consultant as it requires deep clinical training. However, I contend that trained or not, it is important to acknowledge the promise that psychological and psychiatric assessment tools hold for companies who are experiencing havoc due to deeply troubled leaders.

LEADERS WITH MENTAL AND EMOTIONAL DURESS

As illustrated in the Dr. Vangella case, organizations may encounter leaders who are experiencing serious mental and emotional duress. Dr. Vangella was able to maintain her leadership role and be quite productive up until the point where the mental, emotional and interpersonal dimensions of her personality disorder became detrimental and prohibitive – most likely a nexus in the three failed surgeries and the subsequent grievances and medical malpractice suits. Once diagnosed, Dr. Vangella, similar to the majority of leaders I have worked with, required extensive outpatient care. It is well documented that narcissists can be extraordinarily productive as leaders in the workplace (Kets de Vries & Miller, 1984a,b; Maccoby, 2003). Future research may pursue whether leaders suffering from narcissistic personality disorder can bring added value to their organizations.

Since it only takes one sick leader to bring down an organization it is critical that companies consider their readiness to deal with the inevitable. An inability to deal with toxic leaders can be highly detrimental to the organizational system. In a volatile workplace already embroiled in bullying, aggression, violence, and what has recently been identified as organizational terrorism it is mandatory that we maintain the psychological and emotional well-being of our leaders (Van Fleet & Van Fleet, 2006). Surely, undiagnosed or misdiagnosed pathologies in our leaders are precursors to ever-escalating organizational dysfunction. Just one failure to timely assess may yield dramatic interpersonal and systemic repercussions including sabotage, plunging motivation and productivity, increased turnover, and a high incidence of internal grievances, formal complaints and litigation.

Leader sabotage and the dysfunctional organization: the fish rots from the head down

> Destructive interaction, in which individuals move either toward
> self-destruction or towards breaking down the system in which they
> participate, may be due to ... incomplete information about the self, the
> other person, or the system ... in special cases, the self-destruction of
> the smaller entity is instrumental to the survival of the larger system ...
> For such delineation an observer is necessary.
>
> (Ruesch & Bateson, 1968, pp. 288–289).

ERATIC AND DEFIANT CEO BEHAVIOR

Leadership sets the tone and the agenda. Erratic, defiant and reckless behavior of a CEO or vice president reverberates throughout organizational culture (e.g., see Kellerman, 2004). Sterling, exemplary decision making from the top emanates throughout the organizational chart (e.g., see Cameron & Lavine, 2006; Whetten & Cameron, 2007), but the hubris, flippant and condescending demagoguery of a corporate or political president metastasizes at every level of company existence (Gabriel, 1991, 1999; Kets de Vries and Associates, 1991; Kets de Vries & Miller, 1984a,b; Levinson, 1976).

Inundated with variables and overwhelmed by stimuli it can be quite challenging for the external consultant to make serious sense out of the misbehavior, misconstruals and misrepresentation of leadership. When the corporate client and the mouth of leadership mislead, problem solving becomes increasingly complex.

FAILURES OF A DEEPLY TOXIC CULTURE

A staggering 100 percent failure rate in Black Valley's recruitment and hiring (thirty-two hires and thirty-two failures over a sixteen-month period) signaled a looming crisis in human resources. Black Valley leadership was so alarmed by its dreadful HR track record that it

retained the Zenton Group, external recruitment and selection specialists. Unexpectedly, the Zenton consultants were soon to be side-
tracked and engrossed in what was increasingly identified as a
"deeply toxic Black Valley culture." The Zenton group faltered and
floundered. Following the disappointing relationship with Zenton, the
company found itself further mired in a "selection failure and breakdown." In an attempt to unravel its difficulties Black Valley Inc.
retained Goldman & Associates to rapid-cycle some short-term, incremental turnarounds and results in hiring and selection. All fingers
pointed toward the entry portals. Black Valley had become quite cynical about any hires. Managers assumed that the further entry of new
employees into the corporate family was doomed to failure and they
portrayed hiring and selection as a "diseased process."

UPPER-ECHELON SABOTAGE

At the time of its contract with Goldman & Associates Black Valley
was unable to diagnose and anticipate the many faces of toxicity
impacting its selection process and day-to-day operations. Moreover,
leadership struggled with objective reality and had difficulties distinguishing between the truth as opposed to manufactured narratives.
In Black Valley, the client organization was consumed in destructive
patterns of behavior, but leadership was extremely "selective about
what it was willing to hear." According to an unnamed source in
HR, Black Valley leadership expected "a false but confirming mantra
of illusions and fantasy." Denial and resistance from the President,
Dr. Hudson Blackman, and his closest ally, the unflinching and 100
percent loyal VP Sidney Graystone, was a daunting and difficult challenge for the consultants. Lacking a fully functional and empowered
human resources department and devoid of any employee assistance
program, Black Valley leadership was deeply vested in protecting
and defending its dysfunctional behavior and collective misrepresen-
tations of toxic processes and operations. Another unnamed manager
in HR offered that there was upper-echelon sabotage.

> The fantasy factory at the top of this organization is untouchable; it is the source of all Black Valley holy commandments and legitimized lunacy ... no rules apply to CEO Blackman or Vice President Graystone ... their sick example poisons all of our corporate clones and buries common sense in broad daylight ... they are corporate clowns ... playboys who fantasize that they are actors and talent scouts ... it's too weird to even try to convey ... they think they're Gable and Flynn ... go figure ...

In the struggle for a workable reality, leadership reluctantly turned to external management consultants for remedies befitting a patient. Yet even as the patient sought diagnosis and treatment it was stubbornly predisposed to reject any data that reflected negatively upon its own spin on leadership.

The consultants pondered the dilemma. Abrupt, arational and radically impulsive behavior all pointed towards an organization stricken by psychological issues and clandestine agendas. How could this be approached and handled? How can destructive patterns of behavior emanating from leadership be identified, arrested and transitioned toward a more functional company existence? How can the organizational disease level be sufficiently lowered to provide glimpses of a functional normalcy and the promise of corporate and individual wellness? Or are some companies doomed to follow in the footsteps of disturbed leadership and at best struggle to escape from a despotic and irrational grip?

SKEWED CASE HISTORY

Black Valley Enterprises Inc. was founded in 1994 by its CEO and President, Dr. Harlin "Hudson" Blackman. Blackman's vision was to provide the immediate metropolitan area with upscale luxury apartment homes – something the market was currently lacking. The first property bought was a 114-unit community located in the prestigious Zanemore Estates zipcode. It was renovated, managed and then sold for a record price per door in 2006 – narrowly avoiding the mortgage and real estate collapse. Following this highly successful transaction, Mr. Blackman decided that he would reconceptualize and limit his operations to the designing, building and marketing of upscale properties, $1.5 million and up. This marked a departure from the earlier focus on buying, renovating and reselling pre-existing apartment-homes complexes of 200-plus units per parcel.

This represented a challenge to Dr. Blackman and Black Valley as it was unexplored territory. Dr. Blackman had built a strong team consisting of five partners and five departments: operations, development, construction, architecture, and marketing. These partners brought a compilation of high-level education and broad, diverse marketplace experience – all committed to excellence in a novel and innovative enterprise. Between 2005 and 2006, the company lost two of its partners for undisclosed reasons. The company started to show what Blackstone later described as "toxic signs" that would turn out to be increasingly detrimental to the company culture and objectives.

In 2008 there were a total of five vice presidents, a chief operating officer and a president. Each was hired on the basis of "their own innovative and independent agendas" and all five had an extensive array of ideas of how Black Valley Enterprises could expand and continuously improve. In retrospect, a major problem was that all of the senior managers were moving in different directions and not working toward accomplishing a unified and collaborative vision of Black Valley Enterprises. The turmoil of the multiple visions brought dissention and resulted in two of the vice presidents jumping ship. Overall, the company saw a significant amount of turnover in 2008. Black Valley Enterprises also had to suffer its way through a rising number of employee grievances and escalating distrust among employees and senior managers. This resulted in discrimination and sexual harassment lawsuits and filings with the EEOC.

Currently, there are 417 employees working for Black Valley. Of those, twenty have been there longer than six years, eighty from three to four years, 227 less than three years – the remaining employees have come on board during the last two years. A few of the most common complaints spoken about by employees include:

1. no respect from leadership;
2. far too much turnover – life is very unstable at Black Valley;
3. remaining employees who have escaped the ongoing downsizings are in constant fear of "whether they will be next";
4. Human Resources is not a safe haven for voicing complaints;
5. each employee is treated differently and there are gender-based, sexual orientation and racially motivated decisions constantly made in the workplace despite the fact that anti-discrimination policies are firmly in place to the letter of the law; and
6. there is a constant, ongoing climate of distrust among employees and senior managers.

CONSULTATION WITH VICE PRESIDENT GRAYSTONE

Prompted by mounting grievances, litigation and faltering teams, motivation and production, the vice president, Mr. Sidney Graystone, hoped that Goldman & Associates "could provide insights into Black Valley's pressing selection and hiring issues." During my interviews with Graystone it became quite evident that senior management was fully aware of the prevailing personnel issues within their organization. Curiously, however, they chose to have as little involvement as possible with these issues. Graystone mentioned that he personally believed that top-tier leaders should try to stay away from personnel issues unless it was absolutely unavoidable. In Graystone's view:

> upper-echelon leadership ... good leadership ... must have incredible doses of patience ... enough patience to keep their noses out of people conflicts in the workplace.

In response to questions asked of Graystone regarding how workplace conflict was to be resolved if leadership would not enter in, the VP offered his spin on Black Valley.

What is required? That is incredibly simple. Too simple in this day of theories about leadership and all of that swimming with the sharks stuff ... and all of that seven habits and leadership soundbite junk. What top leadership needs when dealing with the people side of the equation is nothing more or less than patience, patience and more patience ... and then another helping of patience. Eventually you want to wait and see whether the issues resolve themselves. They usually do if you keep your big paws and little brains off of the employees.

In fact, Mr. Graystone was quite demonstrative in his view.

There is a hierarchy in place for a reason. Mid managers, line and staff managers are the ones on the firing line. If senior leadership gets involved they will only succeed in undermining their mid-level managers.

During the course of directing this initial interview toward a needs assessment and differential diagnosis of what was ailing this company, the VP offered that "we have a sick company at present. But our illness is transparent. I diagnosed it some time ago." Surprised, I pressed for an explanation. Graystone offered his analysis.

All of the grievances and litigation threats we're facing lead back to square one ... to genesis. It all leads back to the entry portal ... our hiring process. It is fatally flawed and we are hiring rotten apples, bad eggs and people who are not even a remote fit with our Black Valley culture. It's been abominable. We have to clear this up or this cancer or this corporate AIDS virus will take grip and spread and we'll go down from a sick, sick, sick hiring process!

Before I could begin my battery of questions, Graystone steamrolled further into his diagnosis and prescription for his company. He reflected on two of the employees he had recently hired. One of those employees was hired as the vice president of construction. Graystone boasted that he had hired him in a bar over cocktails. Apparently, they exchanged business cards as strangers and several rounds of drinks later Justin Conner was in charge of all construction operations, A to Z, throughout Black Valley Enterprises Inc.

A second person hired by Graystone was also brought in at a senior management level, specifically as the vice president of property management. Pamela Stewart was hired at the same nightclub as Justin Conner and in the midst of similar late night social circumstances. In the initial assessment session Graystone repeatedly boasted of his "talent scout" powers, asserting that he knew "at first sight" that Stewart was "drop dead gorgeous" and the "one female who would stunningly occupy a leadership slot at Black Valley." Some six months after the barroom hire, Pamela Stewart left Black Valley in the midst of media controversy and conflict. She proceeded to file a sexual harassment grievance against the senior VP of construction, Justin Conner, the gentleman hired by Graystone at the same bar. Conner, VP of construction, is now the target of a "prime time media law suit" involving off color and "blatantly sexist remarks" he allegedly made to Ms. Stewart in front of a number of stunned employees. The verbal abuses were also allegedly accompanied by inappropriate "touchy feely behavior" publicly and physically addressed to Pamela Stewart. Unfortunately, human resources did not play an active role in the handling, negotiation or resolution of these complaints. In my initial interview Graystone repeatedly portrayed his human resource employees as weak.

> Those HR people are paper pushers. They are weak and ineffective. They don't know crisis management. They certainly can't handle people issues involving our employees at Black Valley. They are incompetent and incredibly stupid. Can you imagine thirty-two hires over about a year and a half and we didn't retain a single one of those people? Isn't that staggering? Embarrassing? Zero retention? Am I dreaming? Dr. Blackman implored me to call up "Ripley's Believe It or Not." I wanted to call up "Twilight Zone" or "Outer Limits." But my CEO didn't want me to breathe a word of it to the

> *Wall Street Journal.* That would be too embarrassing for us within the business community ... that we have an HR department that needs to be leveled and eliminated ... stupid and incompetent beyond belief!!

Vice president Graystone was particularly striking and memorable in his flamboyant and extremely emotional outbursts on behalf of the absentee Dr. Blackman and himself. Whenever Graystone felt the passion, and that affliction came quite frequently, the Black Valley consensus was that the vice president was melodramatic, full of himself and bordering on a preacher with a life-threatening message. In this case the sheer outrage of the HR failures ignited Graystone and reverberated throughout the organization. I took private note that when wearing my counseling psychology hat and referring to the diagnostic manual for evaluation of psychopathology I would have been seriously inclined to have considered VP Graystone as a possible candidate for a histrionic personality disorder (American Psychiatric Association, 2000).

NO EMPLOYEE ASSISTANCE PROGRAM

Further questioning targeted the behavior of human resources and an elaboration on the department and its leadership. In the process of the needs assessment and overall discovery process I learned that there was no EAP in place at Black Valley and that there had never been a functioning EAP either on or off site. Offering that the establishment of an EAP could be valuable, I reasoned that counselors and specialists might in fact serve as internal coaches and consultants and possibly bridge some of the gap between the HR department and employees, ultimately providing assessment and intervention en route to addressing the insidious spread of grievances and looming litigation. In response, Graystone appeared very agitated, annoyed and anxious. He exclaimed,

> I've had my experiences with an EAP in the past ... at other companies. I can tell you one thing, doctor, it's that EAPs are

practically worthless. They peddle all of this squishy, touchy feely crap and get all of the employees going with this positive thinking, inner motivation psycho-babble junk. Since Black Valley is a smaller company there is no real need for an EAP. And frankly, doctor, I will do everything in my power to make sure that an EAP is never contracted with. I don't care whether they are on premises or off-site. They are worthless and will make shit worse. They will side with my unfortunate group of lazy, suspicious employees and get the women and minorities all pumped up. As it is, look what happened with that lady VP that I hired, Ms. Pamela Stewart! That has been a disaster. So much for liberation – I find it hard to believe that my boy, Justin Conner, is a sexist. He's just a good ol' construction boy … a young man who uses a little bit of foul language now and then – but if you're in this racket … who doesn't? In any event, concerning that EAP proposal, Dr. Goldman. Thanks but no thanks. Let's not go there. If you do, this meeting is already over, sir. And come to think of it … our consultation would be in serious, serious jeopardy!

The vice president's rant and rave against any talk of a future Black Valley EAP was so pronounced that it bordered on being melodramatic and sounded somewhat threatening and foreboding. Clearly the hostility throughout the company was at times concentrated and centered in leadership as the degree of upper-echelon spewing and negativity could be overwhelming at times. Moreover, there was no talking or reasoning with Mr. Graystone. He was a one-way communicator, a one-way ticket to the Graystone view of reality. All roads into Black Valley came through Graystone. To make matters worse, it became abundantly clear that the actual chances of going face-to-face with Dr. Blackman or bringing him into this consultation were less than nil. Apparently Graystone was the "one and only spokesperson for Mr. Hudson Blackman." The word was that all roads to Blackman had to go through Graystone. Clearly, Graystone protected Blackman, shielding him from trouble, toxicity and the unpleasantries of hostile organizational realities.

A DEFIANT, RESISTANT CLIENT

The initial two-and-a-half-hour interview was essentially Graystone's curtain call. It was a one-way communication and mandate. He delivered an edict that was devoid of any inkling of listening, give and take, or feedback from the vice president. Of particular relevance was the fact that Mr. Graystone had everything figured out ahead of time. Although he found reason to turn to an external consultant after realizing that Human Resources had failed his employees, this did not signify that he was in an exploratory or investigative frame of mind. Far from it. Graystone dictated his diagnosis to the consultant. Moreover, Graystone proudly carried the burden of his disastrous hire of the Zenton recruiting group. Zenton was an expensive collection of consultants briefly retained to provide "sound hires of middle to upper managers – since HR has been incapable of sober decision making." Ironically, the Zenton hire only made hiring and selection matters worse. Black Valley, led by Graystone and Dr. Blackman, impulsively brought Zenton on board. The shotgun decision and short-term relationship turned quite dysfunctional and "drove Black Valley further into a black and toxic hole."

For Graystone, Black Valley's incompetency at hiring and selection was "compounded by Zenton's high class and pricey services." It was a very simple world for the vice president. Black Valley had a sorry interviewing process and leadership had mistakenly contracted with a sick group of so-called selection experts. Graystone called in the Zenton doctors and they failed miserably. In the words of Dr. Blackman, Zenton was "guilty of blatant and willful malpractice." Now Black Valley was turning to another doctor to find the medicine and treatment to turn around the hiring debacle. Enter Goldman & Associates. I wondered whether we were working for a grateful client or whether they were jilted, angry and on the rebound from the brazen and deadly one night stand with Zenton.

It was abundantly clear to Vice President Graystone that once the hiring process was healthy, the whole organization would no longer be on a downslide. So through it all, it was now up to

Goldman & Associates to turn it around and get it right. Despite patient and careful prodding that "perhaps a more comprehensive, differential diagnosis was in order," there was no support, whatsoever, from the VP. In fact it triggered another rant and rave,

> Doctor, please, please, please. I have an MBA. I've sat through all of those egg-head organizational behavior, strategy and leadership courses. I know where you professors are coming from. You want these mega consulting jobs that require two-and-a-half years of assessment. And in 2012 or 2015 you'll do me a favor and deliver on my desk a color coded very, very thick report on everything that's right and wrong in my company, A to Z. Thanks, but no thanks, Doctor. And you'll probably bring in at least a half a dozen of your expensive suits to ring up hourly rates for you with the goal of inching toward a six-figure consultation. Believe me, I know the routine. It's like the ancient Greeks or Romans or whatever. You know that Trojan Horse routine? A bunch of your high priced, clueless consultants will climb out of that damn Trojan Horse and you'll run up bills for everything imaginable. I'm Mom and Pop around here. You're probably too young for "Ma and Pa Kettle," but that's Black Valley. Multi-millions on the line but a very small operation. Get small and modest with me and we'll do business ... get small ... get small. Remember Steve Martin? Let's get small!

To state that Graystone was overwhelming is an understatement. Leadership had it all figured out despite the fact that nothing much was working around Black Valley. Somehow in Graystone's twisted way of seeing things he was both the patient and the doctor. His company was sick and he was the internal doctor who put the stethoscope to the organizational patient. But wait. For some reason or other he decided that he could not in fact effectively handle the doctoring of his own company, requiring the services of external experts. So he called in our consulting group to simulate a set of external experts. Go figure. Suffice to say that Graystone blew a lot of smoke. His line of reasoning was beyond enigmatic; it was problematic, contradictory and toxic. When the dust finally settled, there was no question that Graystone was intent on one and only one assessment and only one intervention. A differential diagnosis was out. Graystone required a "human resources is sick" diagnosis and a prescription and intervention honed and targeted for a makeover of recruiting, interviewing and selection of employees. This time around he was looking for retention. He wanted to get to the nexus of the organizational ills.

Graystone epitomized the know-it-all defiant and resistant client. In the terminology of Douglas McGregor (1985), Graystone was an extreme "theory X." In addition, the VP carried this hierarchical, dictatorial manner into the heart and soul of the company and consultation. Did I need to walk away and tell Graystone to "find someone else?" Or was I going to figure out a way to deal with this bully and make inroads toward an intervention? If there was one interpretation that I wholeheartedly shared with Graystone it was his "Trojan Horse" view of traditional consultancies. Curiously, I couldn't agree more. In a subconscious manner this worked on my psyche and appealed to an idealistic streak deep inside. I fully believed that Graystone was not on the cheap but was rather a bright VP with some blind spots as large as the Grand Canyon. But his bright side was laser sharp. Yes, perhaps I could break bread with this loud-mouthed vice president and create a hook up and a line in. Was a genuine dialogue between consultant and client actually possible?

A DEEPER, TOXIC WELLSPRING

Lurking, however, was the fact that a much deeper wellspring of toxicity was undoubtedly underlying many of Black Valley's organizational symptoms. Dysfunction does not spring from the hiring process, alone. I suspected that the thoroughly unavailable and invisible Chairman and President, Dr. Hudson Blackman, was a key player in the widespread toxicity. Clearly, Blackman originally approved of and extended his blessings for the Zenton miscue. Blackman also approved of the "no EAP clause." Moreover, there were issues surrounding the employees' poor views of the human resource department and their reluctance to utilize its services even in the face of bullying in the workplace and a growing incidence of grievances and EEOC complaints. Other concerns pointed toward the distrust between management and employees and the troubling phenomenon of unorthodox and seemingly grossly negligent leadership hires.

But first things first. Perhaps Black Valley was exactly the type of consultancy Goldman & Associates was looking for. It offered a unique opportunity to work with a company headed by leaders practicing extraordinary degrees of denial and resistance and engulfed in fantasy. Black Valley leadership was at times inept when faced with reasonable lines of inquiry and doses of stark organizational reality. As the consultant I was initially afforded precious little opportunity to investigate or proceed with a diagnosis. Any thoughts of a comprehensive needs assessment were out of the question. What was left? It so happened that in the early stages of the Black Valley case I was in the process of communicating and partnering at an upcoming convention with the master of rapid results and the incremental approach to systems consulting. It appeared to me as if a Schaffer-styled approach (e.g., see Schaffer, 2002; Schaffer & Ashkenas, 2005) might be applicable to a client who only wanted the consultant to tackle one restricted dysfunctional area of the organization. I began having serious thoughts of somehow pursuing a consulting relationship with Graystone in the hope of seriously scrutinizing and leading interventions within the hiring process at Black Valley. If I was crystal clear in my objectives it could help me survive an extremely totalitarian styled bully of a client and leader.

NEGOTIATING SMALL WINS: RAPID-CYCLE
CONSULTATION

At the close of the initial consultative interview and "fact-finding mission" with Graystone we agreed to a "five-day incubation period" whereby we would gather our thoughts, work through our impressions of each other and the prospective consultation, and come together for a second meeting on day six. Once upon a time, back in the 1980s, Kets de Vries and Danny Miller likened the investigative work of the consultant to that of the hero of detective fiction, Sherlock Holmes (e.g., see Kets de Vries & Miller, 1984a,b). Yes, it is difficult to deny that the consultant (who is not limited to administering tests and measurements and generating metrics and is rather engaged in the thick process of unraveling dark narratives and destructive behavior) is an investigative detective in the most serious sense of the term. I was seriously intrigued by the Black Valley Enterprises case. Beyond all doubt, there was far more than met the eye. I expected that the whodunnit and unraveling of the extremely toxic patterns would reveal a few surprises and professional lessons.

Infused with the vision of a detective and the quests of a psychoanalyst anthropologist on in-depth missions (e.g., see Armstrong, 2005; Hirschhorn, 1988), I entered into a second meeting with Mr. Graystone. During the incubation period I emailed the VP offering that "perhaps Mr. Blackman would like to join us as there will undoubtedly be issues coming up of direct concern to him." I received a rapid-fire response within approximately three minutes:

> Mr. Blackman cordially declines. I will see you at our meeting. Rest assured that the Black Valley Enterprises Chairman will be apprised of all relevant matters pertaining to our upcoming conference ...

The response was not unexpected but I was specifically concerned with securing documentation establishing an electronic trail of the missing-in-action Chairman. It was not yet appropriate to assign any specific interpretation to this behavior, only a tally of behaviors to be revisited at a later point in the relationship.

At the onset of the second meeting I surprised Graystone by immediately agreeing to the limited scope of the consultation whereby I would "concentrate 101 percent of my efforts on the hiring process at Black Valley Enterprises." This made him curious when I offered that:

> there are a vast array of approaches to consulting and coaching and in the case of Black Valley I see the sense in initially limiting our scope and gathering our first victory ... Rapid results are in order!

In fact, I was speaking to my belief in, and experience with, the incremental consulting practices expounded upon by Schaffer in his high-impact approach (2002). It seemed particularly fitting at Black Valley to stop the bleeding by creating some rapid results through a narrow and highly focused intervention. A few small wins were in order.

POINT/COUNTERPOINT: INCREMENTAL AND SYSTEMS VIEWS

Graystone took the bait and immediately requested "clarification of what is meant by the phrase 'initially limiting our scope?'" Although a bit testy, I was very pleased with the first genuine semblance of dialogue. It was a vast improvement over the one-sided monologue and dictatorial assessment by the VP of what was wrong with his company – to the exclusion of any words edgewise. I pointedly replied to Graystone:

> I am deeply committed to small wins and rapid results. I would like to set a framework of 100 short days – say a week beyond three months – in order to reach a significant turnaround in the Black Valley hiring process. Once this is achieved and quantified I will be ready to tackle project number two ...

Once again, Graystone was perplexed. He was noticeably pleased with the 100-day rapid results pledge but unsettled by the announcement of a second project and the implication of more projects down the line.

> One hundred days is excellent. It is music to my ears if you turn that dysfunctional operation into a viable, normally functioning unit able to hire sane people who are sober, qualified and a cultural fit for our organization. But you got me bewildered on this numbering of projects and the implication of more to come? What in the world are you referring to?

I welcomed the chance to attempt to voice in plain language the rapid results approach that I recently incorporated into my management consulting and coaching repertoire – with no small thanks due to the seminal voice for "high impact" and "incremental consulting," Robert Schaffer of Schaffer & Associates.

> Let me put it this way. We still have to see the success that I am pledging you with the hiring process. If you see major results in a 100-day rapid-cycled project I can promise you more. For example, a complete healing of the hiring process and the removal of disease from your entry portals. But this will still not fully rid your company of what ails it. There are deeper sources of toxicity in your midst. Even the hiring process will most likely entail some examination of the earlier Zenton consultation and players in other parts of the company who take marching orders and follow a *toxic hiring protocol*. I will successfully revamp your hiring process. Ad hoc hires will most likely be a thing of the past ... But suffice to say ... once we have our first success it should become abundantly clear that we have more work to do to detoxify your company ... but I'm more than happy to let that unfold ...

> Graystone appeared to have a revelation. His face lit up.

> I get it. You are working with me on first fixing the basic, smaller problems. Let's say you are the doctor and you find that the disease began with the ineptness of our own people doing our own hiring. How could we screw this up so royally, so completely? You come in with your social science stethoscope and diagnose, give us the medicine and we get healthier. But you further diagnose and discover that we are still even sicker? Our illness extends above and beyond the hiring process. You know, Goldman, in disguise you are still playing the systemic, companywide consultation game with me. Aren't you? You'll be looking under rocks? You'll wind up shrinking my head and snooping around Dr. Blackman's world. You got me worried, good man. Sooner or later you'll put me under the interrogation lights to answer for me hiring that idiot VP in a night club under the influence? Am I right? You won't even stop there. You'll drill me on the Zenton contract, won't you?

In response to Graystone's speech and insights I gave it to him straight.

> Yes. You are on target. The doctor does do a differential diagnosis. There is no other way. I see illness in a number of possible areas at Black Valley. But the most immediate and urgent is your hiring process. I'll start there. And we will be successful. But we will have to proceed further and conduct a 360 degree differential diagnosis. I am afraid that cleaning up the virus in hiring points me in several directions and does not completely eradicate the toxicity. Yes, you are right. But let's get the lowest hanging fruit, our most obvious area for organizational pain, fully assessed and treated.

A dialogue along these lines proceeded for approximately an hour or more. At the core it was a basic philosophy of science debate. In the final analysis Graystone was very much on board with a systems analysis and his reasoning skills quickly grasped that an incremental, rapid results approach to smaller projects could definitely be viewed as small wins along a path toward treating toxicity throughout Black Valley Enterprises. Consistent with this blend of an incremental and systemic approach to the consultancy Graystone and his attorney proposed a contractual arrangement that reflected this step-by-step process predicated on small wins and incremental successes. The contractual agreement mandated a third session prior to formal commencement of the consultation. We reached a cordial understanding. But still no Chairman Blackman. He was nowhere in sight.

BLACK VALLEY CONSULTATION, ASSESSMENT

Human resources operated in its own constellation. Entering Black Valley HR was akin to admission to a culture within a culture. HR was peculiar. I began with field observations, dialogues with key HR officials, examination of audio and video taped interviews and a comprehensive review of HR documents and decision making for the past three years. The HR track record was not good. Strikingly, the last thirty-two employees hired over a period of seventeen months resulted in 0 percent retention! Thirty-two out of thirty-two new staff, sales and entry-level employees were fired, downsized, quit or requested and received a transfer to Black Valley's North Country location in Boise, Idaho. This abysmal statistic served as a genuine threat to HR as well as to leadership. It had led to the disastrous contract with Zenton, with the embarrassing external hiring and selection experts who were bona fide idiots. The dark data reverberated throughout Black Valley and signified an atrocious hiring and retention process, questions of serious organizational instability and an urgent need to address these weaknesses – the sooner the better. How was it possible that thirty-two strategic decisions went 100 percent awry? Surely these failures were indicative of a toxic recruiting, interviewing and hiring process. How could this not be the case in the face of such lopsided metrics?

Black Valley had not fared much better in its recruitment, interviewing and hiring of upper level management. Hoping to bring stellar individuals on board, HR and leadership placed much hope in choosing and grooming the next generation of upper-echelon leaders. Research revealed that the Chairman himself, Dr. Hudson Blackman (Doctorate in Business), had extremely low regard for his HR personnel and with the blessings of his VP, Graystone, they decided to take high-level decisions out of the hands of HR and outsource top hires to Zenton, the external executive recruitment firm. HR leadership felt humiliated but could neither gain the ear nor confidence of Blackman or Graystone. Both leaders were 101 percent closed and opposed to considering HR as credible or capable of engagement in executive hires. To a large degree this was due to the fact that HR had already managed to overwhelmingly establish just how dysfunctional they were, based upon their recent 100 percent failure rate for low-level, staff, administrative and entry hires. Quite simply, the recruitment, interviewing and hiring processes fell upon hard times as turbulence and turnover were constants. This destructive statistic and trend was further compounded and magnified by upper-echelon management's blatant disregard for hiring protocol, jurisdiction and procedure. As indicated, Graystone's infamous ad hoc, barroom hires of two soon-to-be-failed vice presidents bypassed both his own HR department and the parameters of the contract with the external executive recruiters, Zenton. Particularly problematic was the fact the hires occurred at a local nightclub under less than optimum interviewing and hiring conditions – resulting in an ongoing sea of gossip further undermining leadership, calling attention to a dysfunctional hiring process and fueling organizational toxicity.

DYSFUNCTIONAL "ZENTON" CONSULTATION

The distrust and lack of leadership's trust in HR had led to the initial contracting with and empowerment of the Zenton Consulting Group. Raphael Zenton, president of the recruitment consultants, could not find his way through the maze of the convoluted Black Valley culture. At a later date, both Dr. Blackman and VP Sidney Graystone revealed that they made the decision to hire Zenton in approximately fifteen seconds. Precious little if any research and checking in the construction community preceded their hire. It was in essence a "shotgun wedding" between corporate client and consultants. As the consultant who later followed the Zenton–Black Valley debacle (Goldman & Associates) I was both mildly shocked and profoundly amused to discern that the interviewing and selection of their recruitment specialists closely mirrored the same toxic pattern that the company professed to be seeking relief from! *In the process of weeding through the riff raff and identifying the barroom styled "pickup" or "hookup" with employees I found a similar "scotch on the rocks" hire of the Zenton Group at an airport lounge – courtesy of Dr. Blackman and Vice President Graystone!*

I discovered that Dr. Blackman and VP Graystone were not one bit amused when their "pickup behavior" and poor judgment was presented to them. They were intent upon the "bad guy" behavior being outside themselves – pointing anywhere other than at their own actions and decision making. In fact, they refused to participate and implored me to "put together a complete package" and let them know "how their company was sick, the prescription, medicine and recovery needed." It was all unclear at the time of our entry as to whether the CEO and VP were still playing the blame game and gunning for the Zenton Group. Hopefully Black Valley leadership had matured and they were looking for an overall shakeup and deep structure cleansing? In the process of unloading his second assault on a consulting group, Blackman set an authoritarian and agitated tone as he shifted into his favorite theory X posturing and challenged me – as I occupied dual roles of potential savior and demonic force. Which would it be? Could an outside consultant manage to successfully probe and accurately read this incestuous, raucous construction culture? Without an accurate needs assessment Goldman & Associates would be destined to join the Zenton Group as collaborators in the empowerment of Black Valley's imploding toxicity.

SURPRISE ME WITH SUCCESS

CEO Blackman fired away at me after addressing his disdain and disgust for the Zenton Group and his utter disappointment in what he termed "all of my incompetent, dilly dallying, latte drinking dilettantes who are masterful with inane existential and philosophical conversation – certainly not in serious work." Blackman unloaded his objectives.

> Surprise me with success. You're the doctor. I'm the patient. The whole of Black Valley is your patient. Do your mumbo jumbo diagnosis. Put your stethoscope to us. Tell me what's ticking and not ticking inside us. But whatever you do doctor, and please listen ever so carefully while you're on our payroll ... do not, and I repeat ... do not involve me, VP Graystone or any Black Valley leaders or employees in any chit chat before you have done your crazy investigation and diagnosis of HR. Do your thing. Do not engage us in mid stream unless it is part of diagnosis of corporate illness ... I demand a complete HR package from you to me. Is that clear, Doctor? What part of this are we not connecting on? ...

We proceeded with a honed and chiseled investigation into Black Valley's overall mismanagement of the recruitment and interviewing process including the dysfunctional Zenton consultation. The Goldman team carefully accessed the day-to-day workings of HR specifically as it pertained to the most recent hires of new employees. Careful observation and questioning of leaders and employees within HR and throughout the company yielded both day-to-day infractions and aberrations as well as further context for the alarming metrics of the recent past. Sorting through numerous narratives we found that "the fish rots from the head down" in the sense that the toxic behavior displayed by VP Graystone appeared to be mirrored and duplicated on a daily basis in the official channels of HR practices. Not surprisingly, there was much in common across the rich and textured descriptions of life at Black Valley as dysfunctional behavior appeared to be the norm in the recruitment and hiring of professionals. Within several weeks of the onset of our assessment we discovered pronounced and ongoing patterns of HR misbehavior in progress. Throughout the recruitment and hiring process, there appeared to be a reluctance to access a full range of recruitment venues and a lack of innovation in attempting to locate potential interviewees. Investigation yielded troublesome patterns strategically deleting any 360 degree attempts at tapping into comprehensive sources for candidates in favor of incestuous gamesmanship, cronyism and organizational inbreeding. At best, human resources' interviewing process was uneven, highly ad hoc and lacking in consistency. Pointedly speaking, disturbing patterns of unevenness and favoritism emerged in interviewer responses to and preferences for certain "types" of candidates. Had Vice President Graystone and President Blackman set an agenda for toxic practices in HR?

TOXIC NEXUS IN LEADERSHIP

The consultants unveiled what they had suspected and what CEO Blackman and Vice President Graystone did not want to hear. The destructive center of dysfunctional hiring practices pointed back toward the top. The idiosyncratic and turbulent decision making could be ultimately traced back to the example set by Dr. Blackman and reiterated by Vice President Graystone. Blackman and Graystone both featured themselves to be impromptu, emphatic and impulsive leaders who were among the very few capable of making major decisions and corporate hires while under the influence at a nightclub. Close analysis of 360 degree evaluations for a three years period (administered twice) of both Blackman and Graystone unveiled fairly consistent and similar patterns of feedback from colleagues and employees emphasizing ego, hubris, impulsiveness, erratic decision making, uneven policy making, lack of involvement in daily operations of the business, and an overall "Disney World" and "screenwriter" approach to how the dual leaders ran the organization. Two unnamed vice presidents (six in total) individually stated during the discovery and assessments that "Graystone lived in a magical, turbulent, dream world where he is the movie director and we are all bit players ..." And the second offered that "both Blackman and Graystone are one of a kind ... they confuse their fantasy of the company with the reality of the company ... this is our life, it's not an extension of their egos or dream worlds ..."

This psychological terrain of the subconscious and dream worlds of the leaders continued to surface even in interviews with Blackman and Graystone. Graystone in particular was more than open and was rather bold in his belief that:

> Black Valley goes as Graystone and Blackman go. If we left this company on its own it would be swallowed up by competitors and fall flat on its face. It's my dreams and my visions and the making of a fantasy into a reality that gives us gusto. I dream and conjure up a better company and I do something about it. My venue might be my executive suite or a strip club, a barroom or a golf course – this upsets small minds. But I'm a big dreamer and Dr. Blackman backs me 101 percent.

Faced with this subjective data there was no way to limit the consultation to the fiscal HR facts, the collection of objective data or a purely metric driven approach to interventions.

Once faced with this darker side of leadership I was reminded of the influence of psychodynamic, psychoanalytic and Tavistock-influenced bodies of research and consulting work. Surely, the psychological forces at work in Black Valley were inseparable from the failures of the human service department's track record at hires, leadership's impulsive and disastrous arrangement with the Zenton Consulting Group, and the sham hires in a barroom fueled by hubris and a lack of any tangible evidence of embarrassment or remorse.

BEYOND HUBRIS AND LEADERSHIP FANTASIES

Unfortunately, the dual leaders did not acknowledge that an organization is "not the external dramatization of our wishes and whims. On the contrary, it possesses a resilience and recalcitrance that will mock the dreamer..." (Schwartz, 1990, p. 90). It is rather the case that organizations can only sustain so much imposition from the fantasy world "before disaster becomes inevitable" (Schwartz, 1990, p. 90). Bringing to mind the group think of NASA, Graystone & Blackman paved the way for ad hoc, collective, company-wide off-the-cuff recruitment, interviewing and hires and they were not about to be questioned surrounding their own impulsivity and erratic decision making without regard to the detrimental outcomes for the company-at-large. It became apparent when we gingerly questioned Graystone and Blackman on their barroom hiring techniques that they firmly warned that any "second guessing of upper-echelon leadership might very well result in instant dismissal of our consulting group." The visceral rejection or indictment of any "false move" by the consultants was in no uncertain terms proclaimed by leadership. They were quite graphic regarding what was "taboo and deeply unacceptable." Light bulbs went off as the consultants increasingly realized that Black Valley leadership behavior pointed toward what Schwartz identified as the "great temptation toward rejecting any who do not conform to the story ... in this way, organizational power becomes enlisted in the process of fantasy ..." (Schwartz, 1990, p. 90).

Goldman & Associates found it no simple matter to communicate the fact that the multiple systemic flaws in the Black Valley Enterprises hiring and selection process did in fact house a toxic nexus in top-tier leadership. Graystone and Blackman were heavily invested in a storyline that pitched toxicity as being neatly centered within the human resources division. HR, of course, was the convenient scapegoat. Heaven forbid that leadership consider that it was they, themselves, who instigated the very organizational disease that they had hired outside consultants to diagnose and treat!

RAPID INTERVENTIONS: SIX–TEN HIRES OVER A THREE-MONTH PERIOD

Lest we forget the original objective of this consultation and get swept away in the drama and complexities of a differential systems diagnosis, the goal agreed upon was that of launching a rapid intervention to turn around the dreadful trend in employee selection. Already equipped with knowledge of possible psychopathology emanating from leadership and the ongoing debacles of human resources, the assessment and intervention could not proceed with all organizational processes and players "as is." The consultation involved HR *and* leadership.

There were three dimensions to the rapid results consultation proposal placed on the table by Goldman & Associates.

Phase One required that all dimensions of the recruitment and selection process had to follow precise protocol and be centralized in HR, with lines of communication and feedback preestablished for Blackman, Graystone, additional top leaders, the consultants and other players all identified in the articulation. Central to this first phase was the caveat that there were to be no ad hoc, impromptu or executive-level "surprises or improvised hires." This centralization of the process and official mandating that there were to be no off-site or ad hoc hires raised the ire of both Graystone and Blackman. Negotiations initially went poorly, but after early bullying and threats of terminating the consultancy and "aborting the contractual agreement" the two leaders reluctantly agreed. Their final affirmatives were based more on "giving the consultants a chance" rather than any public agreement with the assessment that ad hoc hires in barroom venues were dysfunctional or could have any widespread toxic affects.

Phase Two required that HR, leadership and the consultants would partner in the recruitment and selection process for an initial period of 100 days following an agreed-upon template of interview techniques and behaviors. There was full participation in the determination of the template for the process although the consultants contributed approximately 75% of the material finally agreed upon. Full participation at all meetings was mandated for leadership, illustrating a breaking of the former trend of little or no input from Blackman and Graystone. It was fully agreed that all parties were responsible for the process, with the consultants taking the initial brunt of the responsibility as a temporary measure during the launch of the prototype. Moreover, phase two also established recruitment venues previously unexplored and untapped. During the agreed 100-day period the selection and interviewing team were to attend one professional HR conference with a "hiring and selection" theme, attend to a newly developed recruiting website, and work on honing and chiseling their prospects for recruiting the best people in the field.

Phase Three established that in a departure from the past, a goal of six and only six hires was to be achieved during the 100-day period. These were to be the result of an extremely rigorous process involving three sets of interviews (rather than a single interview as in the past) and the need for an all-inclusive decision-making process on hires mandating full agreement from Blackman and Graystone. Disagreements and conflicts over candidates would follow principles introduced from the Harvard Negotiation Project, with much effort going into the reaching of complete consensus and a company-wide "getting to yes." The six hires were to be for a 360-day "conditional hiring period." As a means for assessing this process it was agreed that any and all hires successfully surviving the 360-day period would indicate a success for the company and its new recruitment process and moreover point toward confirmation for the consultants. Specifically, although the recruitment and selection process would require a rapid cycle of 100 days for the six hires to be made, the full results would take 360 days. Between days 101 and 360 the consultants would be available for troubleshooting, coaching, assessments and other activities supporting the six hires and maximizing the survival of the organization's choices.

RESULTS

While it is outside the scope of this chapter to get into the many detailed accounts of the process, the rapid results consultation was 100 percent successful and initially represented a complete turnaround from the 100 percent failure of the pre-Goldman & Associates selection process. Two subsequent rounds of hires followed a similar format and the number of employees selected was upped to ten per 100-day period. Out of the twenty new employees hired, including twelve managerial hires, the failure rate was 5 percent with one out of the twenty hires not surviving the 360-day conditional hire period. In this one case a male manager in his early forties was going through a contested child custody battle in the courts as part and parcel of a high-conflict divorce.

Black Valley was extremely pleased with the results, with accolades and testimonials issued by Dr. Blackman and Vice President Graystone. Submerged in this consultation was the effort of the external experts to both invalidate and terminate the ad hoc, impromptu barroom hires of the dual leaders – as these actions had a toxic impact throughout the organization. This was achieved with a delicate behind-the-scenes negotiation process eventually overcoming extreme resistance. *Decorum was deemed critical as there was to be no public loss of face for the leaders.*

COMPLEX PROBING OF PSYCHOPATHOLOGY
IN LEADERSHIP

Dr. Blackman was quite elusive and strategically unavailable during much of the consultation. The gentleman occupying the dual roles of CEO and president of Black Valley Enterprises Inc. appeared to many of his sales and construction employees as quiet and seemingly bordering on passive. Particularly striking was Dr. Blackman's poor attendance at critical meetings, venues and occasions as his pattern of absenteeism served to deflate and confuse subordinates and colleagues. Overall it would not be unfair to state that Dr. Blackman more than Mr. Graystone presented a somewhat enigmatic figure to his company. Follow-up to 360 degree feedback evaluations over recent years yielded such descriptions as "the leader who lurks in the shadows" and the "man in the long black coat." An aura of mystery and suspense followed Dr. Blackman throughout Black Valley. Notable, however, were very occasional outbursts witnessed by what Mr. Graystone referred to as "the privileged few of the Black Valley family." Specifically, I call attention to Blackman's outbursts whereby the mild mannered executive became loud, aggressive, blaming, condescending and outraged at negative news targeted at his person. What immediately comes to mind are Dr. Blackman's own rants and raves directed toward human resources for their 100 percent selection failure in the hires of thirty-two new employees over the original sixteen-month period.

Judging from the poor selection and retention track record it was evident from the early moments of the consultation that much needed to be addressed. There was a dire need for consultant–client dialogue, debate and research surrounding unseen injustice and incivility (e.g., see Cortina *et al.*, 2001), stigma and stigmatization in the company (e.g., see Paetzold, Dipboye & Elsbach, 2008) and organizational corruption (e.g. see Ashforth, Gioia, Robinson & Trevino, 2008; Lang, 2008; Misangyi, Weaver & Elms, 2008; Pfarrer, DeCelles, Smith & Taylor, 2008; Pinto, Leanna & Pil, 2008). The consultants recognized that the injustices, incivility, stigmatization and corruption in the selection process coupled with subsequently outlandish turnover required serious assessment. Goldman & Associates were committed to engaging Blackman, Graystone, HR and Black Valley staff and professionals in candid client disclosure, extensive narratives, organizational therapy and a search for best practices and solutions. Much of this proved to be approachable via the negotiation and scripting approach adapted from the Harvard system (Fisher, Ury & Patton, 1991). The assessment and negotiation provided a blueprint for intervention and hopefully yielded stronger recruitment procedures, a vastly overhauled interviewing agenda and a significant turnaround in selection and retention rates (e.g., see Shaw *et al.*, 2005).

Particularly in the early stages of the consultation, the VP and CEO were slow to warm up to the significant issues placed on the table. Rather than comply with requests for disclosure, Graystone and the "phantom CEO" appeared to be far more concerned with poisoning any rational account of the toxic Black Valley scenario. Before the negotiation agenda was approved, the two leaders attempted to derail the Goldman & Associates assessment by relentlessly returning to past failures. Leadership could only see a dependency gap and could not respond to the prospect of an abundancy gap (Cameron & Lavine, 2006). The dysfunctional organization closely followed suit. Armed with the behind-the-scenes bitterness of his CEO, VP Graystone continuously attacked the previous Zenton consultancy. A serious obstacle entailed overcoming Graystone's extremely agitated response to Goldman & Associates' questioning of "dysfunctional barroom executive hires" by the vice president. *It was later discovered that Dr. Blackman was physically on location with Graystone for both hires and the inebriated leadership duo shared in this debacle.*

The troubling composite of Dr. Blackman's style of leadership began with his elusiveness and lack of availability in the organization for strategic decision making. This was compounded by Blackman's tendency toward passive–aggressive behavior as he assumed a very mild mannered, cultured and passive veneer in his everyday business life, but intermittently housed a highly explosive demeanor. Blackman typically resisted any attempt at asking him to recognize or assume responsibility for toxic behavior in the organization that was in part traceable to his leadership. Everyone else in the organization was to blame except himself for the dysfunctional barroom hires, for his destructive pattern of absenteeism and for the abysmal track record of employee selection prior to the Goldman & Associates consultation. Blame could never be attributed to Dr. Blackman. He was beyond reproach but he was fully capable of going through a somewhat shocking transformation from passive to aggressive and hostile.

Mr. Graystone clearly served as Dr. Blackman's protector and buffer. In fact it appeared as if Graystone had been strategically placed in Black Valley to absorb the majority of the toxicity naturally directed toward the desk of the CEO and vice president. Graystone continuously covered for Blackman, made each and every one of his absences credible and explained away his CEO's avoidance of conflict situations to the point where no one questioned his behavior. For Black Valley employees Dr. Blackman could do no wrong. Thanks to Mr. Graystone.

Mr. Graystone, with the blessing of Dr. Blackman, was at the hub of the upper-echelon sabotage and dysfunctional behavior at Black Valley. Suffice to say that the two barroom hires both overtly and subconsciously sent out the message that hiring and selection was hardly a serious business. *Human resources were happy to comply and became the poster child for inept recruitment – following the lead of the vice president.* Particularly troublesome in dealing with Graystone was an extreme hubris and impulsiveness that he deemed above law and order or metrics. If Graystone wanted to hire a beautiful lady to fill a managerial position in his company, there was no reason in the world why his having consumed five cocktails should impair his judgment! Moreover, with the CEO and President sitting by his side at the barroom table, all was right with the world and their decision making. In a fairly flamboyant display of uncontrolled hubris compounded by an exalted fantasy world that he believed he could will into fruition, Mr. Graystone uncomfortably pointed in the direction of the histrionic personality. But based upon my structured clinical interview he fell one symptom short of a full-blown *histrionic personality disorder.* Yes, this leader demanded attention twenty-four hours a day and reveled in his own impulsive brilliance and funny version of reality.

DOES THE FISH ROT FROM THE HEAD DOWN?

In a word, "yes." Despite the fact that as managers, CEOs, consultants, coaches and professors we have become consumed in complex organizational systems and systemic analysis, the power of leadership is still enormous. In the case of Black Valley we find an organization submerged in a hiring and selection debacle and a collection of employees in constant fear of "who will be next?" Despite the fact that this chapter focused on the use of a short-term, rapid-cycle intervention to turn around a toxic hiring process, the troubles experienced by the company were symptomatic of deeper pathology. The source of the toxicity can be traced back to the two big fish: Dr. Hudson Blackman and Mr. Sidney Graystone.

The biggest fish, Dr. Blackman, was a lethal force to overcome. He never suffered for lack of creative interpretations of the injustices and corruption of the disastrous Black Valley selection and retention debacles. It was unveiled that Blackman fed Graystone the formidable negativity and resistance that initially disrupted and slowed down the consultation. I was perhaps most struck by the vice president's attempt at explaining the injustices perpetuated by leadership with an analogy to "black swans." Drawing ridiculous analogies to Taleb's brilliant book, *The Black Swan* (2007), Graystone used his best CEO doublespeak and sophistry to proclaim that "it was the law of improbability that resulted in some unlucky hires in this insane executive recruiting lottery." I was flabbergasted.

As a management consultant who utilizes and integrates counseling psychology in his work I directed an assessment and intervention that ultimately was intent upon identifying both the visible and the invisible. The consult was designed to provide rapid-cycle treatment as an incremental measure en route to longer-term company-wide interventions, change and development. On the visible and incremental side of the consultancy it was necessary to stop the hiring failures as soon as humanly possible. In contrast, the invisible and systemic dimensions increasingly addressed the deeper-rooted pathologies in leadership and the toxicity largely originating in upper-echelon leaders and diffusing throughout the company. Although the depth of the psychological assessment and the longer-term treatment and leadership coaching of both CEO Dr. Blackman and Vice President Graystone are beyond the scope of this chapter, it is nevertheless fair to state that in the case of Black Valley Enterprises *the fish does indeed rot from the head down.*

5 The obsessive compulsive leader: a manager's mandate for perfection or destruction

Individuals with obsessive compulsive personality disorder (OCPD) attempt to maintain a sense of control through painstaking attention to rules, trivial details, procedures, lists, schedules ... to the extent that the major point of the activity is lost. They are excessively careful and prone to repetition and ... oblivious to the fact that other people tend to become very annoyed at the delays and inconveniences that result from this behavior.

(APA, 2000, p. 725)

TOXICITY SUMMONS

The need to assess and respond to the dysfunctional organizational system and destructive leader becomes particularly pressing when toxicity sets in and threatens workplace stability (e.g., see Goldman, 2006a,b; Hirschhorn, 1988; Kets de Vries, 2006; Kets de Vries & Associates, 1991; Lubit, 2004; Korzybski, 1950; Minuchin, 1974). At Johnstone-Mumford International Bank a change in leadership signaled ensuing turbulence. Upheaval came in the form of an expatriate senior manager, Dr. Raymond Gaston. Abruptly hired from a competitor without a thorough background check, Johnstone-Mumford became increasingly perplexed by the obsessive perfectionism of the new leader. Colleagues and subordinates debated behind closed doors whether his seemingly destructive behavior was deeply embedded in the personality of Dr. Gaston or whether it was more a function of a discombobulated organizational restructuring and a traumatic and failing expatriation.

Fully committed to hiring leaders from within the ranks of their own organizational system, the hiring of Dr. Gaston marked a complete departure from Johnstone-Mumford protocol. Gaston had previously worked for an industry competitor in São Paulo, Brazil, an organization bound to a rigid, old-school and hierarchical approach to management. In sharp contrast, the recently arrived expatriate found himself in an alien environment marked by an extremely horizontal, team-oriented, theory Y management style featuring employee empowerment. Gaston appeared to be both unable and unwilling to adapt to Johnstone-Mumford's longstanding management style – preferring to "correct the shortcomings and inadequacies of an inept bottom-up scenario."

There was no getting-to-know-each-other or honeymoon period for the expatriate leader and workforce – the senior manager steamrolled directly into his leadership role. Behind the scenes Gaston had received the carte blanche blessing of Tom Grimes, as the vice president wanted "all the judgment calls on leadership to be made by my new leader ... there will be no standing in his way." Dr. Gaston immediately imposed his severe brand of theory X styled leadership on the Johnstone-Mumford tellers, officers and staff. As a staunch perfectionist who mandated 100 percent compliance with all of his inflexible rules, Dr. Gaston was met with much resistance and disrespect from employees. Reactions ranging from silent brooding all the way to angry outbursts were not unusual. Swearing and gossip filled the back rooms and corridors, occasionally resulting in abusive verbal displays before customers of the bank. A handful of employees deliberately plotted to undermine client relations and actively connived to sabotage Gaston whenever possible. Hostility and conflict increasingly became the norm during banking hours as a growing minority of employees vocally wreaked havoc with their boss's authority.

All attempts at subordinate communication with Dr. Gaston were to no avail as the newly ordained senior manager of operations belittled and "disallowed negative criticism of a superior." As a result, a stream of complaints eventually inundated human resources. The combination of clandestine, behind the scenes sabotage mixed in with overt verbal conflict reached a crescendo with approximately fifteen employees knocking on the door of the employee assistance program's counselors. The word out in the corridors of Johnstone-Mumford was that "Dr. Gaston was an alien who should pack his bags and head back to São Paulo."

CONSULTATION WITH A STRUGGLING ORGANIZATION

Once upper-echelon leadership was unable to look the other way and operations and customer service became increasingly dysfunctional a decision was made to seek external experts. The VP reluctantly accepted the recommendations of the directors of human resources, and the employee assistance program, and the Goldman Management Consulting Group were retained. By the time the external consultants arrived, Johnstone-Mumford perceived itself as a struggling organization with an ill-fitting and deeply troubled expatriate senior manager. The EAP made it immediately clear to the Goldman Consulting Group that its head counselor had seriously entertained the possibility that "Dr. Gaston was either going through an incredibly stressful time or that he may be suffering from a psychiatric disability." In addition to "making sense out of the overall organizational upheaval" HR and the EAP red flagged the psychological state of Dr. Gaston to the point where they wondered whether it might have been a significant contributing factor in the mutiny, defiance and sabotage spreading through an increasingly toxic workplace. The external consultants promised a differential diagnosis and series of interventions that would in fact take into account organizational policies and strategy as well as the interpersonal relations and the psychological state of Gaston.

On the surface, a warm, congenial, relationship-oriented banking culture had been blindsided when it allowed its highly regarded Ms. Francine Oster to be transferred to the Johnstone-Mumford Amsterdam branch and concurrently welcomed the new Senior Operations Manager from a competitor, Sergio Santos International Bank of São Paulo, Brazil. The "swap" of leaders was perceived of as an overnight changing of the guard as Johnstone-Mumford offered in retrospect that "we had no choice as we had to respond hastily to the urgency of replacing Ms. Oster."

When the consultants arrived, Johnstone-Mumford questioned whether it had sufficiently explored the temperament, personality and psychological characteristics of the new leader. HR was self-conscious and doubtful whether the shotgun interviewing process leading to the overnight replacement for Ms. Oster was a source of the toxicity. HR perceived itself as having been cornered into a severe timeline and deadline for the replacement of Oster. Had HR in fact focused on a skill set and shallow reading of credentials? What was at the core of their future senior manager remained a mystery. The interviewers had made no effort to seriously find out what made Dr. Gaston tick. At the time of his wildly rushed hiring, Dr. Gaston was a complete and utter enigma. As more than a few Fortune 500s have recently discovered, the hire of an enigmatic and mysterious figure into a leadership position carries with it a laundry list of potential perils. Such was the fate of Johnstone-Mumford.

BACKGROUND NARRATIVE: CASE HISTORY OF A UNIQUE BANKING CULTURE

Johnstone-Mumford International Bank with offices in New York, San Francisco, Miami, London, Stockholm, Amsterdam and Brussels took pride in growing into a global organization able to seamlessly cross borders and provide a myriad of financial links between the North American and European business communities. A follower of Six Sigma and dedicated to "top shelf customer service," the Johnstone-Mumford upper echelon promoted a culture of "escalating continental excellence in service of the customer."

Entrenched in Fortune 500 corporate dealings as well as occupying a strategic role in cross-border real estate investment, JM not only "waved the international flags of excellence and quality" but also invested in leaders and employees who were innovators and "forever exercised their right brain creativity." Along these lines there were formal procedures for recognition of the "artistic leader of the month." Somewhat tongue in cheek, leadership wanted to convey to all members of the JM family of banking that there was not only room for artistry – but also outright encouragement and reward for thinking and innovating outside the box. Awards, bonuses, sizeable promotions and skyrocketing annual salaries were not unusual if an employee stepped forward with a new idea able to actively improve any dimension of customer service. Suffice to say that Johnstone-Mumford was able to instill a "culture of caring" to the banking world – in a phrase it was "the artistry of banking." Through all phases of banking operations, JM stressed the artistic and creative as the heart and soul of doing business, fulfilling tasks and operationalizing the daily flow of banking with the verve possible through emotional intelligence (e.g., see Frost, 2003; Goleman, 1995). Accordingly, JM deeply valued the "whole brain" and the emotionally intelligent leader able to infuse a myriad of difficult-to-measure subjective elements into the essence of banking service. It was hardly surprising that the former senior manager of operations, Ms. Oster, epitomized the relationship qualities and priorities prized at JM.

A CHANGING OF THE GUARD AT JOHNSTONE-MUMFORD

The ability to combine a savvy, global approach to banking blended with an empathic, relationship-oriented, customer-centric approach to service increasingly established a unique niche market for Johnstone-Mumford. Central to the establishment of a global family culture was the importance of cross-fertilizing the EC and US branches with the best offerings from selected JM leaders. Specifically, this entailed that upper level managers enter into the JM "expatriation–repatriation" culture required to fully immerse leadership in the operations of a minimum of three branch locations over a lifetime of service. It was expected that leadership would aspire to cross the Atlantic during the course of their career and become fluid in both North American and European dimensions of banking.

In Miami, Florida it was time for the operations manager, Francine Oster, to prepare for her departure and an expatriation to the Amsterdam branch. Although there was a certain degree of consistency of organizational culture on both sides of the Atlantic, there were also national culture issues to be addressed. Ms. Oster received leadership coaching from two experts – one in the substantive operations issues succinct to Dutch and EC banking and a second from a cross-cultural expert committed to socially transitioning her from Miami to Amsterdam.

Concurrently, the Miami bank was on notice and eager to meet its new replacement for the highly esteemed Ms. Oster. Dr. Raymond Gaston (a Ph.D. in Business) most recently held a leadership role at the Sergio Santos International Bank of São Paulo. A native of pre-Castro Havana, Cuba, Dr. Gaston had served in a management role in a major Brazilian banking institution and established himself as "an up and coming force in international banking" in his last four years at Sergio Santos International. Unclear to employees, however, was the behind the scenes story of why Mr. Gaston had elected to leave Sergio Santos and decided to come to Johnstone-Mumford. Was it about salary? Culture? Escaping conflict? Expanding his expertise from the Americas into the European Community? Despite the positive and enthusiastic reception, there was a troublesome undertow.

On the surface, the announcement of the transition from Oster to Gaston appeared to come down fairly smoothly. In typical JM fashion, the organization felt that a significant change in leadership should coincide with the fresh start of a new year. And so it was. The new year was initiated with the introduction of Dr. Raymond Gaston, Senior Manager of Banking Operations at the Miami, Florida branch of Johnstone-Mumford International. Away from the public eye, however, the changing of the guard was not without its doubters and skeptics. A growing number of whispers prevailed and filled the hallways – mostly conjecture as to why corporate had decided to bring a Sergio Santos manager suddenly into the JM family. Wasn't there a JM expatriate available from another branch? Did Gaston, the outsider, receive full expatriate training before his entrance into JM Miami? Why not? An assortment of cynical and sarcastic questions flowed. Responses were promised but did not quite arrive.

NEW LEADERSHIP: NO HONEYMOON, WHATSOEVER
The early days of Dr. Raymond Gaston were testy and troublesome. First word out was that Gaston was hardly touchy feely. He was

substantively a completely different breed than the recently departed Francine Oster. Oster always seemed to have an extra five minutes or an extra hour or two to devote to the human drama and interpersonal dynamics. In contrast, Gaston gave all the early signs that he seemed to be 98 percent about task and the tangibles and perhaps 1 percent or 2 percent at most about the people side of the equation. Tellers, loan officers, financial specialists and professionals throughout the Miami branch increasingly questioned the incoming leader. At "internal customer" and "colleague building" meetings Gaston appeared to have ample measures of intuition, insight and even provided a few glimpses into a reservoir of emotional intelligence and some indicators of warmth of character. But once the banking day was in full swing there was an overwhelming consensus that Dr. Gaston was a "nuts and bolts" leader who wanted to crunch the numbers and had little if any interest in the quality of the interaction between bank officer and customer. For the first time, employees felt that there was a reversal of company values and priorities. People skills appeared to be devalued and trivialized. Were employees seeing accurately or just being over-reactive to change? How could their new leader have missed the core of the Johnstone-Mumford operation – service built around rock solid, customized customer relationships?

INITIAL INTERNAL ASSESSMENT: CULTURE SHOCK

Talk and criticism diffused rapidly throughout the Miami branch. What was up with this new Dr. Gaston? One financial advisor took it upon herself to research Gaston's former employer, Sergio Santos International Bank of the Americas, to see how he had functioned in São Paulo. Johnstone-Mumford asked itself whether it was experiencing an old fashioned dose of culture clash – a battlefield with the culture of Sergio Santos – as exported by Dr. Gaston. On the other hand, employees feared that their obsessive and compulsive perfectionist of a boss was perhaps unstable – mentally and emotionally. It was in fact somewhat reassuring when Julia Smythe (financial advisor) discovered that within the US-based branches of Sergio Santos there was in fact a hard-nosed approach to "minimizing excessive human interaction" and "keeping extraneous communication with customers to a minimum." Apparently, a "time is money" philosophy permeated Sergio Santos. Fully schooled in a predominantly left brain, analytic, task-oriented culture, it became instantly more understandable how Dr. Gaston had reached his state of excessive concern for task and the perception of relationship building as an ensuing threat to productivity. Maybe Gaston had just internalized the Sergio Santos culture and was in fact of sound mind and body.

The word spread surrounding Dr. Gaston's past banking history. Gaston was a stranger in a strange land at Johnstone-Mumford. He came out of a theory X, authoritarian, task-oriented culture and subordinates wondered whether he could even begin to fathom or appreciate the fact that Johnstone-Mumford was the antithesis of Sergio Santos' highly vertical leadership. Both sides (Johnstone-Mumford and Sergio Santos) were experiencing culture shock. Communication had to be the key. Why was Dr. Gaston reluctant to address the relationship side of managing? Was this consistent with the Sergio Santos culture or a reflection and extension of his professional history and personality?

SELF-DISCLOSURE AND BRIEFING

In an effort to talk about the lack of talk and express suppressed feelings that had been rendered obsolete by their new boss, employees in concert with the Director of Human Resources called for a meeting with Dr. Gaston.

Informally called and headed by HR, the topic of the meeting was "The Johnstone-Mumford Corporate Family," an allegedly goodwill-building subject matter that would allow people to speak about the relationship dimensions of the workplace without explicit, high-priority concerns for metrics and productivity.

Gaston was very polite and respectful. He acknowledged many issues pertaining to emotional intelligence while at the same time quietly calling attention to the "numbers and the tangibles that we have to live or die with."

After a number of probes the facts of Gaston's previous position and banking culture (in Brazil) began to unfold. It became clear that Gaston had in fact lived with serious levels of accountability at Sergio Santos – where it was not unusual to micromanage employees to the extent of timing their interactions with customers – face-to-face, over the phone, and via the bank's website and email system. Concise, constrained communication was mandated whereas conversations that exceeded preestablished time limits were viewed as serious infractions "worthy of discipline." Gaston, himself, closely monitored these exchanges and was the "watchdog" for excessive verbiage and "sloppy slush time" allotted to customer transactions.

Although perhaps understandable, the JM employees and managers were a bit taken aback by this information as it represented old-school banking – in stark contrast to their highly conscious relationship-building orientation toward customers.

In response, HR and mid-level managers offered to Gaston that at Johnstone-Mumford they had made a concerted effort to move the organizational culture from the classic "theory X" to a far more "theory Y" orientation. Empowerment of employees was held at a premium and the watchful eye of the micromanaging leader was at least for JM a relic of the past.

The exchange proved to be very amiable and there appeared to be ample reason to believe that Gaston was no stranger to the people-oriented culture of JM but was rather a product and devout proponent of a more classical and authoritarian brand of leadership. No promises were made. Conversation and self-disclosure was the goal and so did it prevail. There were several indications that Gaston could in fact be flexible or more situational than he had shown in his early months. Despite an abundance of skepticism – doubts over Gaston's micromanaging was prevalent among his subordinates – there was a concerted effort to sidestep any loss of face or overt criticism of their new leader or any of the JM players. Suffice to say that discontent with Dr. Gaston was submerged and lurked at times just below the surface niceties.

A FOREWARNING OF TOXICITY

Yes, there were pleasantries, etiquette and social graces. Dr. Raymond Gaston's early months were in fact both perplexing and disarming. The word was out that the new leader was a bean counter, a metrics man and the kind of boss who assessed his tellers and home mortgage experts by the numbers they had generated over the past two weeks. What have you done for me lately? Gaston wanted to see tangible results. In stark contrast to his predecessor, Francine Oster, there was no recognition or appreciation for reaching new heights in customer service. The buzz around the bank was that "Gaston might time you on his stopwatch and see whether you exceeded the one hundred and fifty second limit placed on standard customer interactions." If a first-year teller dared go six or seven minutes on a routine deposit, withdrawal or mortgage payment, Dr. Gaston was apt to put the poor soul on strict probation!

This radical departure and deviation from the longstanding relationship culture under Oster was a growing and constant source of distress. The more generous employees attributed Gaston's sharp, time-conscious, task orientation and subsequent belittlement of the human service dimension as indicative of a "clueless expatriate" and the result of the "importation of a hostile culture into the JM sanctuary." Others were less generous in their interpretation of the outsider leadership of Dr. Gaston. It became commonplace to hear the tellers and officers constantly mutter about the "genuinely mean-spirited leader" and how Gaston "had a black heart." On several occasions high-performing mid-level managers let it be known at a luncheon that "when Oster left we lost our heart, soul and emotions. We are left with an analytical, obsessive robot of a leader." One teller cited Gaston as being "a negative and pessimistic boss who is programmed to mistrust and see us fail." Another teller put her dismay in the form of a written grievance offering that "Dr. Gaston's eyes strip me of my dignity and his facial expressions get me seething. I'm not sure that he's really my leader. He seems more like my adversary and enemy." Also worth mentioning is the fact that a young financial advisor confessed to

HR and the EAP that "Dr. Gaston humiliated me on three occasions in front of all of my peers – just when I was late due to our babysitter and nursery glitches with my babies." She went on to describe how on a particular occasion Gaston announced out loud in front of her co-workers that 'Ms. Morton is six minutes and twenty-two seconds late. But maybe we should rejoice ... she is here ... she did arrive ... bravo!!'"

Little by little, resentment seemed to build. Dr. Gaston's type A personality had come into plain view and there was consensus over this authoritarianism and rigidity. Difficult and inflexible standards continued to surface as the legal tender in the workplace. A growing number of employees were beginning to view Gaston as threatening and predisposed to undermine the best of their efforts and work product. In retrospect I later interpreted these early weeks of Gaston's leadership as the *forewarning of toxicity* and a cancerous state of organizational behavior that increasingly metastasized throughout Johnstone-Mumford. Destructive signals and tendencies continued to appear at all work stations. And in most instances Dr. Gaston was physically present and inseparable from the ensuing organizational toxicity (e.g., see Whicker, 1996).

Growing numbers of employees questioned whether the clash of Gaston's old Sergio Santos culture with the more decentralized workplace of Miami's Johnstone-Mumford bank could actually be the source of the brooding dissatisfaction and frustration. Growing ranks of employees felt that they were in fact dealing with the difficult behavior of a single leader who was an independent agent above and beyond the grip or influence of his former organization. In plain language employees wanted to know – "Is Dr. Gaston a mental case?" The game became one of watching and decoding the unsettling behavior of their leader. No more excuses.

DESTRUCTIVE BEHAVIOR EMERGES ON THE SHOP FLOOR

Although the clash of organizational cultures was a clear and present threat as was evident in the contrast of Sergio Santos and

Johnstone-Mumford, there was far more in play than initially met the collective eye. It wasn't until the ninth month, however, that Mr. Gaston's destructive behavior and toxic influence became overtly and overwhelmingly obvious on the shop floor as well as to the vice president and the upper echelon. The dysfunctional tailspin of the Miami branch could not be separated from the sometimes puzzling but consistently adversarial and annoying behavior of Gaston. Several overt, loud altercations had caught employees, management, customers and security guards by surprise. All three of the hostile verbal exchanges directly involved Raymond Gaston and were characterized by shouting, angry voices, filthy language, physical threats, taunts and attacks on personal character. The entire bank abruptly altered operations on all three occasions as if a robbery or natural disaster had impinged upon the flow of the daily workplace. Employees and customers were dumbfounded.

Consistently micromanaging daily operations and spot checking random transactions, Gaston turned some employees nervous and hostile. Routine matters were all subject to a fine-tooth comb. Trust was a precious commodity and there was little of it to go around. Gaston assumed he was going to find mistakes wherever he looked. His hovering presence seemed to incense tellers and officers to the point that they were losing their rational track and analytic logic was crumbling. Rather than playing a supportive team role Gaston was determined to find fault and tear his employees down. In order to understand the groundswell of discontent and conflict that led to three public altercations, it is necessary to digress a bit farther into what was truly disturbing the workforce.

Gaston required meticulousness in all of the bank's printed and written transactions to the point where it drove his employees to the brink. Let me be specific. Gaston obsessively critiqued documents and forms for any stray marks, cross outs, creases in the paper, folds, changes of ink color on the same document, the mixing of pen and pencil, and a long list of further minutiae. If there was any deviation, whatsoever, from his strict requirements of "absolute, utter perfection," then the entire document had to be discarded and started over again from scratch – regardless of the minutes or hours already spent on the project and the bank's client! The extreme public displays of anxiety and loss of face from some of the bank's officers – in front of customers – did not appear to faze Dr. Gaston, whatsoever. Such trivial customer service concerns were always besides-the-point for this Senior Operations Manager. If perfection was not achieved the transaction was worthless. Inferior documents and other such abominations all had to be deleted despite any human capital or customer service costs.

Hour after hour, day after day and week after week this extreme and incessant micromanagement chipped away at the collective psyche and emotional life of employees. By the ninth month, the month of September, a few employees started to snap. Formal grievances were filed with HR and kicked across town to the employee assistance program. But little satisfaction was achieved. HR and the EAP hesitated, stalled, expressed concern and offered very little resolution or satisfaction. Dr. Gaston was sanctioned and approved by default. The more adventuresome and adversarial employees considered taking justice into their own hands once their appeals to the upper echelon were just shuffled aside. They were looking the other way on Dr. Gaston. The vice president figured that they would get around to enculturating Gaston with some of the right brain, theory Y, empowerment principles in due time. But leadership and subordinates were running on different time clocks – and for the employees the clock was running out on Gaston.

To compound matters, Gaston's excessively type A personality and need to be in utter control were further accelerated by odd recurring behaviors that increasingly took a toll on daily operations. At first it wasn't exactly clear, but with time it became evident that Gaston had a personal and physical aversion toward handling money. Gaston specifically avoided touching paper money or coins and when he had no choice he pulled out a pair of nylon gloves that he always put on before he handled currency. A red flag went up around the office. What was this? One teller spread the word that Gaston was "a freak who suffered from an insane phobia – a banker afraid of touching money? No way!" Moreover, Gaston was extremely defensive and embarrassed about this behavior and the perception of same. When questioned about his avoidance of money Gaston would typically turn hostile, walk away or abruptly change the subject.

In retrospect, the disturbing altercations that arose during September appeared to be inseparable from employees' perceptions of and reactions to Gaston's excessive behavior. Entry level tellers as well as middle managers were upset by a leader who hovered, incessantly criticized subordinates and was prone to shred hours of his officers' paperwork, contracts and documentation due to a perceived minor flaw or irregularity. In the view of one middle manager, Gaston micromanaged employees to the edge. In fact, the publicly destructive displays were passed along to HR who in turn made recommendations to the employee assistance program. Both HR and the EAP were perplexed. After four months of investigation and deliberation the issue was walked into the vice president's office. The consensus that emerged was that an external consulting and coaching group should be retained.

ASSESSING DESTRUCTIVE LEADER BEHAVIOR

The Goldman Management Consulting Group received a call regarding a possible consulting job from the head of Johnstone-Mumford's HR department. Expressing fear of potential violence in the workplace (based upon the three public altercations at the bank during September) she wanted to proceed as rapidly as possible. The following morning I met with the HR and EAP directors who briefed me on several of the grievances filed against Dr. Gaston and described the destructive behavior spreading throughout the bank.

Ms. Charmine Holden expressed broad concerns from her vantage point as HR director. The Johnstone-Mumford workplace had little experience with serious conflict or destructive behavior during the five years that Oster served in the leadership role over banking operations. Holden was quick to offer that there was "at very least comparative negligence on the part of the bank." Apparently, the Amsterdam branch placed an urgent request into Miami for an expatriation transfer of Oster due to a terminal illness faced by their longstanding operations head. Having allegedly spent two summers in Amsterdam with the bank, Ms. Oster was a known entity and constituted a high-level and appropriate request for transfer. Consistent with Johnstone-Mumford's leadership culture it was within reason for Ms. Oster to participate in an expatriation. Francine Oster was completely in favor of the move. In contrast, however, the Miami branch did not have an available expatriate from the JM family to welcome in place of Ms. Oster. After a thorough search for options in San Francisco, Manhattan, London, Stockholm and Brussels there was no alternative other than to recruit from outside. This led to the recruitment of Gaston from Sergio Santos International of São Paulo, Brazil. Gaston was apparently displeased with his managerial position at Sergio Santos and had been on the market in search of another appointment. At the time of the interview he had already given notice and was in his last two weeks with Sergio Santos.

Due to the urgency of the situation for Johnstone-Mumford, there was a helter-skelter quality about the departure of Oster and the hire of Gaston. The comparative negligence referred to by Ms. Holden referred to the fact that Johnstone-Mumford did not have the time to put Gaston through the "family culture training" and hired him without the benefit of adequate briefings and enculturation. At the time of the hire, upper-echelon management and HR agreed that within the first six to eight months they would set up a customized coaching regimen for Gaston – enabling him to learn about JM management style and organizational culture, from A to Z. Unfortunately, an unanticipated crash on Wall Street and dire financial straits due to an economic recession preoccupied top brass and HR, and Gaston was glossed over during his first year. Despite the extreme misfit of Gaston within JM organizational culture, there was no denying that he did bring pedigree in the form of impeccable credentials – graduating from a top five MBA program. Moreover, due to what was later found out to be non-disclosure on the part of his previous employer, Dr. Gaston brought a less than sterling reputation from Sergio Santos. The company had completely failed to mention the serious conflict and destructive behavior that led to his departure.

In retrospect and with much hindsight, HR recognized that it did not sufficiently scrutinize Gaston's past at Sergio Santos. Moreover, there was no denying that little attention was paid during the interviewing to what typically constituted the highest-priority criteria in Johnstone-Mumford hires – the people and relationship skills of the candidate. Looking back, Ms. Holden was quite certain that this was an unfortunate oversight that could not be separated from the destructive behavior in the workplace and the altercations in which Mr. Gaston had been a direct participant.

After conducting two lengthy needs assessment interviews with Ms. Holden, I provided some initial impressions as to what would be required in order to appropriately enter into a consultation. I required introductions to key players in the organization, access to arrange and conduct strategic interviews, an ability to engage in longstanding observations of the workplace, and subsequent question and answer sessions with employees. Of particular interest was the ability to obtain clearance for possible one-on-one leadership coaching and therapy with Dr. Gaston – contingent upon his agreement. All conditions were discussed, negotiated and satisfactorily agreed upon.

INITIAL IMPRESSIONS

In the early weeks of the consultation, there was reason to believe that there was a clash of organizational cultures. Clearly, Johnstone-Mumford had been negligent in preparing their outgoing leader for her transfer to Amsterdam, but not preparing their incoming leader for JM culture in Miami, Florida. Yes, Mr. Gaston was a stranger in a strange land. There certainly was a pronounced clash of banking cultures between Sergio Santos and Johnstone-Mumford. But that was hardly all there was to it.

As an extremely bright, MBA, Dr. Gaston intellectually grasped every nuance of information handed to him about JM culture. He was well read on organizational behavior to the point where I would not have thought twice about asking him to visit my MBA class and talk about contrasts between organizational cultures in South, Central and North American Fortune 500s. Gaston was astute and even professorial in his knowledge. Undoubtedly, he was behaving in a type A, condescending, micromanaging, and obsessive manner for a reason. What was his reason?

I anticipated successful "leadership coaching" sessions with Gaston. He was quite amenable to a personalized approach – contingent upon his request for privileged communication. This was granted after clearance with Ms. Holden.

LEADERSHIP COACHING

Build up your client. Bring dignity to your patient. Emerging from management and psychology traditions I knew that it was paramount for Dr. Gaston to be allowed to save face and be treated with the utmost dignity. Coaching was not about tearing the man down. It was about gathering information, securing data, and obtaining an extensive narrative that included both objective and subjective terrain.

Gaston was resistant for the first three sessions. He almost completely refused to discuss his own behavior and rather chose to speak of his "defective subordinates" and "disappointing colleagues." It was as if he was performing on a stage for an audience. Gaston repeatedly stated that he "refused to back down from excellence" or "make excuses and cower away from perfection." During the fourth session it slipped out that Gaston had suffered through a number of grievances and he was in the early stages of litigation dating back to his time as a leader at his previous organization, Sergio Santos International Bank of the Americas. What emerged as a constant was a repetitive, long-term pattern of behavior. Gaston was not just responding to exigencies in the Johnstone-Mumford workplace or attempting to use strong-armed measures to motivate non-productive employees. His excessively authoritarian, type A style of micromanaging was somehow deeply etched into his personality and past.

By the fifth session there was entrée to begin a line of questioning that dug deeper into the grievances and allegations that had arisen at Johnstone-Mumford and had been part and parcel of the three altercations during the month of September.

What was behind Gaston's public hostility and destructive incidents with subordinates? Dr. Gaston readily admitted and even boasted that he expected "somewhere in the vicinity of 95 percent to 100 percent precision when it came to paperwork and documents compiled by his banking staff and officers." Two out of the three altercations could be traced back to Gaston's finding flaws in the paperwork for mortgage loans. The two bank officials in question had crossed out mistakes, shifted between two ink colors, had a misspelling or two, and both documents were folded and one had a three-inch scotch taped tear along the bottom. Although the documents were legible and complied with regulations in the banking and loan industry, Gaston was livid when he discovered the "third class, embarrassing documentation that is far beneath the dignity of Johnstone-Mumford International!" In both instances Dr. Gaston discovered the documents by peering over the shoulders of his two employees and politely requesting that they relinquish them so that he would be able to do a "spot review" and "impromptu critique" of their work.

Both officers felt demeaned in front of their fellow employees inasmuch as the public reprimands and condemnations expressed by Gaston were uttered in a loud, forceful and condescending voice – sufficient to cause considerable trauma and loss of face.

In both instances Dr. Gaston proceeded to make photocopies of the documents and then defiantly and mockingly shredded them in front of his officers. While both were taken aback by the confrontation and unexpected embarrassment, the second officer became quite outraged, thus leading to a public altercation.

Reflecting on the precursors of the confrontations, I entered into a dialogue with Gaston on the subject of "perfection." After perhaps ten minutes of establishing common ground and validating a need for "certain degrees of precision," I entered into a line of reasoning zeroing in on "precision as a question of degree." Clearly, we both agreed that certain strict standards should and must be followed in the workplace. Generically speaking, for example, the TQM and Six Sigma movements both demanded regularity, meticulous attention to detail and a precision approach to repeatable, standardized quality control. But how were Gaston's demands for perfection different? An aberration? A destructive undermining of his employees with toxic, system-wide implications?

Gaston was quick to recognize – although he stood 101 percent behind his perfectionism – that his expectations were personalized and even idiosyncratic. In other words, Gaston was a one-man, self-anointed quality control movement at Johnstone-Mumford.

While grappling with Gaston's excessive perfectionism we seemed to be stuck on an analytic, left brain level of analysis. The promise of an emotional breakthrough finally appeared in the form of Gaston's cognizance of his responsibility for the pain experienced by his subordinates as a result of his destructive behavior.

FROM EMOTIONAL DENIAL TO EMOTIONAL INTELLIGENCE

Destructive behavior in organizations inevitably contains toxic emotional dimensions (Frost, 2003). Thought and verbiage alone are only part of what breaks down as tempers flare and indignation rises. The whole gamut of human emotional experience is inevitably unleashed even within the contained demeanor and conservative culture of a banking institution. Gaston was faced not only with the emotional life of injured subordinates, but also (and quite reluctantly), with his own inner turmoil and demons. Obsessed with "the perfect form" and unwilling to negotiate, Gaston's rigid, cerebral, left brain center of control dictated that destruction was superior to making allowances for a defective document. But at what emotional cost to self? Subordinates? Colleagues? Institution?

LEADERSHIP THERAPY FOR "PERFECTION OR DESTRUCTION"

As the consultant and coach on site, for three months I gathered data in personal sessions with Gaston as well as through my increasing access to the everyday workplace as a participant observer. My ability to personally observe the workplace-in-action rather than limiting myself to observations of only Gaston or a few others was critical. As an organizational behavior professional I proceeded as an anthropologist and analyst of sorts in the tradition of Armstrong (2005) and Hirschhorn (1988). Committed to the ebb and flow of a field study, I turned into a participant observer in the everyday unfolding of events within the bank: by walking around; listening to classified conversation behind closed doors; gossiping in the hallways; watching astutely on the firing line between employees and customers; immersing myself in bank meetings and at team and decision-making sessions – whenever and wherever Dr. Gaston interacted with colleagues, superiors, subordinates and customers. Over time, elements of Dr. Gaston's personality and leadership style became more transparent through the variety of workplace venues. Moreover, the behavioral patterns of colleagues around Gaston and the people side of the organization unfolded.

In part due to in-house training and the emphasis on "people skills" emanating from HR, the importance of emotional intelligence as well as the emergence of toxic emotions in the workplace (Frost, 2003; Frost & Robinson, 1999; Goleman, 1995) did not go unnoticed by the Johnstone-Mumford corporate community. This sensibility opened doors for assessment and treatment. HR and the EAP had in effect "greased the way" for the fine line between conflict and psychopathology and between coaching and therapy (e.g., see Rowley, 2007). More than anything there was consensus that "something had gone wrong with leadership" and that this coincided with the departure of Oster and the arrival of Gaston. Beyond that, little was said and conjecture levels were high and churning. Any light in the way of an assessment or intervention that a consultant could offer was bound to be met with at least some level of interest and sensitivity.

As a result of my participation in the daily work life of Johnstone-Mumford I enhanced my status and stock value with Dr. Gaston as he became increasingly amenable to coaching. His early resistance gradually subsided and he turned more confessional during sessions. After I had successfully moved the coaching into a more personalized and therapeutic mode, Gaston finally included his inner life and subjectivity into the sessions. Gaston's core was beginning to emerge.

It surfaced that Gaston had similar issues in his past leadership role with Sergio Santos and had been "unable to shut off an incessant demand for the perfect document." In a phrase borrowed from Gaston, he articulated that his policy at both Sergio Santos and Johnstone-Mumford had been one of "perfection or destruction." Not only were Gaston's subordinates victimized by his compulsive and polarized approach to "excellence," Gaston, himself was a casualty of his own making. Unable to modify or temper his demands for perfectionism, Gaston not only accumulated employee resistance and adversaries, but was also enmeshed in his own private civil war. Entrapped in a prison of obsessively irrational and alogical demands, Gaston was on automatic pilot. When it came to how documents and procedures were carried out at Johnstone-Mumford, there was only one right way to conduct business relations and the keys to this perfection were deeply locked within Gaston's mind. In the face of this manic and obsessive demand for 100 percent excellence and compliance, all other functions and operations came in a distant second. As expressed in a leadership therapy session, "Dr. Gaston was unable to shut off an incessant demand for a perfect document – regardless of the human cost, waste or breakdown in the workplace."

The document or mortgage loan with a single irregularity, correction or flaw (according to Gaston's standards) was shredded in broad daylight for all to see. In addition, the teller or officer who went over the allotted 150 seconds recommended for customer service interactions was devalued, demoralized and docked. On a few occasions Dr. Gaston humiliated such "excessive customer service agents" on the spot. Gaston was on a witch hunt for imperfections. Subordinates reported that "Dr. Gaston appeared to be filled with venom and driven to fulfill a vendetta." Gaston cultivated a relentlessness and grit needed to both demean and repeatedly call to task his subordinates. He turned his back on attempts by his officers to plead their case for some greater measure of customer service or a prioritizing of human capital building. Rational, reasonable explanations of why officers required more time with their clients were automatically dismissed as "academic" and "frivolous frou-frous." Gaston was extremely quick on the draw whenever his perfectionism and type A leadership style were questioned. Emails addressing the people side of business and requests for exceptions to Gaston's time constraints on specific customer transactions were immediately discarded, deleted and ostracized. Communication was one way – from Gaston to his subordinates. The upward flow of communication was considered a sacrilege. Feedback was something that employees recalled from their pre-Gaston days.

Based on months of observation and the transition from coaching to therapy sessions, a clinical diagnosis emerged. The symptoms and indicators all pointed in the direction of a DSM-IV-TR diagnosis 301.4 of Obsessive Compulsive Personality Disorder (American Psychiatric Association, 2000, pp. 725–729). In addition there was a second diagnosis of 300.3, Obsessive Compulsive Disorder (American Psychiatric Association, 2000, pp. 456–463). At the core, Gaston suffered from an Obsessive Compulsive Personality Disorder structured around an extreme "preoccupation with details, rules, lists, order, organization, and schedules to the extent that the major point of the activity is lost" (American Psychiatric Association, 2000, p. 729). Moreover, Gaston's dysfunctional brand of perfectionism contaminated his workplace, negatively impacting productivity and all phases of internal and client-centered operations. In the words of the DSM-IV-TR, Gaston was living proof of a "perfectionism that interferes with task completion." He was "reluctant to delegate tasks to work with others unless they submit to exactly his way of doing things … " (American Psychiatric Association, 2000, p. 729).

DECODING A "PERFECTION OR DESTRUCTION" LEADER

Focusing on the "perfection or destruction" origin of the three work-place confrontations, I was able to shed light on the pivotal role of a key leader in shaping workplace incivility. Although the original intention of Dr. Gaston's action was to reach higher levels of customer service, the results were incivility, destructive behavior and toxicity. In the third incident in question the altercation expanded beyond Gaston and his loan officer and directly impacted one of the bank's high-end clients. Ironically, Gaston was quite intellectually aware of the destructive impact of his "perfection or destruction" assault on subordinates. But as already indicated, the obsessive compulsive leader was caught in an affective, emotionally unintelligent quagmire and was unable to control his own behavior when on the firing line.

Gaston experienced similar extremes and pain in his personal life, leading to two contested divorces and a myriad of unsettling personal issues. Moreover, his obsessive compulsive personality disorder was further compounded by a closely related obsessive compulsive disorder (see American Psychiatric Association, 2000). Gaston did not limit his control to micromanaging employee time allotted to customer service or his demands for a radical perfectionism in all documents and printed and computerized forms at work. His obsessions extended to compulsive avoidance of "dirty money" which caused varying degrees of internal havoc at Johnstone-Mumford. Money was obviously the name of the game and the organization was attempting to adjust to an upper-echelon leader who had major issues when it came to physically handling the most treasured and central asset – the legal tender. Unable to rectify his obsessive avoidance behavior, Gaston lived in a state of fear and guilt over the dreaded "dirty money." Not surprisingly, his avoidance of money only served to compound the overall state of toxicity in banking operations.

The impact of Gaston's behavior on his leadership and the workings of the entire Johnstone-Mumford organization was critical. As a leader, Gaston was largely controlled by his obsessions and his colleagues bore the brunt of this. The obsessive compulsive nature of Gaston's destructive behavior increasingly contaminated the Johnstone-Mumford work environment, cutting deeply into production, motivation, morale, teamwork and the overall organizational culture.

CONSULTING AND THERAPEUTIC INTERVENTIONS: PHASE I

At first or second glance, Johnstone-Mumford was experiencing a difficult transition, moving from a culture of predominantly theory Y leadership under Francine Oster and into the more theory X, authoritarian leadership of Raymond Gaston. Slightly below the surface and lurking in the shadows of this changing of the guard was a leader who imported a significant propensity for hostility, resentment and toxicity. Situated outside the ordinary boundaries of organizational conflict, the Johnstone-Mumford breakdowns were in fact inseparable from and largely driven by Dr. Gaston's longstanding Obsessive Compulsive Personality Disorder (e.g., see Grayson, 2003). Faced with a toxic organizational system, the consultant was able to locate the nexus of the destructive behavior within Dr. Gaston. *Working on the assumption that systemic repairs of dysfunctional organizations need to be directed toward detoxifying human capital, the initial intervention required was treatment for Dr. Gaston's obsessive compulsive personality disorder.* Systemically speaking, Johnstone-Mumford did not have the luxury of suspending or limiting operations. They had to choose between interventions that could radically modify Gaston's behavior and replacing him.

After Gaston began his prescription medication and psychotherapy regime for controlling OCPD, I worked with the vice president of the Miami branch of Johnstone-Mumford to generate options for both Dr. Gaston and the organization. Recognizing that at minimum Gaston required approximately nine months of medication accompanied by intensive leadership coaching and therapy, it was readily apparent that a temporary or longer-term replacement was necessary. Over a period of two lengthy "options and restructuring" sessions, the consultant, HR and upper-echelon leadership agreed that there were no officers or managers currently working at the Miami branch of the bank experienced enough to immediately replace Gaston. Furthermore, based on HR's recent experience with an outside managerial hire (Gaston), the consensus was that every effort should be made to keep the current leadership appointment within the Johnstone-Mumford family.

I suggested that the leadership challenge be posed in the form of a conference phone call between senior members of the six Johnstone-Mumford campuses. Agreement was immediately procured. During this conversation, an unexpected option arose during the conference call. Francine Oster, formerly of the Miami branch and currently placed in Amsterdam, said that she was highly impressed with a mid-level operations manager on her leadership team who had recently completed the five-year mark of his appointment. Winston Chambers, the manager in question, was in fact currently being reviewed for promotion and potential expatriation to another JM locale. In Oster's view, Mr. Chambers would be more than suitably qualified to fill in for Dr. Gaston during his executive coaching and treatment. If it were to be later determined that a long-term replacement would be needed for Dr. Gaston, Oster offered that Chambers would be "an extraordinary candidate for the longer-term appointment." As a former MBA student at an Ivy League university in the US, Chambers was sufficiently briefed on US business etiquette and banking culture and would be in a position to step right in and hit the ground running. As a life-long dedicated team player, Francine Oster offered to provide several intensive one-on-one training and briefing sessions for Chambers in support of a smooth transition and expatriation.

CONSULTING AND THERAPEUTIC INTERVENTIONS: PHASE II

Following the dual diagnosis of Obsessive Compulsive Personality Disorder and Obsessive Compulsive Disorder a series of leadership therapy sessions focused on the projected restructuring of leadership, the replacement of Gaston, and the need for Gaston to get "unstuck." Dr. Gaston's therapy addressed both highly personal and organizational issues focusing on how the senior manager had been a major instigator in the depreciation of human capital at Johnstone-Mumford. Much talk centered about the precursors leading up to the three verbal conflicts in the workplace and subsequent grievances filed against Gaston. Reflecting on the toxic impact of these incidents and how they diffused throughout the workplace, Gaston carefully decided to waive his confidentiality and privileged communication status during therapy – permitting me to share vital information-as-needed with JM leadership – in turn maximizing the systemic implications of the therapeutic approach. Gaston confided that this waiving of confidentiality was in part triggered by his negative experiences with the Sergio Santos International Bank of the Americas. During the later stages of his previous employment with Sergio Santos, Gaston was under psychological treatment for what was vaguely identified as "a stress disorder" but he had decided at the time to maintain confidentiality and not share the information with his superiors. Yet, despite Gaston's confrontations with Johnstone-Mumford subordinates and the grievances filed, Gaston was "committed to making it work with JM and sorting my way through these obsessions and compulsions." Although it was difficult at first for Gaston to lower his defenses and acknowledge the destructiveness of his leadership, in the third month of therapy he did an about face and expressed a complete commitment to treatment. Gaston turned over a new leaf and took complete ownership of his diagnosis. He was no longer defiant in therapy.

In conjunction with drug therapy and counseling I worked with Gaston to attempt to "refit him with Johnstone-Mumford culture." We worked to achieve a lower-risk alternative to his high profile and human capital-intensive leadership role. Quite simply, Gaston required a little time away from the relationship and people side of the business. Johnstone-Mumford's commitment to Gaston was both fair and generous and consisted of two options: (1) a paid administrative leave while the "issues were sorted out"; or (2) the alternative of "providing Gaston a back or side door option in the company where he would be able to maintain a low profile during his recovery period." In an effort to utilize and build upon his unique information systems background, Dr. Gaston opted to continue on with Johnstone-Mumford and accepted a mid-level management role in the Information Services Department. The position provided a behind-the-scenes financial and IT appointment away from the public eye. It was a numbers-intensive appointment and a stark alternative to the constant human interaction demands of his former role.

Appreciative of the 360 degree effort to create an alternative to a dismissal, Dr. Gaston graciously offered to quietly work with his incoming replacement.

IMPLICATIONS FOR LEADERS AND ORGANIZATIONS

A change in senior level leadership requires careful preparation and transitioning. Caught in the winds of change, the Johnstone-Mumford International Bank was blindsided by the transfer of leadership at its Miami branch. Whereas the outgoing senior operations manager, Ms. Francine Oster, had set a highly collegial and theory Y oriented tone for the institution, the incoming replacement, Dr. Raymond Gaston, was more of an afterthought, a ninth-inning replacement, an ill-conceived psychological and cultural misfit and clash with Johnstone-Mumford culture rather than a strategic and compatible hire. By serving up Dr. Gaston as a prototype I remind companies that the prospects for trouble at the top are increased significantly when your personnel door swings open too hastily, too wide and too often. JM's failure to carefully monitor and adequately scrutinize its key hire allowed destructive behavior through the front door during the light of day.

6 The borderline leader: when brilliance and psychopathology coexist

> How much freedom should be given to the entrepreneur, to the person
> with the high need for achievement, to the organizer, to the initiator, to the
> person who enjoys running things, being boss, wielding power? ... Who
> will collect the garbage? How will the strong and the weak relate to each
> other? The more capable and the less capable? How do we achieve love,
> respect, and gratitude for authority?

(Maslow, 1971, pp. 219–220)

BRILLIANCE AND PATHOLOGY COEXIST

Far beyond our usual concerns with difficult people in the workplace, bullies and irritating bosses lurks a shadowy, dark world of high-toxicity leaders. *Successfully climbing up the company ladder does not exclude the possibility that brilliance and pathology exist side-by-side.* In some cases leaders exhibit highly personable interpersonal and emotional behaviors that are the attractive, alluring outer shell of their disorder (e.g., see Kets de Vries and Associates, 1991; Lowman, 2002; Lubit, 2004). Subordinates and colleagues are drawn to their charm and style (Lipman-Blumen, 2001, 2005). In comparison, other bosses appear flat and dull, lacking the grace, pizzazz and intoxicating qualities that make for extraordinary people connections.

Favio Burnstein is a high-profile and extremely successful leader in the fashion industry who rocked the status quo in the US and Europe. Favio's productivity and creativity is exemplary. When he is on his game he is unstoppable. But there is another side to Mr. Burnstein – he is a white-collar toxic. Despite his brilliance, he can be a seriously dysfunctional boss. While his sophisticated, entrancing relationship management skills are renowned in the fashion world of models and designers, so is his reputation as a high-maintenance leader who has a few "serious issues."

As Favio goes, so goes his company. Emotions are highly contagious. The high workplace drama of Favio Burnstein both inspires and infects the entire organization; he is a supreme motivationalist and a lethal contaminant. Favio makes for a memorable study of disturbed leadership and an extraordinary subject for consultation and executive coaching.

DYSFUNCTIONAL BACKGROUND NARRATIVE

Favio Burnstein is a very strong personality at Sergio Mondo Fashion House in Miami Beach, Florida. As Senior Manager of the Creative Designs R&D Division, Burnstein has achieved legendary status. As some of the designers put it, "when Favio is good, he is very, very good, and when he is bad, he is wicked." The "good" Favio has brought Sergio Mondo Fashion House (SMFH) from obscurity to international acclaim in a period of five years. When Favio first walked in the door he took on a new wave, punk, hip hop, MTV styled fashion house with a clientele in their late teens and early twenties. Favio brought a sleek international mentality and energy to SMFH, combining the best of high couture from houses in Milan, Rome, Manhattan, London and Paris. Under the tutelage of Burnstein, SMFH graduated from the MTV genre into a sophisticated, high-end, mature, world-class universe of high fashion and international runways. Within a matter of a few years, Hollywood starlets, European royalty, and players around the globe wanted to step onto the red carpet in Favio's Fashions. Favio Burnstein made such a splash that his designs were more associated with "Favio" than with Sergio Mondo. But the CEO and CFO of Sergio Mondo Fashion House were tickled with the newly found status and success and were more concerned with keeping their celebrated leader happy than with questions surrounding who was upstaging whom. This was not about who took the bows and got the recognition. SMFH's top brass lived and breathed success and they were enamored with Favio Burnstein. Favio was their ticket to be discussed in the same breath with Armani, Versace and the top international fashion houses.

Concerning his personal demeanor and physical presence at SMFH, Favio was "hard not to notice." As stated by Joyce Ferber, one of the designers, "Favio was all business but seemed to wear his personality and private life on his sleeve." Burnstein made it perfectly clear that he was a frequent gambler. He talked of his escapades at the dog track, with the ponies and in Las Vegas and Atlantic City. On some Monday mornings, Favio was on top of the world and other Mondays he was in the dog house. It all depended on how his impulsive and chronic gambling habit went that weekend. And he always bragged about his "speeding tickets" and the "scam of photo radar."

There were some days that Favio shifted into his "soccer identity" and spoke of how he used to play goalie in "the old country" and he questioned "what in the world am I doing in this selfish fashion industry?" It was curious to hear a leader openly discuss what he had made of his life and whether he was in the right profession. There were days when Favio appeared very manly in his dress and manner and other days when he was in the words of Joyce Ferber, "south of a metrosexual." As Morty, a colleague, put it, "there are days when Favio claims to be a man's man and other days when he tries to convince everyone that he is bisexual or gay." It wasn't so much that anyone in the workplace really cared. It was just that Favio made a spectacle of himself. According to Morty, "Favio is so colorful and full of personality, but he also seems so unsure of who he really is. Will the real Favio please stand!" In his relationships with staff and designers, one day Favio put subordinates on a pedestal. Morty offered that, "first you walk on water and you're a saint and a week later Favio speaks to you in front of all your peers like you were a lower life form emerging from middle earth." There were many times when Favio was the center of attention and kept all conversations going. Other times, he appeared lonely and very depressed. He had been abandoned by his wife, his best friends, and "booted in the butt" by the company in Rome that "he put on the map." Any talk about Favio has to recall that infamous "prime time" evening when Favio and everybody were frantically working on designs for a "through-the-roof" client from Paris. The stress level was surreal and Favio pulled another one of his many all nighters. The next morning, the workplace discovered that Favio had turned suicidal, slit his wrists, and that 911 was called by Charlie Cement, the night-time janitor. Favio survived that one, but suffice to say, he is high risk and highest maintenance! After that drama, Favio's reputation became quite dark and legendary around Sergio Mondo.

FAVIO'S PERSONALITY DIFFUSES THROUGH THE ORGANIZATION

As a leader, Favio was obviously flamboyant, dramatic, deeply troubled and enigmatic. He engulfed, lifted and confused his work-force. In the final analysis, Favio took his employees on a wild, steep-lechase ride, through praise, hyper compassion and wild success, to depression, anger and despair. *The workplace seemed to take on characteristics of Favio's personality.* Francesca, a former model turned fashion designer, in her late thirties, was initially put on a pedestal by Favio. She was beautiful and brilliantly creative. Favio raved incessantly about Francesca's designs at SMFH meetings and wrote emails to the entire staff inviting them to emulate the "elegant and innovative Ms. Francesca Jarry," and follow suit. She was treated as if she was a princess, and a brilliant one at that. Favio clearly idealized Francesca and held her up as a role model. Although other designers might come up with an excellent innovation, it was always a question of "finally reaching Francesca standards." Favio would say, "for us to break through the fashion industry's roof and sail toward the sky and rain on the design world, we do as Favio and Francesca does." But, when it was a bleak day and mood, Favio turned around and trashed his own designs and entire career and pulled Francesca down with him. The workplace was flabbergasted.

EXTREME CRUELTY: BARBARISM IN THE WORKPLACE

Ironically, it was Francesca who first spoke up with human resources by expressing her "deep concerns about Favio and what the hell is going on around here." Francesca later filed an internal grievance against Favio Burnstein for "extreme cruelty and barbarism in the workplace" and for "harassment, sexism and discrimination that I wouldn't wish on a dog or a pig." The grievances filed with the human resources department were questionably handled, and according to the plaintiff, Francesca received little if any satisfaction. Ms. Francesca Jarry followed with a civil lawsuit alleging harassment, workplace discrimination and cruelty against Sergio Mondo Fashion House and Favio Burnstein.

At the point where Ms. Jarry filed her lawsuit, the CEO, Calvin Rodriguez attempted to more directly engage HR and the employee assistance program in conflict resolution and in a possible assessment or counseling of Mr. Burnstein. Favio appeared to be stigmatized by any questioning of his sanity and made it perfectly clear to the CEO and HR that he did not want "to be seen in EAP or anywhere near the seventh floor or everyone would think that I went postal and I'm a lunatic." Apparently, the EAP offices were located on the seventh floor and any time spent on this floor of the SMFH building earned you an instant reputation as "loco en la cabeza." In response to their inability to initiate any internal remedies and the escalating grievances and charges against Favio, Sergio Mondo were not only concerned, they were very perplexed. Apparently, Ms. Jarry's experiences were not unique. It was reported by HR that Favio Burnstein had a "very erratic personality and way of dealing with employees." It was stated that Favio alternated between praising employee accomplishments in a grandiose fashion and devaluating and outrageously humiliating and belittling these same designers on other occasions.

To make the company crisis even more acute, Favio's outbursts of adoring adulation and disgust and debunking were always conducted in public. Saving face for employees was not high on his list of leadership skills. Another staff member reported that "Favio turned livid and totally crazy when I was exactly nine minutes late to a meeting due to the fact that they closed part of the highway that I drive on to get to work." The employee stated that she attempted to state her reason for being late to Favio but he "refused to hear me and ranted and raved and acted like I killed his father or something by coming late. He was screaming in front of everyone and he scared the holy ghost out of me. He scared everybody! You could hear his wild, screaming, ranting psycho voice fourteen miles from here!"

In narrative interviews with employees, anecdotal evidence revealed that Favio was equally unpredictable in his socializing with subordinates. Some days he would spring for lunch, take two employees out and treat them like they were international movie stars. Three weeks later, the same employees were out at lunch with Favio and he sneered, treated them like inferiors and dogs, and snickered about the "fifth class designs" that they were turning out. He humiliated his employees in public. He was widely known for kicking his voice up several octaves and screaming obscenities at the top of his lungs. Francesca Jarry added that Favio got irate with her at a weekly designers' meeting and cried out in public that she was a "third class human being who should go back to the third world." Jarry stated that "Favio was so angry that he spit on the floor behind me. I was walking out of the room to get away from him and the whole humiliation." The "third world" ranting was of particular concern to Francesca since she was originally from Quito, Ecuador, and felt that she "was being demeaned and diversity laws were being trampled on." Overall, designers and staff interviewed reported that Favio's personality was "beyond bizarre" and was "unpredictable and erratic in the most dramatic, unbelievable and scariest kind of way."

A DYSFUNCTIONAL COMPANY IN SEARCH OF TREATMENT

Sergio Mondo Fashion House has 711 employees. A total of 212 were under the leadership of Favio Burnstein's "design division." Over a period of approximately ten months, nine complaints and five formal grievances were filed with HR. Some of these were also in consultation with the employee assistance program. Of these, two escalated into pending formal litigation. The majority of the allegations contained references to the type of behavior already referenced. HR and the Sergio Mondo CEO, Calvin Rodriguez, wanted to handle this problem "in the most discreet manner possible." Rodriguez had been concerned all along about the Americans with Disabilities Act rights afforded to Favio, and the fact that if he had any "official" mental or emotional problems this was all protected as privileged information. Meanwhile, HR and the EAP attempted on numerous occasions to sit down with disgruntled employees and with Mr. Burnstein to attempt to find reasons and solutions for these workplace conflicts.

The disturbances reached a crescendo when there were allegations from a top designer, Miles Berish, that "Favio purposefully gave me six assignments over two days so that I would fall on my face. When I questioned him, he told me, and I quote 'you should forget about your personal life, Miles, if you want to be a designer under me. You are lucky I am even giving you three seconds of my time, you gnat.'" Once again, Favio got so angry that he spit on the ground near Mr. Berish and slammed his fist through a thin wood door, drilling a hole through the wood and fracturing a bone in his right hand. Another grievant alleged that "Favio complimented my work at our weekly meeting and later that same day called me vile names in an email that he sent to about 90 people in our division that I work with every day!" Yet another grievance reported that Favio Burnstein "cursed me out in front of two of our biggest clients and accounts and he set me and our company up for failure. We lost the clients because he had an indignant tantrum! Am I dreaming or is this sucker sick?"

THE EXECUTIVE COACH ASSESSES "TWISTED LEADERSHIP"

The HR department contacted me after thirteen months of complaints and two potential legal cases. They invited me in for a series of three long talks that included the CEO, Calvin Rodriguez, and a representative of the EAP. They were extremely concerned with internal grievances, pending litigation, and a massive, destructive trend in the design division. Clearly making the point that design was their "bread and butter," CEO Rodriguez disclosed that Sergio Mondo had lost four "very substantial accounts" over the last six months. Over the past year-and-a-half, "since Favio got weird," they had a net loss of approximately twelve key clients. Their company was "going in the dumpers" and "all roads seemed to point back to Favio Burnstein." They were convinced that there was no quick solution, and they had tried to talk with Favio on numerous occasions and they came up "empty." They were still struck by his track record and talents and dumbfounded by the downward spiral. *Since the Favio problem emerged turnover had reached epidemic proportions.* Turnover was always high in the design division but it had "gone through the roof" since Favio "turned psycho."

In the process of conducting a limited organizational needs assessment, including semi-structured narrative interviews of chief officers and the director of HR, I found out that despite everything, Sergio Mondo did not necessarily want to fire Favio. I uncovered little if any client or organizational resistance from executive management and HR, and rather found an extraordinarily high level of support for a consultation. Clearly, the top brass had already conducted their own needs assessment, but this turned out to be fairly consistent with my own. CEO Rodriguez and the director of HR, Manny White, felt "strangely stuck with the loco genius" and wanted to see whether they could "salvage his brilliant and innovative side and get his personal garbage out of the picture." They genuinely wanted to explore and get to the bottom of all the conflicts and see whether Burnstein could be salvaged. CEO Rodriguez made it crystal clear that "Favio is a remarkable yet troubled man. Whatever is going on, I want to save him and make him a fixture at Sergio Mondo. The good and brilliant Favio is absolutely, positively irreplaceable." Rodriguez was very much swayed by "the first two golden years with Favio when Sergio netted in excess of fifty-five million dollars under his twisted leadership and brilliance." I was struck by the "twisted leadership" reference.

The consultation may have been initiated by a series of internal organizational crises within the fashion division of Sergio Mondo, a condition that spread to HR and the grievance system, but our collective needs assessment pointed toward a single, primary source – Favio Burnstein. The next issue in the consultation strategy was how to make initial contact with Favio. Was it going to be "required" by the CEO and/or HR that Favio see me as a client? The decision was that HR would make a "strong recommendation" that Favio consider "talking with an outside expert." Since I alternatively wear hats of psychotherapist, management consultant and leadership coach, how would I identify myself to Sergio Mondo, Favio and other members of the organization? Would I risk stigmatizing Favio by referring to myself as a psychotherapist, and positioning him as "patient?" Or would it be more comforting to identify myself as "executive coach" or "management consultant" with Favio occupying the role of a "client?" *We collectively decided on the "executive coach" hat.* But HR had some reservations. In the event that my clinical psychology expertise pointed the intervention in the direction of a psychopathology, then this would have to be appropriately addressed and might entail a changing of hats. These concerns were due to the company's preoccupation over the Americans with Disabilities Act. In the event that Favio did have "official mental or emotional problems" and "there was a psychological diagnosis," they recognized that the coaching might morph into a therapeutic consultation bound by privileged communication and the fact that Favio had significant "rights" as a mentally disabled worker who just happened to be functioning in a leadership role. HR and the CEO asked a number of questions concerning whether Favio would wind up being a "protected class of employee" if he was "mental." I referred these very delicate issues to their company attorneys and stayed closely in the loop. I assured Rodriguez and HR that everything would remain completely confidential and that we would consider options once we got further down the road into the coaching situation. Inasmuch as I approached coaching with a strong affinity for trust, relationship building and therapeutic dialogue, I anticipated that any conversion into the psychotherapeutic realm would be fairly seamless.

A WILDLY CREATIVE LEADER STEEPED
IN PSYCHOPATHOLOGY

Mr. Burnstein contacted me via email and we set up a first appointment in my professional office, miles away from Sergio Mondo. Favio was candid and savvy. He knew something was really the matter. Favio felt "empty" and in rapid fashion disclosed some of his concerns in the workplace and in his private life. Favio was graphic about his substance abuse history, reckless driving record, sexual escapades with numerous "love partners" and what he labeled as a "somewhat reckless and unstable past history." Burnstein had a pattern of very hot and cold workplace and personal relationships, fleetingly intense and then out the door. He idealized lovers and workers and alternatively shattered them in public, bringing them down in fits of anger. Favio's world was very "black and white." His real self or identity was very shaky and he gravitated toward extremes in his personality. You were either completely on his side or a mortal enemy and to be scorned and shunned. Favio felt very vulnerable in the workplace and in his personal life. He claimed that "everyone walks out the door on me. I can't trust that anyone will stay." He went on to disclose details of this pattern throughout his love and family life, and also at Sergio Mondo. Clearly there was a pattern of turnover and instability throughout the fashion industry and particularly in the design division of Sergio Mondo. He said it "made him feel insecure." He confessed that "I read in a paperback romance book about SAD, you know, separation anxiety disorder, and I bet I have that." Favio desperately wanted stability in his workplace and this was connected to his "feelings of emptiness" and several incidents where he "slit his wrists" because "it was all crap and I couldn't stand the stress and I desperately wanted everyone to salute Favio and tell him I will stay with you forever." When he suspected that there was going to be a revolving door at Sergio Mondo, he subconsciously empowered himself to be abrasive and abusive and kick designers and staff out the door before they would have a chance to abandon him. Favio wanted to beat his subordinates to the punch.

Working with Favio's psychological issues as cues and prompters I gradually made the transition from coach to psychotherapist, explaining to Favio that I "wore both hats" and that "the therapy hat would allow me to do a better, more comprehensive job." Favio was a bit baffled but pretty much unconcerned. At this point he needed the professional attention and was in a state of quiet desperation. I explained that in the event that it was necessary, I might come up with a psychological diagnosis at some point in time. Favio was agreeable. I officially announced my identity as psychotherapist. I believe that by virtue of initially dealing with an "executive coach" Favio was more at ease, less stigmatized, able to open up, take down his defenses and let the personal issues gush out. At a later point, it was not that difficult to transition to what I termed as "the therapist" inasmuch as the territory had already been entered and for Favio it was only a slight alteration in the semantics and identity of the professional he was disclosing to.

COMPANY AND LEADER ON THE COUCH

Over the course of several months of sessions conducted three times per week, I increasingly recognized that Favio Burnstein's erratic and destructive style of leadership, and deeply troubled intrapersonal and interpersonal behavior was centered in a pre-existing (prior to Sergio Mondo) "borderline personality disorder." This disorder (DSM-IV-TR 301.83) is characterized by "a pervasive pattern of instability of interpersonal relationships, self-image, and affects, and marked impulsivity that begins by early adulthood and is present in a variety of contexts ..." (American Psychiatric Association, 2000, p. 706).

Favio had a longstanding pattern of undermining his achievements just when he was about to reach his goal. His borderline personality disorder was prevalent when he first dropped out of high school in the last month of his senior year and returned to obtain his GED some five years later. Similarly, he dropped out of his Bachelor's degree program in college in the last semester of his senior year and returned later to obtain that degree. This predictable pattern was repeated yet again in his MFA program when he withdrew his senior year and returned some seven years later to complete the degree. Ironically, after his first two years at Sergio Mondo, Favio was reaching his goals and was very successful, exceeding all personal and company expectations in innovation, design, expansion into an international client base, world markets and profitability. But in typical, undermining, borderline personality disordered fashion, Favio jumped ship and started to sabotage his efforts and the workings of his designers and staff. His troubling and self-defeating interpersonal patterns of destructive behavior, severe doubts regarding identity, self-worth and abandonment, and lethal driving, gambling and promiscuity took over. The active borderline personality disorder was boldly expressed throughout the Sergio Mondo workplace and *Favio emanated toxicity*. Favio was contagious!

In addition to his pre-existing borderline personality disorder, there were precipitating factors in the organizational environment that contributed to the reappearance of Favio's older symptoms. The "trigger" was the instability of the designer world and how this played into the many insecurities and abandonment issues faced by Burnstein. Clearly, *Favio's personality disorder made him a poor fit for a transient organizational culture*. Favio was desperate for stability and a workplace that was not in constant upheaval. Although he was a world-class innovator in design and thrived on constant change in the clothing industry, a closer examination revealed that he always favored the "classics that never go out of style." In the interpersonal realm, Favio was extraordinarily vulnerable to turnover. In examining the interface between individual leader and organizational system it is fairly clear that in cases of leaders with pre-existing personality disorders, extremely stressful and disruptive forces in the daily workings of company life will necessarily reset and fuel the pathology. The coach or consultant addresses the issues of "organizational fit" and "triggers" and attempts to negotiate more favorable conditions alongside treatment of the personality disorder. It is an example of blending individual differences research with a more systems dynamics approach – in other words, how do I pay serious attention to the needs of both the individual leader and the company as a whole (e.g., see Senge, 1990; Von Bertalanffy, 1950, 1968)? In this case, Favio was extraordinarily valuable as a leader to his company and Sergio Mondo were amenable to becoming more of a "learning organization" (Senge, 1990) to preserve their eccentric and troubled meal ticket.

INDIVIDUAL AND ORGANIZATIONAL PATHOLOGY

The fact that Favio suffered from a long-term personality disorder in no way diminished the severity of the abusive and harassing behavior he dished out. Many of Favio's subordinates viewed themselves as targets of emotionally abusive behavior characterized by "hostile verbal and nonverbal behaviors (excluding physical contact)" (e.g., see Keashly & Harvey, 2005, p. 203). Some anecdotal reports of the effects of emotionally abusive behavior by Favio's subordinates included: negative mood, anger and resentment (see Ashforth, 1997; Richman et al., 1999); anxiety (see Tepper, 2000); decreased psychological well-being and lowered self-esteem (see Cortina et al., 2001); reduced organizational functioning and decreased job satisfaction (e.g., see Keashly & Jagatic, 2000); job tension and greater turnover; work withdrawal behaviors and greater intention to leave (e.g., see Ashforth, 1994); increased absenteeism; decreased productivity (Ashforth, 1997); and plummeting organizational commitment (Duffy et al., 2002).

Through a high-impact, incremental approach to executive coaching (see Schaffer, 2002) and rational–emotive psychotherapy (see Ellis, 1993), I increasingly understood some of Favio's internal locus of control issues and how his disordered world is ordered. We were still left with decisions regarding individual and organizational interventions for both Favio and Sergio Mondo Fashion House. After diagnosing Favio with borderline personality disorder and referring him to his internist, medication was prescribed for his personality disorder and he began a drug treatment regime conducted in concert with our agenda of behavioral therapy.

After extensive communication with Sergio Mondo's HR department and CEO, Calvin Rodriguez, Favio decided that he wanted to "open up a dialogue about his Borderline Personality Disorder" with key employees who had filed grievances against him. He said that he "wanted to be a man, not give excuses, but face the facts and clear up the mess and move on to greater things." There was a month-long delay due to ADA, Title I issues handled by the attorneys. Finally, Favio "received clearance to communicate and open up." In a series of meetings and group sessions, Favio, myself, and members of HR and the CEO all participated in key "psychological" and "management consulting" issues aimed at reinstating the "golden era of Favio's first two years at Sergio Mondo." The agenda promoted was one of advancing positive psychological capital (e.g., see Luthans *et al.*, 2007).

An improvement in Favio's mental and emotional health was anecdotally tied to an increase in overall Sergio Mondo motivation and profits, and a decrease in hostility, turnover and retaliation from his staff. I viewed the coaching and psychotherapy with Burnstein and employees as part of a broader systems consultation with Sergio Mondo. Assuming that Sergio Mondo Fashion House was a living organizational organism and an open system (e.g., see Von Bertalanffy, 1950), I perceived Favio as a pathological part and nexus of a systemic problem engulfing a significant number of employees. My continuing work with Favio led to more systems consultations with Sergio Mondo, in an effort to integrate both the atomistic or parts problems and the organizational system and processes (see Levinson, 1981, 1987, 1991, 2002). I worked on the assumption that the individual progress made with Favio alleviated not only mental and emotional pain and anguish but gradually cleared the way for personal productivity in his position as a leader within his company. In essence, it is not too much of a stretch to hear the executive consultant or organizational psychotherapist reflect on the treatment and successes with an individual leader and state that "this increased productivity is potentially leverageable for the increased productivity of the entire organization" (Lowman, 2002, p. 153).

DUAL LEADERSHIP INTERVENTION

In a series of "escalations," I moved from a more individually focused coaching and psychotherapy orientation to a primarily company-wide, systemic consultation. Once Favio convincingly came out of the closet, loud and proud about his "disorder," a series of team consultations followed. After several months of healing talks and team sessions I attempted to strategically propose significant organizational change in the form of a plan to consider a "dual leadership" approach to the design division. As Favio felt progressively stronger and his symptoms went further into remission, I came up with a conflict resolution and systemic change strategy initially pitched to Rodriguez and then to HR. Francesca Jarry's litigation was still pending with a court date rapidly approaching – but her persistence and drive was dissipating due to the progress being made with Favio and the entire division. Healing was underway. Francesca was at first reluctant to attend our management consultation sessions (later to be termed "conflict resolution meetings"), but finally did check in for a few breakthrough sessions. The ice was broken and she began a minimal dialogue with Favio. Influenced by the fact that Francesca had been in leadership positions in the past and that Favio was wounded but improving, my proposal was that Francesca would serve as a co-leader with Favio. I hoped to approach some conflict resolution first via our consultations and dialogues and secondly through our new therapeutically guided partnership in leadership.

With the assistance of HR and the attorneys, I drafted a plan for a six-month trial period of dual leadership. Meanwhile, HR and the CEO further negotiated with Jarry's attorney that if this co-leadership experiment was successful and Burnstein satisfied Jarry's request for apologies, the lawsuit would be dropped. In addition, for a period of six months, team consultations and conflict resolution meetings with the division would precede en route to a longer-term and deeper healing. During this period of time I was also engaging two counselors from the employee assistance program of Sergio Mondo, attempting to put into place a train-the-trainer agenda. I view this ongoing commitment as a vital part of the consultation. Following best practices of high-impact consulting (Schaffer, 2002), I was engaged in an incremental, sub-project within a larger systemic and organizational consultation. We were collaborating in the individual and group healing process and were all emerging from dysfunctionality into a more functional and learning organization.

The once fatally flawed Favio showed strong signs of improvement. He realized that this company was in it for the long haul. Half of his healing was due to the fact that his CEO and his company were committed to him. He had never experienced a boss like CEO Calvin Rodriguez. Favio was surrounded by caring, compassionate individuals and it appeared as if he had gotten to the root of his old problems that were destroying both him and Sergio Mondo. Sergio Mondo were extremely pleased to have a new, improved model of Favio on board, and eventually they were able to amiably resolve all but two of the grievances. These were settled out of court. The dysfunctional behavior characterized by plunging motivation, productivity and profits, widespread instability, loss of key clients and a myriad of workplace conflicts was gradually subsiding and we were on an upswing. A fatally flawed Favio was reinvented as a merely flawed and "mildly toxic" Favio. The fashion man began to show that the new model could be brilliant and innovative. He even learned how to share the stage and stress of leadership with Francesca. Curiously, the co-leadership strategy is still in operation, some seven years later. Suffice to say, despite a few altercations and flare-ups it has been quite a successful ensemble.

AT THE FAULT LINE OF LEADER AND
SYSTEMIC TOXICITY

The extreme case of a borderline personality disorder (BPD) is an example of what the DSM-IV-TR describes as "Cluster B Personality Disorders" (American Psychiatric Association, 2000, pp. 701–717). As illustrated in the narrative of Favio Burnstein, characteristic behaviors of Cluster B leaders include: highly dramatic and emotional in the workplace; conflict and crisis prone in social and organizational life; behavior that repeatedly violates cultural norms and players in the organization; suffering from pervasive, inflexible mental, emotional and interpersonal disturbances that are stable over time; and the experience of repetitive patterns of distress or impairment in social and work life. *Personality disorders affect as much as 10–15 percent of the adult population in the US at some point during their life.* There is no reliable data available, however, for the prevalence of personality disorders among US leaders within organizations, in part due to therapist–client confidentiality and the privileged communication status afforded individuals with psychological or psychiatric conditions as protected by the Americans with Disabilities Act (ADA). Lacking data, I am working on the assumption that personality disorders in leaders and organizations will roughly mirror the data generated in the general US adult population. I personally suspect that the percentage would most likely be considerably higher than the norm due in part to the designation of extreme degrees of hubris and narcissism as commonplace in high-achieving climbers and leaders.

The borderline personality disorder case study investigates a "preexisting" personality disorder thought to be at the eye of the high-toxicity organizational storm. The DSM-guided diagnosis of borderline personality disorder is not viewed as a mere by-product of a dysfunctional organizational culture, but rather as a primary result of a "preexisting" individual pathology. This determination was in part based on reports of Favio's history of conflicts with other employers – all pointing toward a long-term pattern of borderline personality disorder separate and apart from Sergio Mondo. As indicated in the consultation, systems variables do interact with the BPD leader, at times triggering and aggravating seemingly dormant or remissive dysfunctional behaviors. The Sergio Mondo organization clearly triggered or activated dimensions of Burnstein's BPD by bringing some separation anxiety issues to the forefront as a result of the Sergio Mondo turnover turnstile. Although another researcher may have focused more on the organizational system as a precipitator of dysfunction, in the Sergio Mondo case I found that the high-toxicity disturbances were far more pronounced and centered predominantly in the leader rather than at the systems level of analysis. In essence, the nexus of dysfunction and highest toxicity levels at Sergio Mondo was in my clinical judgment traceable to the borderline personality disorder and secondly to the separation anxiety disorder and acute depression of Favio Burnstein.

Curiously, any personality disorder or high-toxicity behavior is always in relation to and operant within a larger organization. *Individual toxicity ultimately cannot be separated from a family or organizational system* (e.g., see Armstrong, 2005; Hirschhorn, 1988). Accordingly, the BPD of Favio Burnstein at some point lends itself to a far more complex and all-encompassing entertaining of a BPD diagnosis for the entire Sergio Mondo Fashion House. This was manifest in the response of subordinates and colleagues to Burnstein's erratic behavior as a leader. In essence, the workforce immediately surrounding Burnstein was necessarily engaged in dimensions of a Borderline Personality Disordered system of interaction. The anecdotal reports of the effects of Favio's allegedly emotionally abusive leadership led to a myriad of dysfunctional worker responses as exemplified in: escalating leave-taking behaviors and absenteeism (Harvey, 1996); decreased productivity (see Ashforth 1994, 1997); and decreased commitment to the organization (Duffy *et al.*, 2002).

HIGH-TOXICITY ALERT: LEADERS GO OFF THE DEEP END

As a researcher and consultant trained in both the management and psychology disciplines, I have increasingly employed a growing number of interdisciplinary tools including a recent increased usage of the *Diagnostic and Statistical Manual of Mental Disorders* (American Psychiatric Association, 2000). Bringing the psychological and psychiatric standard for assessment into executive coaching and management consulting assignments, I have been able to extend my repertoire into the farther reaches of toxic leadership and organizational behavior. Particularly in cases characterized by a more serious state of psychopathology or "high toxicity," I have found the DSM particularly useful in sorting out the lighter or milder forms of toxicity from those cases red flagged by Kets de Vries and characterized by leaders who "go far beyond the abnormal ways of functioning ... they go off the deep end" (Kets de Vries, 1995, p. 217). Throughout his tenure at Sergio Mondo, Favio Burnstein was going off the deep end as a lea attempting to productively function despite a Borderline Person Disorder. He was highly guarded and privileged to a point abou pathology – qualifying him as a white-collar toxic. Colleagues subordinates respected Favio, perceived him as special and privi and were quite hesitant to complain or be perceived as whistle bl against a world-renowned boss. When Sergio Mondo failed to and appropriately diagnose and treat the leader, the high toxicit tably encompassed and contaminated large numbers of emplo the case of Favio Burnstein this company-wide poison culmi something roughly approximating a Borderline Personality Di Organization with added dimensions of depression and s anxiety disorder.

This case suggests that in the event of an extrem leader toxicity, the intervention of an external third party necessary for the recovery of both the leader and the organization. *Falling outside the expertise of most managers and human resource specialists, psychopathology is best delegated to psychological and psychiatric-trained EAP therapists or external specialists in these areas. Left undetected, toxicity escalates and permeates organizations.* As indicated by Goldman (2006a,b, 2008a,b), Lipman-Blumen (2005) and Frost (2003), the threat of highly toxic leadership requires advanced scouts or toxin detectors within the organization who are able to initially distinguish whether an individual may require further assessment. Clearly, high-toxicity leadership presents a complex challenge for management to incorporate psychological and psychiatric expertise into an organization's repertoire.

7 Trouble at the top: high-toxicity implications of a leader with antisocial personality disorder

> If psychopathic individuals are consciously aware of their heightened sense of boredom when compared with others, they render it acceptable by redefining it as a superior attribute of their personality. Others may be characterized by them as leading sedentary or mundane lives, yet their benchmark is always risk taking through overt behavior, rather than satisfaction through emotional experiences within themselves and with others.
>
> (Meloy, 1992, p. 111)

A COMPANY FACED WITH AN ABUSIVE LEADER

In this chapter a company finds itself on the couch when it discovers that a high-ranking leader may be suffering from a psychological disorder that is having serious consequences for its workforce. At stake is the need to enhance organizational readiness for dealing with dysfunctional behavior centered in a strong but abusive leader. Of particular concern is the plight of the company faced with physical and emotional assaults on employees rationalized by a leader who contends that he is driving lazy workers toward new levels of motivation and productivity. Despite his many achievements, awards and accolades, the Senior Manager of Operations has also been degrading and "manhandling" employees in a series of physical and verbal altercations that have resulted in grievances and pending litigation.

Particularly troublesome have been the shortcomings of the company's internal experts in addressing the problem with leadership. Following a prolonged and destructive delay marked by an assumption that "the conflicts were quite normal and could be worked out with patience and TLC," verbal confrontation escalated into physical violence.

The case was initially reviewed by human resources and referred to the organization's employee assistance program. The ineffectiveness of internal options meant the company turned towards an external expert. The coaching and consultation that followed focused on the psychopathology of the leader and its direct toxic impact upon his immediate division and the company at large. The consultation required professional level knowledge and utilization of the *Diagnostic and Statistical Manual of Mental Disorders* (DSM-IV-TR) (American Psychiatric Association, 2000) in assessing the high levels of toxicity in the leader – a skill set that was not within the expertise of HR and was lacking in the EAP handling of the case. The narrative of this consultation will go into sufficient detail to offer a blueprint of somewhat commonplace mismanagement of high-level toxicity in the workplace, the ramifications of trivializing serious pathology in leaders, and what constructive alternatives and positive options can be considered and implemented.

ADDRESSING TOXIC LEADERSHIP

In the course of functioning in the worlds of both academia and consulting I am sensitive to the need to provide research studies that point both my university colleagues and the leaders of businesses to the dark or toxic side of behavior. Lacking a fundamental understanding and belief in the impact of the dark side of leadership, it is easier to turn away, proceed with resistance and denial, and trivialize data pointing toward dysfunctional behavior.

Along these lines I find that it is important to note that a growing number of management and organizational behavior experts have in recent years increasingly addressed this darker, toxic side of leadership (e.g., see Armstrong, 2005; Bowles, 1997; Fox & Spector, 2005; Gabriel, 1999; Goldman, 2005; Hirschhorn, 1988; Kellerman, 2004; Kets de Vries & Associates, 1991; Kilburg, 2000; Lawrence, 1998; Levinson, 1972; McLean, 2001; Miller, 1990). Within these ranks there is a group of scholars who have specifically built upon personality research resulting in a robust strand of investigation focused upon dysfunctional leadership and organizational behavior (e.g., see Kets de Vries, 1989, 1995; Lipman-Blumen, 2005; Lowman, 2002; Lubit, 2004). Of particular relevance to this chapter are the research and reports of consultations that address extremes in the form of highly toxic personality disorders in leadership and their implications for organizations (e.g., see Goldman, 2005, 2006a,b; Maccoby, 2000, 2003).

To date, research addressing personality disorders indicates that mental and emotional disorders do not fall within the usual skill set of professionals trained in business and management. It is rather the case that researchers have convincingly pointed toward the relevance and importance of incorporating psychological and psychotherapeutic perspectives into the analysis and consultations. This line of inquiry has been exemplified in: psychodynamic perspectives on organizations (Hirschhorn & Barnett, 1993; Miller, 1997; Parker, 1997); organizational therapy (Matheny, 1998; Schein, 2000); cognitive OD stressing the mental processes of individual organizational members (Matheny, 1998; Matheny & Beauvais, 1996); and the psychoanalytically grounded work of Kets de Vries and Associates (1991) and Kets de Vries and Miller (1984a,b). Unique to Kets de Vries' writings was his announcement that the clinical approach initially utilized in the one-on-one therapeutic relationship between analyst and patient has "now spread to the study of organizational practices" (Kets de Vries and Associates, 1991, pp. 75–76). As subsequently described by Goldman (2005), the ability to articulate and operationalize a clinical approach provides a basis for guiding and structuring action research into leadership pathology and dysfunctional organizations.

HIGH TOXICITY REQUIRES THE DSM-IV-TR

Personality disorders and their organizational contexts point to the presence of pathologies in the workplace generally falling outside of the expertise area of leadership scholars and management consultants. The prospect of DSM assessments of organizational pathology is rather awkwardly situated in between industrial and organizational disciplinary silos of leadership, management, psychology and psychiatry. At stake is the demarcation of mental illness and psychopathology extremes in leadership. This is not to be confused with the recent leadership studies addressing "milder" toxicity (e.g., see Frost, 2003). The majority of the toxicity research is what I term "toxicity light" and is primarily focused upon flawed, difficult leaders (and enabling followers and toxin handlers; e.g., see Frost, 2003; Lipman-Blumen, 2005). It predominantly falls within the range of what Maslow termed "normal pathology" in the workplace (1971). In the course of addressing a need for "organizational therapy" in response to the recent surge of toxicity research into organizations and leaders, Schein (2000) commented that "some level of toxicity is normal. That really has to be hammered home rather than thinking of toxicity as abnormal" (p. 36). But not only is it important to acknowledge the normal or light degrees of toxicity, it is also critical to red flag the farther reaches of toxicity. Extremely destructive and high levels of toxicity in both leader and company (as in a personality disorder) can in fact constitute abnormality and psychopathology.

It is important to note that while this emergence of leadership research addressing toxicity does at times utilize the language or semantics of the DSM, there is an absence of DSM-guided *clinical assessments* of psychopathology in either individual or organizational systems. In contrast, the clinical usage of the DSM-IV-TR in this study will clarify the incidence and clinical assessment of highly toxic, pathological leaders and the implications for the study of dysfunctional organizations.

Quite simply, the failure to incorporate the DSM-IV-TR in the assessment of a highly toxic leader may unwittingly serve to perpetuate and extend the pathology deeper into the organizational system. As will be demonstrated, the deeply rooted personality disorder of Rick Boulder, Senior Operations Management of WinnerWear, has already seeped into the workforce. Lacking an accurate assessment and intervention rooted in the DSM-IV-TR, the toxicity can only metastasize with dire consequences for the company.

"DSM-IV-TR": A SEARCH FOR OBJECTIVE STANDARDS

Despite a groundswell of academic, Fortune 500 and international media interest in toxic leaders and organizations, there is a notable absence of objective standards for assessing or clearly defining what constitutes extremely toxic or pathological behavior in the workplace (e.g., see Fox & Spector, 2005; Goldman, 2005). On the one hand, there is widespread agreement that there will be dire consequences unless organizations grasp and respond to toxic and psychopathological behaviors in individuals that invite danger into their companies (e.g., see Fox & Spector, 2005; Kellerman, 2004; 1995; Kets de Vries and Associates, 1991; Lipman-Blumen, 2005; Lubit, 2004). Shocking incidents of workplace terrorism (e.g., see Van Fleet & Van Fleet, 2006), suicides, sabotage, executive theft and other company crises have triggered more of an inward-looking, psychological awareness of organizations, leaders and employees, and the recognized need for early detection systems. Toxic behavior (e.g., "bullying" and "displays of anger and aggression in the workplace") is under scrutiny and occupies the attention of leadership, HR, employee assistance programs, coaches and consultants. However, there is little consistency or agreement in leadership or management consulting circles concerning how assessments or diagnoses are to be made or even as to what constitutes toxic or dysfunctional behavior in either individuals or organizations. Critical is the ability to discern between more serious pathologies, such as personality disorders, in contrast to the "toxicity-light" focus of the majority of leadership researchers who address "flawed leaders" who have been mentally and emotionally impacted by divorce, child custody battles, accidents, injuries and deaths, and a myriad of psychosocial and environmental stressors experienced during the course of organizational life.

As has been substantiated by the collaborative efforts in the DSM of over 1,000 mental health professionals and numerous professional organizations, personality disorders are characterized by enduring, inflexible, and stable patterns of behavior (American Psychiatric

Association, 2000). When the patterns are identified as recurring destructive behaviors, they result in significant distress or impairment in social and occupational areas of functioning – impacting the individual, significant others, colleagues, associates and subordinates in the workplace. The assessment of a personality disorder requires a differential diagnosis, including but not limited to: a structured case history; clinical interviews and assessments; possible field research into social, family and organizational environments; an assessment of the client's medical, family and psychological history; and a minimum number of personality features that meet the criteria for an official diagnosis. The clinical diagnosis of a personality disorder stands in sharp contrast to the milder personality turbulence faced by leaders who may be experiencing family or occupational conflicts and generalized toxicity. Also important is the difference between clinically destructive leaders (with DSM IV diagnoses) and those who meet only several of the characteristics for a narcissistic or borderline personality disorder but fall short of the minimal criteria. This "short of psychopathology zone" may mimic some of the characteristics of a full-blown personality disorder but will be shorter lived; lack a long-term personal and occupational history; be less severe; and exhibit lower degrees of dysfunction in the individual and the system. This less severe category of flawed leadership falling short of the psychopathology zone appears to be the primary domain of the "toxicity-light" and dysfunctional focus in leadership research and commentary. As a means of gaining greater insight into the broad range of leadership and workplace disturbances, I propose that a study of the DSM-IV-TR can only enrich understanding of the difficult distinctions to be made between the leader who has anger management "issues" in contrast to a leader suffering from an antisocial personality disorder.

In studying more chronic and deeply flawed forms of leadership and organizational conflict, the DSM-IV-TR is also helpful in efforts to come up with something closer to what members of the Harvard Negotiation Project have described as "objective criteria" or "independent standards" (see Fisher, Ury & Patton, 1991). In addition, the DSM is invaluable training in recognizing psychopathology and not treating organizational or leadership pneumonia as if it were an ordinary corporate cold.

Interest in and acknowledgment of the DSM within the management discipline is not new. The leadership and management literature reveals researchers and practitioners who display awareness of the DSM (e.g., see Kets de Vries and Associates, 1991; Levinson, 1976; Lubit, 2004). References to DSM pathologies have been made in the writings of Kets de Vries & Miller (1984a,b) when the authors transposed the semantics of abnormal psychology into the "neurotic organization." Roy Lubit recently provided a myriad of references to DSM categories of pathology in the process of describing symptoms and behaviors of toxic managers, subordinates and difficult people in the workplace (Lubit, 2004).

A CASE STUDY IN HIGH TOXICITY

What follows is an example of an application of the DSM-IV-TR to a scenario of highly toxic leadership and organizational pathology in the workplace. In the consultation narrative, I am the action researcher alternately wearing the hats of management consultant, executive coach and psychotherapist. As a consultant and participant observer, I first assess reported organizational symptoms and anecdotal evidence, conduct an organizational needs assessment and narrative interviews, and engage in extended workplace observation. Based upon consistent reports of chronic interpersonal dysfunctions and "self-problems" involving company leaders, I proceed to the executive coach perspective and ultimately wear the psychotherapist hat – conducting structured clinical interviews as required for DSM-IV-TR differential diagnoses. In the case described, I find a personality disorder within an individual leader at the nexus of company dysfunction.

The following case is based upon actual consultations, with names and players fictionalized. The case is presented as a step towards conceptualizing prototypes of personality disorders in leaders within organizational systems, and distinguishing between general toxicity and psychopathology. In the course of presenting the case study,

I interject information on the composition and usefulness of the DSM-IV-TR as a tool for leadership research, management consulting and coaching. I will be addressing both those with and without specific training in clinical psychology, psychotherapy and psychiatry.

A JERSEY VERSION OF EARLY BRANDO
ON A BAD NIGHT

Rick Boulder is the Senior Manager of WinnerWear International (WWI), a sportswear company primarily involved in innovating, designing and marketing WinnerWear (WW) basketball and athletic shoes.

Boulder is an unlikely Senior Manager, having worked his way up the corporate ladder without the benefit of a college education or an MBA. In fact, Mr. Boulder dropped out of high school in the eleventh grade and returned in his mid-twenties to finally obtain his GED. Boulder started his working career as a factory line worker for a world famous sports shoe and athletic wear Fortune 100 corporation, Berkeley Sports International (BSI). After three years on the factory line, Boulder was promoted to foreman, and eventually was promoted to middle and senior management appointments. Boulder not only knew the sportswear and athletic shoe business from the ground up, he also had street smarts and people skills that he learned on the sidewalks of Newark, New Jersey. Rick Boulder understood the mind of the blue-collar worker, was an alumnus of the mean streets and gang life, and ultimately graduated to upper management due to his ability to combine a big heart with a passion for quality and getting the job done. Boulder could explain Total Quality Management, JIT, and Zero Defects in the language of the street. Boulder spoke directly to factory workers. He was definitively one of them.

Boulder was always known as a motorcycle-riding, long haired, fiercely independent "shit kicker" who "sliced his way to the gut of the matter in seconds." Boulder was a charmer and confidence man. He was a master conversationalist and initially could be quite seductive. Boulder was much admired in BSI, but he also had a reputation as a "rebel without a cause." Some of the line workers used to refer to him as a "Jersey version of early Marlon Brando on a bad night." Boulder earned this reputation by showing a massive temper at times in the workplace when on different occasions he bullied and threatened "lazy" line workers, threw a company cat in a worker's face, and heaved a $2,000 computer through a factory plate glass window – in response to what he identified as "massive screw-ups, assholes and insubordination."

On a more personal note, Boulder was three times divorced. His second wife committed suicide shortly after a messy divorce. Boulder has three children by his ex wives (one per marriage), and prior to his success in manufacturing he was in constant trouble with the law for failure to make child support and spousal payments. Boulder also has a history of clashes with authority. He was arrested on three separate occasions for physical altercations with police officers and he has amassed a record-breaking number of traffic tickets for a two-year period in the State of Colorado. Since his last divorce, five years ago, Boulder, in his own words, "settled into the single life" and is constantly "searching for very young ladies who like to go biking on my BMW Café Racer ... across the Colorado line and into the wilds of New Mexico."

THE PHYSICALLY AND EMOTIONALLY
ABUSIVE LEADER

Boulder wanted everything on the factory lines "to work like a charm" but in the workers' eyes, he contradicted himself. Rick demanded compliance with the rules to the ends of the earth. But when it was about Boulder himself, he broke the rules all the time. He was sued for non-compliance with the Americans with Disabilities Act (ADA) when he openly cussed out a physically handicapped line worker in language that cannot be repeated. Boulder got so angry one morning when line worker Paul Ruff was an hour late, he was waiting for him in the parking lot and was cocked and ready to physically threaten him. There was a memorable altercation. Employees were watching through the windows. There was yelling accompanied by some pushing and shoving. Boulder and Ruff had to be restrained. Ruff vowed "never to forget." Ruff resigned and litigation is pending.

According to factory workers, Boulder's leadership style was paradoxically both admired and perceived to be reprehensible. Many of the workers truly appreciated the in-your-face qualities of Rick's brand of leadership. If he didn't like your work product or thought you were doing a lousy job, he'd let you know in three-tenths of a second. If he saw you "screwing up" at your station, he was very likely to walk right over, grab your arms and manhandle you into the "correct" behavior at the factory line. It didn't matter if you were a male or female line worker. He'd get irritable, aggressive and physical with workers. Boulder was not beyond physically assaulting his employees if he didn't approve of what they were doing. Boulder was quite impulsive and shot from the hip. On one occasion, he shoved a crane into the back of a shocked line worker and pretended that it was an accident. Jasper Johns was in shock. Johns told the personnel department that Boulder "had no respect for the workers' safety and is a monkey and baboon primitive." Mr. Johns required medical treatment and also proceeded to visit the infamous "sixth floor" for a series of sessions with the employee assistance counselors. This consequently led to the filing of a formal grievance and complaint against Boulder.

In what appeared to be directly related to Boulder's disruptive behavior, there was an increase in personal aggression (e.g., see Robinson & Bennett, 1995). Verbal abuse, loud altercations and physical confrontations became commonplace in the factory. Shouting and explosive anger fits became more prevalent. There were incidents of physical violence in the bathroom and the parking lot. Some workers were caught smoking marijuana during breaks. And there was growing talk among some of the younger, macho male line workers about "teaching Boulder a lesson that he'll never forget." One worker warned that he was going to teach Boulder "the mother of all lessons." Boulder heard about it. He got even meaner and more secretive, tougher and increasingly vindictive. If you crossed Boulder, watch out.

Boulder's physically and emotionally abusive behavior sum-
moned increasing acts of revenge and retaliation from his targets.
Subordinates were intent upon getting "an eye for an eye." The workplace became a physical and organizational battlefield that mirrored
the land mines occupying Boulder's mind.

Boulder drove his workers hard. They were very productive and
motivated up until the point when his strange, abusive and dysfunctional behavior was exposed. At first, workers were scared and did not
have a rule book for Boulder's anger and aggression. Personnel was
always hearing about Boulder. The local police department had booked
him numerous times on workplace disturbances. Everyone assumed
something was wrong with him. To say he had an "anger management" problem was to put it very lightly. *The disturbed leader's
venom had proved toxic and had infiltrated the organizational
system.*

A LEADER WITH ANTISOCIAL PERSONALITY
DISORDER

Boulder contacted my offices and said he wanted to make an appointment to see a psychotherapist. He was paying himself. He did not want
his company to know. He did not want to bill it to his insurance
company. He wanted anonymity and privileged communication.

I conducted a series of comprehensive case history interviews
with Mr. Boulder and administered several assessment instruments
including the Global Assessment of Functioning (GAF) Scale
(American Psychiatric Association, 2000, p. 34) and the Minnesota
Multiphasic Personality Inventory–2 (MMPI–2). Despite a long track
record of dishonest, unethical behavior, Boulder made an attempt to be
honest with me. *Yet Boulder was without repentance.* He was
extremely proud of his misbehavior. In his mind he was a brutal
angel "chosen to right some of the wrongs of this disgusting, lazy
world of bums called factory line workers." Boulder was quick to
the draw, confident and even cocky. He boldly informed me on our
first meeting, "Doctor, I want you to know in no uncertain terms,

that I ain't no sociopath, psychopath or fruitcake! Don't you dare tell me no different!"

In a series of interviews consistent with a multiaxial, DSM assessment, I discovered that Boulder did in fact receive an initial diagnosis from his employee assistance program's counselor. The diagnosis can be interpreted in terms of what Ashforth identified as a "petty tyrant" or "abusive supervisor" (Ashforth, 1994, p. 755) According to what Boulder shared of his experience with the EAP counselor, he was told that he "belittled subordinates, lacked consideration, showed extreme inflexibility and rigidity, ridiculed and physically abused employees, discouraged initiative from his workers, was perceived as arbitrary, unfair, played favorites, and used a forcing style of management." Boulder was referred by the EAP to "anger management" counseling and training and this was conducted over a period of ten weeks. Boulder was repeatedly told that he "had to chill out" and "learn to control his emotions." He was further instructed that "sometimes leaders get disgruntled and angry but with proper training and assistance they can get over it." Concerning the repeated incidents of his physical abuse against subordinates in the workplace, it was described to Boulder (by his EAP counselor) as his "lack of emotional intelligence" and his "inability to keep the toxic workplace out of his mind." In essence, Boulder was instructed that he was "suffering from a temporary lapse of civility and ability to maintain in public and that he would soon recover from his fight with anger, aggression and hostility."

After carefully assessing Boulder's mental and emotional health track record within his company, I proceeded with a DSM-guided differential diagnosis. Synthesizing the results of the Global Assessment of Functioning Scale and the MMPI–2 with other assessment tools, I found that Rick Boulder had considerably more than an anger management problem. Boulder was suffering from a long-standing personality disorder that was significantly impacting his performance as a leader in the workplace. Boulder's diagnosis was antisocial personality disorder (DSM-IV-TR 301.7 in American

Psychiatric Association, 2000). He was the son of an abusive, cocaine addicted, alcoholic father who also had been diagnosed and treated for Antisocial Personality Disorder. Boulder's personality as revealed in the testing and clinical interviews was that of someone who is inflexible, maladaptive, and is an ongoing danger to self (DTS) and danger to others (DTO). Boulder's criminal behavior dated back to his pre-teen years and he had a longstanding pattern of failure to conform to social norms with respect to lawful behaviors; deceitful-ness, as indicated by repeated lying, use of aliases, or conning others for personal profit or pleasure; irritability and aggressiveness, as indi-cated by repeated physical fights or assaults; reckless disregard for safety of self or others; consistent irresponsibility; and lack of remorse for injuries caused to others (see American Psychiatric Association, 2000, pp. 701–706).

DANGER TO SELF/DANGER TO OTHERS

Boulder was not happy when I informed him that his confidentiality and privileged communication status was threatened by my assess-ment that he was a danger to self (DTS) and a danger to others (DTO) in the workplace. After spending three weeks and nine sessions (cognitive–behavioral, rational emotive therapy) going round and round on the psychotherapeutic responsibilities related to DTS and DTO, we only started to understand each other. Once he knew that we were playing hardball, Boulder's behavior in therapy mirrored some of his destructive actions in the workplace, including turning on the charm, illustrating extraordinary powers of intuition and rational intellect, and periods of exhilaration and confidence followed by deep, dark depressive moods. Boulder had sophisticated techniques for trying to undermine and overturn the therapist. When his charm and interpersonal techniques did not produce results, Boulder attemp-ted to find protection under the ADA, Title I (Americans with Disabilities Act, specifically targeting Psychological Disorders). Boulder verbally threatened me when he stated that if I "even thought about reporting any of this to anybody … he had harsh solutions in mind." Once Boulder fully comprehended that I wasn't about to back off he decided that he would "cut a deal with me."

As an action researcher, I increasingly understood what it was like to be with Boulder in the workplace. I was a participant observer to his personality disorder and Boulder quickly and methodically attempted to coerce therapist, colleagues, subordinates and the entire workplace into his web of pathology. His force, confidence and magnetism were in my face and the threats were real. Since he already felt that his life as a senior manager at WWI "truly sucked," he decided to negotiate with me. Boulder was extremely concerned about not breaking any of this news to his CEO, Markus Duffy. Boulder finally acknowledged, after many counseling sessions, that he was in the DTS and DTO category and because of this he was not protected by the Americans with Disabilities Act. Boulder recognized that it would be futile to try and turn this around by naming himself as plaintiff and his company as the defendant in a lawsuit. It would more than likely be a losing battle. Boulder even went to the trouble of researching case law and precedent. He eventually decided that he did not want to take any legal action because it would call attention to his personality disorder. He handed in his formal resignation, which was accepted. I will not go into the legal proceedings that followed, but I will offer that it was not particularly favorable for Rick.

THE COMPANY PERPETUATES ITS LEADER'S TOXICITY

In subsequent follow-up to Rick Boulder's departure, I was engaged in company-wide consultation with WinnerWear International. In this systems phase, I conducted a post-Rick Boulder organizational needs assessment, accessed data on productivity and profits, engaged in an extensive observation of the workplace and conducted a series of open-ended narrative interview sessions with former colleagues and subordinates of Boulder. Overall, I noted two trends. The first was the widespread mimicking and mirroring of aspects of Rick Boulder's antisocial personality disorder throughout the organization. Boulder's behavior appeared to have permeated some aspects of the system. The second trend was an organizational period of grief over the loss of Rick Boulder. *Despite abuses suffered, organizational systems are infamous for defending and perpetuating their pathologies, maintaining and sustaining a dysfunctional equilibrium and resisting change and interventions.* Over a period of two years following Rick's departure, the design division went through two leaders before deciding that the third leader was a cultural fit. This was central to the recovery process as the members of the organizational system were responding to losing their familiar source of conflict.

THE THREAT OF A PRE-EXISTING LEADER PATHOLOGY

The study presented is intended to provide a "strategic sampling" of a personality disorder in leadership within its natural organizational context. Utilizing the DSM-IV-TR as a central hub for assessment of pathology, the seriousness of the organizational conflicts and leadership disturbances presented required diagnosis and interventions typically falling outside the expertise of management professionals. In choosing to convey this case, I carefully searched for a consultation epitomizing more extreme, well-defined characteristics of a personality disorder. My action research and case study agenda has been to "utilize extreme cases to develop rich theory" (Elsbach, 2005, p. 10).

The Boulder/WinnerWear case describes a "pre-existing" personality disorder traceable via "911" reports of organizational crises. The organizational red flags pointed back toward leadership as "personality disorders are inevitably manifested in social situations" (Vaillant & Perry, 1980). This in turn led to the singling out of a leader for an individual case history and structured assessment. *In the case study described, the DSM-IV-TR guided diagnosis of a personality disorder was determined not to be a direct or primary outgrowth or product of a dysfunctional, pathological organizational system – hence the "pre-existing" determination.* This does not discount, however, a myriad of mediating and interacting systems-generated stressors, workplace conflicts and organizational variables adversely impacting the troubled leaders and accelerating their symptoms. Moreover, another researcher may have assessed these same cases as exhibiting a nexus of pathology in the organizational culture via a more macro systems dynamics approach (e.g., see Senge, 1990).

A major concern and limitation in framing an individual differences approach based on the DSM is the need to integrate the seemingly old-school traits-influenced perspective within a more holistic systems analysis. From a process or systems view (e.g., see Argyris, 1985; Checkland, 1981; Gallessich, 1983; Schein, 1969, 1987; Senge, 1990) there are limitations to a primary focus upon the individual rather than centering the inquiry on the pathological behaviors and patterns in the larger system itself. Despite my initial holistic scanning of each organization, extensive periods of observation within each workplace, and the compiling of multi-faceted and systemic needs assessments, I settled down to an incremental, more modest focus on a specific individual. Is this not a reductionist methodology supplying only a mere snapshot within a vast pool of systems pathology? In other words, is it not a serious limitation to be focusing upon a nexus of leadership pathology when the organizational system, itself, is in part responsible for the leader's behavior?

INDIVIDUAL OR SYSTEMS PATHOLOGY?

Philosophically, it is impossible to antiseptically or conclusively extract any individual differences or a toxic individual leader from systems influences. Any individual differences assessment would necessarily incorporate systems variables. This is a given. The more important concern is one of degree and professional judgment. In the consultation presented the organizational system stressors were in my clinical opinion not sufficient to warrant a primary or exclusive focus on the broader systems pathology. It was my judgment that despite the fact that the organization did in fact incite, provoke and activate dimensions of the leader's pathology and exhibit some systems-wide dysfunctional patterns, the most immediate 911 fires to be attended to were centered in leadership and specifically in a single leader. *Keep in mind that as a practitioner engaged in action research I have somewhat different constituencies to answer to than does the researcher who functions solely within an academic context.* As a consultant in the field I must take action and this entails risks not typically faced by a pure researcher.

As the executive coach and consultant I specifically answered to the primary sponsor or client who expects ROI, and rapid-cycle, accountable outcomes. Viewed from the necessarily pragmatic positions of the practicing consultant and corporate client, are there many CEOs out there who want to be told that "I diagnosed your organization and I am sorry to inform you that the entire system suffers from borderline personality disorder?" In essence, this systems perspective is a theoretical analysis that may incorporate some seeds of truth. But in Corporate USA it is far more affordable and plausible to avoid the "Trojan horse syndrome" characterized by a myriad of consultants and coaches who descend upon the company, analyze the system from A to Z, deliver an impressive, costly, bulky report and exit prior to implementation (see Schaffer, 2002). In contrast, I provide a high-impact consultation approach utilizing DSM-IV-TR assessment tools en route to identifying the most urgent pressure points and subprojects within the organizational system. This approach entails a rapid-cycle, brief-therapy (e.g., see Walter & Peller, 1992) action agenda of organizational change via a seriously needed assessment of an antisocial personality disorder in a deeply disturbed leader. This seemingly individual differences approach based on the DSM does not negate, whatsoever, a fifth discipline (Senge, 1990) or general systems-influenced orientation (Ruesch & Bateson, 1968; von Bertalanffy, 1950). It rather positions the incremental participatory action research study and consultation within a broader systems campaign tempered to ROI, cost containment and the complex realities of a vast organization in search of treatment. Ultimately the real challenge is one of integrating individual differences and systems models. Providing treatment for a leader with an antisocial personality disorder, for example, does not negate a broader "company on the couch" pattern of systemic defiance, widespread employee arrogance and workplace incivility and hostility also worthy of further assessment and intervention.

Occasionally I have found that divisions or entire organizations appear to inspire a DSM-based personality disorder diagnosis. In the case of Rick Boulder's departure from his company, the entire system displayed clear symptoms of an Antisocial Personality Disorder. It was a pathway from "leader on the couch" to "company on the couch." But this systems application of the DSM presents a myriad of variables and challenges. Can we move from an individual differences approach to an organizational systems adaptation of the DSM? The clinical application of the DSM to organizational assessments presents a golden opportunity to truly put the "company on the couch." Surely, Kets de Vries has been knocking on this door and stimulating research and debate for decades. Hopefully, my analysis may persuade some to take another step in crossing disciplinary lines by investigating criteria for high toxicity or psychopathologies and applying the DSM-IV-TR (and the subsequent DSM V) to systems analysis.

THE CHALLENGES OF THE DSM-IV-TR

There are limitations to this study that point toward the DMS-IV-TR itself, and how it is operationalized. The DSM-IV-TR is obviously not a manual to be pulled off the shelf by the average leadership researcher or management consultant as it requires deep clinical training. However, I contend that trained or not, it is important to acknowledge the promise that it holds for leadership and OD research and applications. But there are significant limitations surrounding the logistics of incorporating the DSM into the leadership and management repertoire. Few leadership researchers or management consultants are significantly trained or credentialed in the DSM-IV-TR. Accordingly, the executive coaching and consultation presented in this chapter may fall outside of their interest or expertise areas. It is not without merit, however, to consider the implications of studying DSM diagnosed leadership pathologies inasmuch as this may be an asset in working with leaders who have narcissistic or antisocial tendencies but fall short of meeting the criteria for a personality disorder.

The DSM-IV-TR presents a disciplinary challenge. How do we overcome disciplinary limitations, move beyond the realm of "milder" or "lighter" toxicity investigations and incorporate the prospect of the study of psychopathology into our research and consultations? While a few leadership scholars have credentials in both management and psychotherapy allowing for reference to and usage of the DSM (e.g., see Goldman, 2005; Lubit, 2004), another promising route is through cross-disciplinary collaborations as recommended by Lowman (2002). Interestingly, it is not just a case of organizational researchers who lack DSM expertise in their investigation of leadership, as our counseling and industrial psychology neighbors conversely need systems and management expertise and are ripe for collaborations (Lowman, 2002).

Another concern of this study surrounds the fact that the credentialed use of the DSM does not eliminate the existence of discretionary, subjective elements throughout the assessment, intervention and implementation process. The DSM-IV-TR is only as good as the clinician and is not a cookbook or set of rules to be applied uniformly. Moreover, there is ongoing debate in the psychological and psychiatric communities over the viability of some of the DSM criteria and the theoretical justification for diagnoses (e.g., see Livesley, 2001). Objective, standardized psychological testing is inadequate as a sole means of data collection (e.g., the MMPI–2) and does not replace clinical judgment and a differential diagnosis. Assessments covering the criteria content for a DSM assessment typically include both testing and the positioning of the expert as a diagnostician and participant action researcher. Researchers considering the incorporation of the DSM into their organizational research and consultation should also note that there are personality assessment tools available such as the MMPI–2 and the Global Assessment Functioning Scale or the "GAF" (American Psychiatric Association, 2000, p. 34) and a myriad of other instruments derivative of various schools of personality research (e.g., the "five-factor model" and the Big Five Theory of personality traits).

A further limitation includes the issue of the generalizability of an action research agenda. I recognize that the soft qualitative data and anecdotal reports generated are not likely to be easily replicated in other settings by other researchers. As an action researcher, however, I am most concerned with generating prospects for rich theory, stimulating strategic dialogue and questioning, serving as a change agent, and challenging current limitations of precedent research.

In selecting more extreme cases of pathology I am examining the farther reaches of leadership dysfunction. Is this a representative case study of dysfunctional leadership? Does the consultation described hold merit for the study of the "dark side" of leadership and organizational systems? Leadership researchers and management consultants may only encounter leaders with less well-defined characteristics than those highlighted in this chapter. Will researchers lacking DSM training confuse aggressive, threatening and inappropriate workplace behaviors with the more extreme antisocial personality disorder? Accordingly, I am concerned that there is the clear and present danger of an uncritical adoption of the DSM-IV-TR, whereby leaders with "normal pathology" and intermittent toxic behavior in the workplace are mistakenly assigned a clinical diagnosis of pathology. Once we consider the possibility of assessing psychopathology in leaders, workers or organizational systems we are entertaining the dangers of misdiagnosis. *Uncritical usage of the DSM may in fact result in the over-diagnosis of a Depressive Personality Disorder for a leader who is temporarily responding to organizational stressors.* Or another DSM failure may be reflected in the inability to grasp the seriousness or gravity of a pathology and its consequences for an organizational system. In the case of Rick Boulder, the EAP initially diagnosed him as a "petty tyrant" and an "abusive supervisor." While both are fitting, this was an under-diagnosis of a far more serious antisocial personality disorder. Boulder's sociopathic and psychopathic personality traits had been unwittingly trivialized and designated as a more commonplace, normal disturbance and source of conflict in his workplace. Sadly, this missed diagnosis resulted in extremely toxic consequences for Boulder's organization.

ARE WE IN THE BUSINESS OF HEALING SICK LEADERS?

A common response heard at the Academy of Management is that "we are not in the business of healing sick leaders and pathological companies; we are not psychiatrists." In response, I find that the specific sub-specialty of personality disorders in leadership as it relates to organizational systems has been on our agenda for quite some time. Surely, if there was any doubt, that was addressed back in 1984 when Kets de Vries and Miller presented us with *The Neurotic Organization* (Kets de Vries & Miller, 1984b). It was now officially out in the mainstream that the management discipline had moved from decades of big five, trait, and individual differences approaches to personality research into the more rarefied and extreme arena of assessing sick leaders and companies. A golden bridge was under construction linking leadership, management and psychology under the shared umbrella of destructive individuals and systems. Upon closer examination I found that this bridge was partial and conditional. It appeared as if the issues of psychopathology or mental and emotional toxicity in leadership were frequently alluded to in the leadership literature but the crux of the research agenda was with leaders who fell short of a DSM diagnosis. In fact, in an interview with Kets de Vries, published in 2004, he stated that "people in mental hospitals are easy to understand because they suffer from extreme conditions. The mental health of senior executives is much more subtle" (Coutu, 2004, p. 66). As illustrated in this book, I have encountered leaders who suffered from serious mental and emotional issues but were able to maintain their leadership roles and be productive up until the point where their personality disorders became detrimental and prohibitive (e.g., see chapter 9).

Once diagnosed, the majority of leaders I have worked with have only received outpatient care and rarely reached a point where they needed to be an inpatient in a mental health facility. Moreover, it is well documented that narcissists, for example, can be quite productive as leaders in the workplace (Kets de Vries & Miller, 1984a,b; Maccoby, 2003). *Future research may in fact pursue whether leaders suffering from antisocial or narcissistic personality disorder can in fact bring added value to their organizations within certain venues and situations.*

Troublesome, however, is the growing incidence in pop leadership publications of pseudo-diagnoses and references to personality disorders, without meeting the DSM criteria. As social scientists, coaches, consultants and business leaders we are more than capable of describing and interpreting *antisocial behavior.* But once we get into the business of talking about narcissistic and borderline executives or we describe entire companies as narcissistic, then we are making sweeping personality assessments and potentially stigmatizing individuals with an unwarranted, flippant, unofficial personality disorder diagnosis. Without a working knowledge and application of the DSM we are constantly confusing and blurring the lines between "antisocial behaviors" or "antisocial traits" and an "abnormal antisocial personality disorder." *Considering the possible consequences of our words for leaders and organizations, I find there is little margin for error. Any error is egregious.* Are we merely borrowing, shaping and molding the DSM-IV-TR in order to extend our management arsenal into the exotic and topical arena of toxicity? Are we not concerned with the precision of DSM language and diagnoses designed by our neighbors over in counseling and industrial psychology and psychiatry?

IT TAKES ONE SICK LEADER TO BRING DOWN A COMPANY

Since it only takes one sick leader to bring down a company are we satisfied with a repertoire of leadership assessment tools that fall short of recognizing the prevalence and inevitability of a personality disorder among our leaders? *Trivializing pathologies and perceiving them as normal disturbances in the workplace is potentially quite detrimental in a volatile workplace* already embroiled in bullying, toxic behaviors, aggression, violence, and what has recently been identified as organizational terrorism (Van Fleet & Van Fleet, 2006). *Surely, undiagnosed or misdiagnosed pathologies in our leaders are a precursor to ever-escalating organizational dysfunction!* Just one failure to timely assess may yield dramatic interpersonal and systemic repercussions including sabotage, plunging motivation and productivity, increased turnover, and a high incidence of internal grievances, formal complaints and litigation.

We may at times be fearful, ourselves, of the unknown. Are we keeping the doors locked on those mysterious psychological disciplines down the road? Perhaps we at times mirror our clients' behavior when we lack readiness and are resistant to assessments, interventions and disciplinary change. *But by virtue of our excursion into unhealthy organizations and leadership it was inevitable that we would follow the trail into full-blown pathology.* The DSM is rapidly within reach by virtue of cross-disciplinary collaborations. Surrounding DSM issues addressed in this chapter, I envision an increasing dialogue between the management and psychology communities. In some instances, there may even be a drive to extend our individual management specializations into the field of psychology resulting in more DSM expertise and psychology credentialing in business schools and management consulting groups.

Future investigations may continue to pursue action research and case studies as presented in this chapter, or choose to move in more empirical and quantitative directions. Along these lines, much needs to be done to bridge "individual differences" and "systems approaches" to leadership pathology and organizational dysfunction. A lofty challenge faces us in attempting to integrate the DSM-IV-TR into leadership, OD and consulting perspectives within the management disciplines. An even loftier challenge centers about the potential viability of the DSM in company-wide, systemic analysis of pathology (e.g., see Minuchin, 1974, for a "family systems" approach). Innovative hybrids of the DSM, fifth discipline systems dynamics, OD, and reinventions of old general systems theory may prove interesting and fruitful.

8   Histrionic leadership: the allure of the toxic leader in a volatile industry

> The anguish of the client, is fundamental to all consultation: No pain, no problem; no problem, no need for a consultant. Despite what anyone may say, no organization undertakes consultation "to make things better" unless someone hurts. Therefore, the basic question for every consultant regardless of the reason for a consultation request is, "Where is the pain?"
>
> (Levinson, 2002, p. 63)

COMPLEX EMOTIONAL CONSTELLATIONS IN A LEADER

A full range of emotional volatility fills every workplace. From the vantage points of organizational behavior, psychology and leadership there is evidence that it is the dark side of emotional expression that solicits an extraordinary amount of attention in the workplace (e.g., see Ashforth & Humphrey, 1995; Goleman, 1995; Kanfer & Kantrowitz, 2002; Lord, Klimoski and Kanfer, 2002). Whereas, the emotionally intelligent leader is correlated with high motivation and productivity (e.g., see Goleman, 1995), it is the perception of emotional negligence and something felt as dysfunctional that brings an organization's affective or feeling side increasingly into consciousness. In essence, the primary attention paid to emotions in organizations is as "a source of disturbance" (Armstrong, 2005, p. 91). While the charming, charismatic, sensitive and empathic boss catches the eye of subordinates, it is the turbulent, excessive and abusive emotional extremes that brings organizations to the offices of coaches and consultants.

In this chapter, complex emotional constellations are embedded in a leader in the fashion industry. Mr. Markus Renee's extraordinary and extreme gamut of highly emotionally charged behavior ultimately cannot be separated from his colleagues and subordinates or the Cavendish & Bodark Haute Couture organizational system.

At what point does the affective behavior of a leader suggest symptoms falling outside the broad boundaries of what is deemed appropriate and acceptable? At stake is the ability of an organization to discern whether they are experiencing only objectionable and difficult behavior or whether a line has been crossed and a workplace has been ushered into a dysfunctional and toxic zone. Who will make this determination: Management? Human resources? An employee assistance program? Or does it require external experts to discern whether an organization has been engaged in merely difficult or substantially dysfunctional leadership? In the following consultation I unveil the difficulties faced by Cavendish & Bodark in their struggle to interpret and detoxify the outlandish emotional displays of their celebrated leader, Mr. Markus Renee. Despite his high-level innovation and unprecedented productivity, the upper echelon was dumbfounded by its fashion leader's capacity to incite extreme responses.

CAVENDISH & BODARK'S ORGANIZATIONAL CULTURE

Cavendish & Bodark Haute Couture is a large upscale apparel store in a major West Coast, US city. Cavendish & Bodark is unique in that it blurs the line between the small boutique and large clothing retailer by specializing in highest-quality, trendy and top designer, haute couture fashion. Celeste Cavendish, president of the company, opened her first small boutique in San Francisco and has expanded to seven large retail outlets, four in the Western US, and three locations in major northern European cities. Cavendish is a widely acknowledged innovator in the fashion industry as she broke with precedent by being one of the first developers of department-sized boutiques. Fashion reigns supreme at Cavendish & Bodark as the top designers are represented on the racks and the competition to earn shelf space is fierce.

The creativity of Cavendish & Bodark extends to its development of both in-house and public fashion shows as designers display their wares on the stores' runways. Conceived of as a "total fashion experience," the fresh approach of combining runway with retail is cutting edge, breaks barriers and defies precedent in the industry. The in-house itinerary includes frequent small showings of new and experimental designs typically modeled by employees for employees. This venue provides what President Cavendish displays as "breakthrough 360 degree involvement of sales representatives in Cavendish & Bodark decision making, A to Z." Sales personnel are literally engaged in voicing their reactions to new designs, limited edition and one of a kind fashions, and first time around "for your eyes only" glimpses of what may soon set the fashion world on fire – or fall flat and bomb. Cavendish seriously empowers her employees to be "invested in strategic fashion decision making" as her horizontal approach extends a degree of leadership to everyone in her company.

Widely viewed as the reigning duchess of a "fashion family," President Cavendish has worked hard at achieving some measure of stability in her organization and providing a more balanced alternative to what she describes as the "wild turnover and infidelity of the fashion industry." In the eight years since conception, turnover initially hovered around 17 to 20 percent but, through an ongoing series of adjustments in hiring and selection and a transition to a family-style culture, the turnover rate dramatically slipped to an industry low of 5.5 percent. Entrance into Cavendish & Bodark is admission into a tightly guarded and closely knit family unit. Commitment to management and leadership, sales representatives, and fashion experts is exceedingly high. Moreover, it is high priority at Cavendish that various expertise areas and divisions regularly cross borders and get to know each other's perspectives, talents and mind sets.

The entrance portal at Cavendish & Bodark is taken quite seriously. Under the tutelage of the president, HR has established a world-class interviewing and research system for potential hires. Interviewees must go through multiple layers of interviews, with a broad representation of Cavendish employees directly engaged as voting members for each and every hire. Once again, President Cavendish deeply believes in the critical nature of a "buy in" and "extreme levels of engagement and commitment to company – achieved through a horizontal democracy of the highest order."

A select and special category at Cavendish & Bodark is that of upper level managers who are hired to provide leadership, vision and transformation, and an ability to be fluidly and frequently engaged with all players including top designers and suppliers. In some cases this includes the engagement of Cavendish leadership in limited edition co-design, as Cavendish & Bodark may partner with a renowned Italian or French designer to create a custom item. In addition, Cavendish & Bodark leaders directly participate in the creation and staging of runway shows and creative input typically reserved for the artist. President Cavendish relishes the prospect of "finding those very few fashion minds who do an eclectic form of leadership truly customized to the high-end clothing industry." Leadership for Cavendish entails:

> not only addressing productivity, human capital, supply chain, purchasing, human resources and customer service but also involves a passion and commitment for fashion design, runway and the whole aesthetic package from conception to delivery.

EXTRAORDINARY HIRES FOR A VOLATILE INDUSTRY

In her six locations Cavendish explained that she has found and hired three "hybrid and seriously eclectic leaders who combine the artistic relationship and the retail specializations." Of the three, Mr. Markus Renee is in Cavendish's words:

> my most talented and unorthodox find. A gentleman with a broad and impressive background in European, Japanese and North American fashion. He is a one of a kind mind and artist who brings extensive world class design and runway experience to our operation. There is no worry that Mr. Renee is confined or restricted inside the box ... he is hopelessly outside the box and bringing daring and potentially contagious prospects to our fashion house.

The unique personality and package known as Markus Renee is both wildly creative and enigmatic. Once on board, the majority of colleagues had multiple reads on Renee. Cavendish, HR and upper-echelon management struggled to interpret his showy and excessive behavior. Extraordinarily talented as an artist and with a flair that ignites customer interest and loyalty, Renee is also a highly complex leader with a dark side.

Markus Renee's first two years at Cavendish & Bodark were marked by breakthroughs in innovative design, articulations with the greatest fashion artists in Western Europe, and unprecedented profits establishing new benchmarks in the industry. As a leader, Renee appeared quite comfortable with the near chaotic state of affairs at Cavendish & Bodark. In the words of upper-echelon management, Cavendish and Renee were a "wonderful and seamless partnership." A veteran of what has alternately been termed the textile, clothing, apparel and fashion industries, Renee was no stranger to the bounded instability around him (e.g., see Stacey, 1992, 1996). He was quick to offer that "fashion is fickle, changeable, hot and cold, up and down, and it's a perfect fit for my flamboyant, impressionable, dramatic personality!" Renee's extreme flexibility allowed him to move very quickly and be instantaneously decisive. When Renee saw a "top shelf assortment of formal lady's suits" he immediately reacted with "it's to die for" and a contract and deal were usually hours away. Exclusivity and timeliness were the holy grail. Renee could be a lightning rod when he needed to be. Contracts were made in what appeared to be minutes. He knew his stuff inside out. Alternatively, he could be quite abrupt and equally decisive when he decided that seventeen racks were going into clearance and "have to be out of my sight in no more than two weeks or I shoot blindly and at will." Renee also made instant u-turns and was known to abort decisions mid-stream. Renee boasted that in one situation:

> I had to renegotiate a new line of young lady's designer dresses and dress shoes when I found out at a minute to midnight that the designer had been cannibalized. We never got a chance to show and sell his designs because there were some spies operating and his fashion was already in the discount houses.

Suffice to say that the fashion industry ironically shares a rapid-fire turnaround time and immediacy with the IT industry. In the words of Renee:

> in the fashion industry, if you blink once you are a generation ago or your stuff is already for sale at the 99 cent shops; and if you blink twice and excuse yourself to go to the little boy's room at the wrong time, you will be three generations ago and your shoes, motherboards and blouses will be from grandma's era – with knockoffs already filling the racks at Kmart and Ross.

THE HONEYMOON PERIOD IS OVER

Gradually, a few problems began to surface at Cavendish & Bodark during Renee's third year. Profits fell and eventually plummeted. Two international designers cut all ties with Cavendish. The newly appointed vice president of operations, Justin Ornish, was hired at the start of Renee's third year with the company, and he appeared to be pointing his finger at Renee as a major source of the organization's recent woes. President Cavendish remained silent. Internal issues arose whereby employees under Renee questioned his leadership style and in some instances filed complaints and grievances.

Was the honeymoon period over? Was this a function of organizational or leadership issues? Questions arose as to Renee's leadership qualities. The talk in the HR department and around the design division was laced with such words as "dysfunctional" and "toxic." Was a downswing getting to the workforce, a fall not atypical in the fashion industry, or was leadership at fault? The VP and HR began asking questions pertaining to Renee's unusual personality and flamboyant way of expressing himself. At this point in the organization's journey there were numerous questions and most lines of inquiry included Mr. Markus Renee. It was a time for probing, self-reflection and attempting to get back on track toward profitability. As a consultant who was brought in to assess the organizational instability I required a full risk assessment and case history. I now concentrate on a full disclosure of the history and role of Mr. Markus Renee as the alleged "center of attention" during the glory years and the decline at Cavendish & Bodark. The historical narrative is strategic to providing interventions and solutions moving Cavendish & Bodark back towards conflict reduction and profitability.

SCRUTINIZING THE LEADERSHIP OF MARKUS RENEE

As a senior manager at Cavendish & Bodark Haute Couture, Mr. Renee is a hands-on leader who is present and available to employees and practices a style of management termed MBWA, or "management by walking around." Mr. Renee frequently states at Cavendish & Bodark meetings that he "does not believe in walls and doors," and consciously "minimizes the distance and time for superiors, subordinates and customers to communicate." He embodies many of the principles of theory Y styled management and greatly values worker empowerment and a horizontal approach to leadership. Markus Renee is an adventurous, innovative and entrepreneurial MBA who emulates the maximum flexibility and trusting approach to employees exemplified in organizations such as Nordstrom's and Neiman Marcus Department Stores. Renee's office has an open door policy and he is constantly chatting with employees and physically roaming through all of Cavendish & Bodark's departments: ladies shoes; men's suits; kitchenware; jewelry; and children's toys. He loves to be called "Mr. Accessible."

When Mr. Renee first occupied a leadership role as the Senior Manager some five years ago (he was recruited from a rival department store chain via executive recruitment consultants) he was immediately popular with employees. Renee was a welcome change from the rigid, old-world management style of his Austrian-born and educated predecessor, Hermann Gunther Gruttman. Renee brought fresh ideas, vitality and a participatory management style. In the first two years of Renee's leadership motivation, productivity and profits soared. But by his third year there were an increasing number of whispers in the workplace concerning Mr. Renee's temperament, personality and leadership style. Even a close supporter of Renee's offered that "our manager has been going through some strange transformations before our very eyes." Allegedly, there was much speculation and informal organizational gossip alleging that Markus Renee's personality had morphed from highly interpersonal, congenial and inspirational to that of an extremely inappropriate and dramatic leader. His behavior in the workplace appeared increasingly wild and erratic, marked by several hysterical outbursts that seemed to come from nowhere. In essence, according to HR director Shirley Tessler, employees were initially shocked and even entertained by Renee's spectacles but this soon turned into a dread of the fearful anticipation of his next explosion. In the words of a colleague, "it was difficult to anticipate when Renee would light up and catch fire and respond in a shockingly inappropriate manner. But you knew it was going to happen sooner or later."

A CONSTANT CENTER OF ATTENTION

Employees were increasingly disturbed and diverted by Mr. Renee's seeming need to be "Mr. Fashion" and the constant center of attention. According to employees interviewed (by the Hans Hanover and Associates Consulting Group), Renee was both flamboyant and redundant in his never-ending stories about his years as a male runway model. Renee got so pumped up in his storytelling that he seemed to vent at times, spewing an extreme rash of excitable emotions. Renee was on a fashion mission fueled by glorious memories and a hyper pulsating emotional state. Based on a broad range of reports from colleagues and subordinates, Mr. Renee constantly wanted to relive his glory days as a model. Once based out of Marseilles, and later, Rome, the Markus Renee of the late 1970s and early 1980s graced the covers of many European and US fashion magazines as a top male model for such designers as Gianni Versace and Giorgio Armani. A self-proclaimed "fashion guru" and "Euro-Narcissist," Mr. Renee transitioned into fashion retail but never quite abandoned his earlier days in front of audiences and the paparazzi.

In Renee's way of seeing his world, wherever his life took him glamour was bound to follow. The senior manager viewed his managerial position at Cavendish & Bodark Haute Couture as a series of opportunities to network with the rich and famous and draw attention to his talented self. At every opportunity, Renee set himself up as a self-anointed fashion expert. He frequently subjected employees to his simulations of catwalk shows starring none other than Mr. Markus Renee! Not only did Mr. Renee cast himself as the prime time Cavendish & Bodark model, he also increasingly turned toward cutting-edge fashions that openly displayed his proclamation of "metro-sexuality" as he purposely blurred the traditional lines between the sexes. Mr. Markus Renee favored skin tight, avant garde Italian clothes that brought to mind some of the lounge lizard outfits of Tom Jones and Elvis Presley during the mid-1970s (early disco period, complete with multi-faceted and layered gold chain ensembles around a hairy chest). He grinded and performed sexually explicit maneuvers under the guise of illustrating why Cavendish & Bodark should or should not carry specific "youth lines" of fashion clothing. This appeared a bit out of the ordinary for a slightly overweight fifty-something senior manager. Reactions were mixed. Some of Renee's subordinates appeared to assume the role of a dedicated fan club committed to empowering his every move.

Surprisingly, Renee's manner and swagger appeared to be oddly contagious in Cavendish & Bodark employee circles. A metro-cool walk and dazzling manner of showbiz-like interaction was increasingly cloned by Renee's young subordinates. Several of the youthful and "Renee inspired" sales personnel increasingly utilized overstatement, affectation and a "gushing emotional quality" in their daily communication with both colleagues and customers. According to the HR direction, "employees appeared to be mimicking aspects of Renee's obsession with being the center of attention." Sales associates increasingly spoke to customers in a manner more appropriate to starlet talk on the Hollywood "red carpet" or the flashy, hyped up conversation on late night talk television shows. The showbusiness attitude that emanated down the organizational chart was accompanied by a distinctive brand of melodrama reeking of Markus Renee. Drama was everywhere on the Bodark floor. There were very high highs and very low lows as associates were one moment overflowing with the affectations of kindness and minutes later openly annoyed, angered and combative.

THE DRAMA KING OR DRAMA QUEEN

At the epicenter of the soap opera was the drama king himself, Cavendish & Bodark's Senior Manager, Markus Renee. Attracting extreme loyalty and humor among followers and bitter and repugnant reactions from detractors, Renee was never boring. The soothsayers complained that Mr. Renee was engaging in provocative and inappropriate behavior – both in his unfortunate runway model simulations and in his minute-by-minute interpersonal interactions in the workplace. In the words of the director of human resources, Ms. Shirley Tessler, Renee looked like a "primping male peacock or an alluring lounge singer who didn't know where to draw the line." The odd behavior extended into alleged "advances" or what Renee described as "innocent touching behaviors" toward Cavendish & Bodark employees. Three employees (one gentleman and two ladies) filed grievances with the Cavendish & Bodark HR department alleging "inappropriate and uncomfortable touching behavior" from Mr. Renee.

The initial vitality and motivational spirit characteristic of Renee's leadership turned into a cautious, defensive atmosphere where a growing number of employees were reluctant to have any encounters with their toxic leader. A significant number of employees alleged that "Mr. Renee is an exhibitionist. It is terribly uncomfortable and distracting to work in his presence." Paradoxically, Markus Renee was also seriously charming, charismatic and alluring to some Cavendish & Bodark employees. But this adulation was waning. Based on individual interviews with all members of Renee's division and a comprehensive 360 degree feedback study it became apparent that the leader's behavior was hotly contested and at the core of all store operations. Overall, it was a surprising split decision for the senior manager. Markus Renee was perceived by his employees as both wildly entertaining and charismatic as well as uncomfortably embarrassing, even threatening. Employees were in majority agreement, however, that Renee was overly theatrical and quite exaggerated in how he expressed emotions to employees, customers, vendors and outside contractors.

Melodrama prevailed and it somehow seemed quite inappropriate within the context of a high-end department store. The high maintenance leader continued to attract the majority of attention. Two freshly hired young female employees complained to HR that Renee had "misunderstood" the meaning of "innocent lunches" in the company cafeteria and considered certain workplace relations to be far more than they actually were. Markus Renee had a knack for embellishing and exaggerating the minute-by-minute exchanges in the workplace into full blown Hollywood movie moments. Even the ordinary or mundane was blown out of proportion and became larger than life. At times Renee's grandiose renditions of reality alternately pumped vigor or outrage into followers around him. Young sales ladies were alternately amused, horrified and repulsed by Renee's amalgam of a Victorian elocutionist and a male lounge singer. HR heard an earful. There was no shortage of gossip, complaints, believers and attackers.

The status quo around Renee and throughout Cavendish & Bodark had grown increasingly rocky. Stability was a distant memory. A wild ride set the stage. Had the people side of the equation gotten totally out of control? What should be done? How could you settle down some of those with grievances and explore the troubling side of the former boy genius, Markus Renee? A senior buyer, Marshall Prague, wondered whether the infamous runway model's EQ would ever match his IQ. Could Renee ever sufficiently step outside himself to truly listen to his once adoring followers? Or was the decadent drama king too far gone, with a closing of his Cavendish & Bodark show inevitable?

The CEO, Celeste Cavendish, made it abundantly clear that she did in fact want me to use all available means of persuasion to salvage Markus. The CEO joined the ranks of believers who saw the innovative genius of Renee but wanted some downside protection along the way. Her simple words were, "yes, he's quite dangerous ... but I believe that he's worth it." Besides, with grievances and litigation lurking, Cavendish did not want to set the stage for some dark media event. Damage control was first on the agenda. Salvage Markus Renee and properly install him as Senior Manager on his way up in the organization.

Moreover, Celeste Cavendish pointed toward the organization as a whole. Even though it was easy to get subsumed in the Renee saga, ultimately she wanted to tame the insidious spread of bad behavior throughout Cavendish & Bodark. Whispers of "Renee's the source; he's the nut job; send him away" did not resonate with the leadership coach or the CEO. Positive leadership had to somehow be red flagged and prevail. Perhaps the troubling issues with Markus Renee could serve as a transformational wake-up call or a "darkest hour just before the dawn" moment.

A CONSULTANT IS CALLED IN

Following several failed attempts by the human resources department and the employee assistance program to intervene, an outside consultancy was retained to assess the conflict-ridden atmosphere permeating Cavendish & Bodark. In the course of a comprehensive needs assessment conducted by Hanover & Associates, questions were asked as to whether the behavior of Renee was negatively impacting worker morale, sales and motivation. Were employees overreacting? Was there a worker conspiracy intent upon collective exaggeration en route to dumping Renee? How did this senior manager who was initially perceived as a breath of fresh air and a "fun guy to work for" turn into a walking deficit and a theatrical plague? The stakes were high. Cavendish & Bodark was terribly concerned about its high-end, impeccable image. Bad press would be devastating. In addition, Cavendish & Bodark's president, Celeste Cavendish, was quite uncomfortable with the mounting number of internal grievances and the threat of looming litigation potentially bringing the company's dirty laundry into the public eye.

A LEADERSHIP COACH AND PSYCHOTHERAPIST IS RETAINED

After five weeks of interviewing and gathering data, Mr. Wilber Hanover expressed that the breakdown of morale, the mounting number of grievances and the threat of litigation required additional support from a leadership coach and psychotherapist. The company's problems extended beyond the typical boundaries of management consulting. It was at this point that both Hanover and secondly Cavendish & Bodark Haute Couture contacted me on behalf of Markus Renee. After a preliminary briefing I tentatively agreed to collaborate with the Hanover group.

A comprehensive briefing provided by the Hanover group was followed by a series of interviews with colleagues and followers who filed grievances and threatened discrimination litigation against Mr. Renee. Consistent patterns of allegedly embarrassing and abusive behavior and accompanying retribution were confirmed. Approximately half of the slighted and angry subordinates could be classified as followers who had great faith in Mr. Renee, placed him on a pedestal and later felt that he was vacuous, shallow and betrayed their trust. One sales associate, Astrid Cunningham, stated that:

> Markus Renee is a magnetic character, a charming, pseudo-sophisticated leader who is a natural born charismatic. He had a lot of us going. We thought he was the second coming. But let me let you in on his fall from grace. Markus Renee fell out of the fashion tower and into the pits of cheap and tawdry exhibitionism ... Markus blows up like a grenade if he isn't the absolute ... I mean the total absolute center of attention. He freaks if he doesn't rule. How do you live with a leader like that? Tell me, what do you do with this high-maintenance clown? Yeah, like he's a legend in the fashion industry but how do we overcome his personality? It's a big "yuk"...

My assessment moved forward with a personal focus on Markus Renee. This was the expectation of both the Hanover group and the Cavendish & Bodark CEO. Working from a hybrid perspective combining leadership coaching and counseling psychology, I entered into an ongoing clinical relationship with Mr. Renee. This process initially included ninety-minute sessions two times a week over a period of ten months. During the early weeks there were frequent phone and email consultations addressing a myriad of workplace, colleague and follower issues as they emerged on the shop floor. A fine line was walked between ongoing coaching consultations for the leader and psychotherapy addressed to the patient. A diagnosis for Markus Renee was determined approximately six weeks into the coaching and therapy. Renee was diagnosed as having "Histrionic Personality Disorder" cited in the Diagnostic and Statistical Manual of the American Psychological Association as DSM–IV 301.50 (American Psychiatric Association, 2000, p. 711–714). Further field study led to the assessment that the histrionic personality disorder had morphed and metastasized within the Cavendish & Bodark organizational system. In other words, a longstanding disorder located in Mr. Renee had spread within the company walls much as an Epstein-Barr virus might physically infiltrate a workplace or second-hand smoke was transmitted from solo smokers and absorbed into the lungs of numerous flight attendants within a closed cabin space.

INTERVENTION WITH A DESTRUCTIVE LEADER

An in-depth investigation of Mr. Renee's past place of employment revealed a similar series of events – a history concealed prior to and during Renee's hire with Cavendish & Bodark. Once provided with the diagnosis (with the consensus of Renee), both Renee-as-an-individual-client and Cavendish & Bodark as the organizational client were in a position to consider some "therapeutic interventions." But the unanimous conclusion was that this was a "problem" outside the realm of "normal conflicts in the workplace" more accurately portrayed as an individual pathology that had in turn affected numerous employees at

Cavendish & Bodark. Once the diagnosis was achieved and interventions chosen by Renee and agreed upon by Cavendish & Bodark, contingency plans were drawn up concerning Renee's future with the company. In addition, Mr. Hanover stepped back into the consultation and worked with his colleagues in Hanover Consulting to provide Cavendish & Bodark with a training program that would effectively move it out of the Histrionic Personality Era of Renee and into a "new morning" of possibilities for high morale, productivity and teamwork.

Once I established the "histrionic personality disorder" it opened the floodgates for both individual and organizational interventions, and provided a basis for a constructive return of Hanover Consulting into the treatment and healing process. The Cavendish & Bodark training fundamentally attempted to de-program employees out of what I described as a system-wide histrionic personality disorder that permeated dimensions of sales, customer service, and those employees who experienced Mr. Renee as a leader and role model.

FOLLOWERSHIP EMPOWERS TOXICITY

It was more than curiosity that led me to ask questions that were formally articulated by Kellerman (2004, 2008) and Lipman-Blumen (2005). Exactly what is the allure of the toxic leader and why do we follow destructive bosses? Even though deeply and adversely impacted by his personality disorder, Renee wielded a significant influence over many Cavendish & Bodark employees and his individual pathology became indecipherable at times from system-wide pathology in Cavendish & Bodark. Employees not only registered complaints against Renee, they also enabled and empowered him, and at times engaged in unwitting transference with the troubled leader, as they felt a "false connection" with him (e.g., see Kets de Vries, 1995, p. 225). Markus Renee had lured many followers into the fascinating, exciting web of his private world of fashion – at the expense of their good judgment and sobriety. Despite his self-possessed rantings, for the longest time followers ignored Renee's faults, glorified his strengths, and gave rise to a dramatic culture with Markus at the center. Make no mistake about it, the overstated and exaggerated self-congratulating prancings of Renee were nourished by his subordinates, and their hopes and desires seemed so intricately tied to his every breath and move. I was equally struck by both Renee's leadership and the role of the follower in the organizational toxicity (e.g., see Kellerman, 2008).

Curious was the pattern shared between Markus Renee and his true believers. Although it originated with Mr. Renee, epidemics of hyperactivity, impulsiveness, make-or-break hunches, quick impressions, and a disdain for facts and detailed analyses contributed to company-wide innovativeness, boldness and aggression.

Some Bodark sales people saw in Renee a rebellious, outside the box, unorthodox, rebel type individual out of their own pasts. Through his antics they celebrated and revisited outrageous behavior from their teens and early twenties; exhibitionism flourished. A few managers even adapted a somewhat narcissistic agenda inadvertently modeled by Renee. Two middle managers mimicked Renee's methods of redecorating and redesigning their offices in a very extravagant and dramatic fashion, engaging in Renee-sanctioned exhibitionism.

DEBRIEFING AND DE-ESCALATION OF DYSFUNCTION

Following ten months of extensive individual leadership coaching and psychotherapy with Markus Renee and accompanying company-wide "debriefing training," Cavendish & Bodark Haute Couture experienced a significant de-escalation of the previously widespread epidemic of histrionic personality disorder symptoms. Of significance is the fact that the allure of Renee as a toxic leader in essence numbed the upper echelon to the dark dimensions of his leadership. Moreover, his consistently destructive behavior – ranging from extreme self-centeredness and sexually seductive and inappropriate public expression to wildly fluctuating emotional extremes and self-dramatization – spread from Renee throughout the workforce. The dual interventions of individual coaching and psychotherapy and team training and the debriefing of subordinates in Renee's division diffused and lessened the dysfunctional patterns of expression.

WHEN TIMELINESS IS DELAYED BY ALLURE AND CHARM

Timeliness in the detection of a destructive leader is significantly delayed by the allures of productivity, charisma, and the exuberance experienced in the presence of an emotionally volatile boss. Eventually, faced with the overwhelmingly toxic dimensions of their leader's behavior, Cavendish & Bodark searched for a way out of a systemic entrapment within which the Histrionic Personality Disorder had in fact broadly metastasized.

Throughout the period of his leadership therapy and coaching, Markus Renee was taking medication for his Histrionic Personality Disorder and taught techniques for increasing his capacity for self-control and de-escalation of his emotionally infringing and toxic behavior.

REDUCING TOXICITY TO FUNCTIONAL LEVELS

This was not a simple case of eliminating histrionic behavior from the workplace and replacing it with healthy behavior – but rather that of negotiating a reasonable blend of fashion industry drama and everyday reason, rationality and appropriateness. Renee, although mostly outside the boundaries of acceptable etiquette, was nevertheless alternately recognizable as a version of the prototypical "Drama King" and "Drama Queen." Rather than being faced with removal of the "malignant leader" it was a case of decreasing Renee's melodramatics and outrageously excessive behavior from 80 percent down to a 20 percent level. Accordingly, it was also an objective of leadership therapy to gradually relinquish Renee's manic need to be the center of attention from 90 percent down into the teens. Clearly the goal of the CEO and president of the company was not to physically eliminate Renee or to disassemble their leader's fashion flair and fire. Deeply entrenched in the runway and "crazy life of high fashion," the top brass only sought medication and the reduction of Renee's difficult behavior to tolerable levels. The hyper-productive and wildly innovative actions of Renee were preserved and not a target of therapy or change.

The "better extremes of Renee's outlandish behavior and drop dead creativity" were to be preserved and not challenged. It was rather a case of smoothing out rough edges and the farther reaches of outlandish behavior to the point where Renee could once again function in the light of day and not drive his once adoring colleagues stone cold crazy. The show must go on.

9 The outer limits of toxic organizational behavior: corporate trauma in the form of disturbed leadership

> Some leaders go far beyond the abnormal ways of functioning ... They go off the deep end.
>
> (Kets de Vries, 1995, p. 217)

THE OUTER LIMITS OF TOXIC LEADERSHIP

This chapter discusses an unusual case. The consultation with Elija Engineering Ltd. morphed into leadership coaching and psychotherapy with the exalted leader of the Research and Development Division, Josh Julia. Under Julia the Elija Engineering company prospered as it expanded its reach into European and Asian markets. Julia's rising star gradually began to falter. Numerous reports came in respectfully inquiring as to the baffling, odd behavior of their leader and as to why he was increasingly absent and managing from a distance via his cell phone and email. Patience gradually gave way to impatience as world-class Japanese clients would not accept any substitute for their beloved Julia and Elija Engineers become increasingly dysfunctional and began to drift without his presence. As will be revealed, the enigma of Julia escalated to the point of my appearance as the external expert. The findings were totally unexpected and represented a first in my consulting work. The fate of Elija Engineering was in the hands of their wildly successful chief R&D engineer. The company CEO was in dire straits during our first meeting. Perhaps shell-shocked is the appropriate phrase to describe how he and many of the engineers felt about the "Julia situation." Was there any rhyme or reason behind Julia's incredibly strange and troublesome behavior?

Suffice to say that Elija Engineering was completely blindsided by the dark and bizarre behavior of its beloved leader. The more obsessive and disturbed his behavior, the deeper his colleagues and subordinates sank into an R&D depression. The CEO suspected an undisclosed source for Julia's "shadow behavior." I was given carte blanche to diagnose what ailed the company.

EXEMPLARY LEADER OR DISTURBED STRANGER?

Why was Elija Engineering Ltd. completely blindsided by the behavior of its chief R&D engineer? Its exemplary leader had increasingly turned into a disturbed stranger.

Management researchers and practitioners concur that organizations are inadequately prepared for employees who are difficult to deal with due to deeply rooted psychological disturbances (e.g., see Frost, 2003; Frost & Robinson, 1999; Goldman, 2006a, 2008a; Kellerman, 2004; Kets de Vries and Associates, 1991; Kilburg, 2000; Levinson, 1972; Lubit, 2004; Robinson & Bennett, 1995). Mild toxicity, everyday interpersonal conflicts and organizational misbehavior (OMB) are increasingly familiar territory (Ashforth, 1997; Barsade & Gibson 2007; Fox & Spector, 2005; Vardi & Weitz 2004), whereas employees with long-term, repetitive patterns of disturbed behavior typically fall outside an organization's range of expertise (Goldman, 2006b; Lowman, 2002). The challenge from the disturbed employee is significantly increased when he or she occupies an upper-echelon leadership role (Coutu, 2004; Kellerman, 2004; Kets de Vries, 1995; Litzky, Eddleston & Kidder, 2006).

To date, the management literature has primarily addressed psychological disturbances in leaders from the vantage points of trait psychology (e.g., see Barrick & Mount, 1991) and personality disorders (e.g., see Goldman 2006a,b; Livesley, 2001; Vaillant & Perry, 1980). Within these contexts researchers have emphasized narcissistic leadership, focusing on both positive and negative deviance (e.g., see Baumeister *et al.*, 1996; Kets de Vries & Miller, 1984a,b; Maccoby, 2000, 2003; Penney & Spector, 2002; Schwartz, 1990; Spector & Fox, 2005). There has been a notable absence, however, of investigation into the broader range of disorders afflicting leadership and organizations (Lubit, 2004). In response, in this chapter I identify an under-explored aspect of disturbed leadership behavior identified in the DSM-IV-TR as "somatoform disorders," characterized by the presence of destructive, self-defeating physical symptoms (American Psychiatric Association, 2000, p. 485).

The body dysmorphic disorder to be disclosed in this chapter brought an organization to the outer limits of toxic behavior. As the external consultant and coach I was contracted to assess the morphing of a brilliant leader into a deeply disturbed stranger who was the nexus of organizational triumphs, upheaval and trauma.

A LEADER WITH BODY DYSMORPHIC DISORDER

Of particular interest in this study is the somotoform disorder 300.7, body dysmorphic disorder, defined as "a preoccupation with an imagined or exaggerated defect in physical appearance" (American Psychiatric Association, 2000, p. 485). Occupying the roles of action researcher and management consultant I present a case study of a deeply disturbed leader who is at the nexus of escalating company toxicity. (*Due to confidentiality and the privileged communication status of clients, the names of individuals and organizations have been changed and scenarios sufficiently altered to preserve anonymity.*)

The central figure in the case study is chief R&D engineer Josh Julia, a perplexing high achiever who also exhibits extremely unusual behavior in the workplace. Julia imported a lesser-known pathology into Elija Engineering Ltd., to be identified as somotoform disorder 300.7, or body dysmorphic disorder. Initially Julia was perceived as bringing extraordinary creativity, brilliance and groundbreaking deal-making skills into his company. Eventually a darker side of Julia's leadership emerged as his disorder negatively affected his colleagues and division. The ramifications for the R&D engineering division and the entire company were unexpected, unprecedented and debilitating.

A CASE STUDY IN DISTURBED LEADERSHIP: ELIJA LTD.

Elija Engineering prides itself on breeding a special "think tank" of engineers who are on the cutting edge of aerospace innovation. Throughout the 1980s and halfway into the 1990s, Elija made the engineering community around the world take notice. Elija R&D was unstoppable; they excelled in major aerospace breakthrough innovations. New engine designs had been sold to the US government, commercial airliners in the US and Western Europe, and ground was being broken with Nippon Airlines of Japan. Elija was synonymous with aerospace innovation.

In 1996, Elija brought in a much heralded engineer from its chief competitor to head the R&D division, responsible for new designs and innovations for high-profile clients. Josh Julia brought an incredibly enthusiastic thrust to Elija and expectations were extremely high. During the period of 1996–1998 Julia and his division bristled with excitement and he appeared to be an extraordinary motivator for a world-class fleet of engineers. Under Julia's leadership four unprecedented engine design breakthroughs emerged and they were embraced by commercial airline clients in the US, Europe and Japan. Noteworthy was the fact that under Julia's guidance a US company had penetrated the Japanese aerospace market for the first time. This was no small feat considering that this meant that the Japanese break with their traditional *keiretsu* protocol (e.g., see Goldman, 1994). Julia essentially negotiated what was previously thought to be non-negotiable. He persuaded the Japanese company to modify their longstanding precedent and protocol by stepping outside of their infamously tightly woven corporate family or conglomerate of companies, the *Nippon Keiretsu*. The charming Julia won the Japanese over in part due to his ability to converse in the Japanese language and spearhead a trust relationship at the negotiating table. Shortly after the deal was finalized the Elija Engineering revenue stream roared and Julia's stock soared. The confidence level of the R&D division of Elija could hardly be contained. R&D at Elija seemed to be indecipherable from

Julia's own extraordinarily confident "can do" personality. Mr. Julia certainly dressed the part for his success. He regularly walked into work with another new $4,000 or $5,000 Armani, Brioni, or Versace suit accessorized with silk shirts, gold cuff links and tie pin, a $20,000 solid gold watch and crocodile shoes and belt. Among the engineers there was some playful gossip along the lines of "perhaps Julia is a narcissist?"

THE EMERGENCE OF DYSFUNCTIONAL BEHAVIOR

Gradually, Julia's colleagues took notice of some of his questionable, troubling and strange behavior. Occasionally, Julia disappeared for a week or more at a time. Once he returned with noticeable "plugs" on his scalp, placed strategically throughout his thinning hair. Apparently, he was having a hair transplant. Although this was as plain as day to his workplace, Julia never mentioned a word about it and neither did his colleagues. On another occasion, in the midst of a particularly stunning innovation and deal headed up by Julia with a South Korean corporate aerospace customer, he pulled off another disappearing act. This time he came back to the workplace some thirteen days later with a noticeably different nose and chin. His nose was considerably smaller and narrower and his chin seemed to be far more prominent. There were facial bruises and other signs of plastic surgery.

Engineers noticed that Julia repeatedly ran off to the company bathrooms. He appeared to be checking himself out about every twenty or thirty minutes in the mirrors. How was his new hair looking? How was his nose doing? What did his hair plugs look like? Could they be detected? If so, in what type of lighting? He came to work with several portable mirrors and used them regularly to see himself in profile, from the rear and from every angle. He quickly hid his mirrors when employees walked into the bathroom. Due to a reported theft (which had nothing to do with Julia) top brass wound up viewing some videos of Julia's bathroom scenario. It was quite strange and troublesome to witness. On some occasions Julia seemed to be quite happy with his reflections in the multiple mirrors. In other instances he appeared very disturbed, angry and with deep grimaces. What was overwhelming was the length of time that he spent examining himself in the mirrors. It reached approximately two to three hours per day.

Despite his "issues," Julia's successes marched on; he continued to be the prize of Elija. Another innovation brought Nippon and Hong Kong Airlines back to the Elija tables as multi-million dollar customers. At the top of their game, in winter of 1999, Julia and Elija were flying far in excess of 40,000 feet off the ground. They could do no wrong. They were the darlings of the media and the engineering and aerospace communities. But sometime during the late spring of that year, Julia's swagger started to falter. The two or three hours in front of the mirror turned into four or five. Eventually, Julia was nowhere to be seen. He started to run his division from his laptop at home. He came in only during evening hours when employees were long gone. He wore thicker makeup on his face. The staff and the entire organization began to be very concerned. What was going on?

One evening a colleague was catching up on an overdue assignment and he caught a glimpse of Julia. His nose looked extremely small, much smaller than in the past. It appeared as if he had had another surgery. His chin looked even larger and more pronounced. Julia pulled a scarf partially over the bottom half of his face to hide his features. It was clear that the extroverted "can do" charismatic leader was increasingly avoiding face-to-face interaction with his colleagues.

Talk around the aerospace teams started to turn ugly. What happened to the high and mighty genius? The think tank man who was the leader among leaders? Gossip around the company was incessant. Someone came up with the brilliant analogy that Julia was another Michael Jackson. Was he in fact addicted to plastic surgery? His fellow engineers were perplexed. Why was a perfectly decent looking guy, a powerful man who cut quite a figure, obsessed with his appearance to the tune of a series of plastic surgeries and major, drastic alterations to his appearance? Moreover, it started to appear as if Julia had no solution, status quo or end in sight.

Ultimately, Julia's golden boy status began to wane. There were fewer innovations and diminishing deals at the negotiating table. The heights of Julia's creativity were a benchmark of the past. Innovation in the R&D department was sparse. Julia's strange behavior and faltering productivity appeared to be contagious. Once an avid people person, Julia was no longer available for employees. The emails sent by Julia to staff and colleagues were all received from off-site locations. It reached a point where the R&D team had not physically seen Julia for several months. Reports of "Julia sightings" surfaced. One night janitor reported seeing him in the shadows near his R&D office suite sometime around midnight. He was allegedly wearing a "half face mask." Whenever he did grace the company with his presence, Julia strategically lowered lighting to cut down on the prospects of video cameras filming him when he was on location. Major clients around the world were clamoring for Josh Julia and it reached a point where they were no longer willing to wait. Julia had psychologically and physically checked out.

THE LEADER RETREATS INTO A "BLACK BOX"

The ramifications for the aerospace engineers were devastating. They were a leaderless crew in search of their MIA (missing in action) platoon sergeant. Julia was magnificent during the upswing of his reign. Who was this other Julia? Who was this brilliant but infinitely strange engineer who was nowhere to be seen and appeared to be dedicating his life to rearranging his face? Motivation, productivity and morale plunged. Turnover raised its ugly head. Elija Ltd.'s aerospace engineering division was unwittingly drawn into a *body dysmorphic system of disturbed behavior.*

Max Elija, CEO, increasingly turned to the HR department and the employee assistance program for answers. Julia did not have an immediate superior in his division and it was extraordinarily difficult for the CEO to initiate dialogue on matters of this nature. Mr. Elija felt extremely awkward about approaching Julia on such personal and embarrassing issues. To compound matters, HR received numerous reports and grievances alleging the presence of "a disturbed leader and a dysfunctional R&D workplace." When questioned by HR, Julia retreated into a "black box" of mystery and non-replies. He was the interviewee from hell. He provided no substantive disclosure and denied that there was any problem whatsoever. He immediately offered that "I had to have a nose realignment and nasal passage reconstruction because I had some damage done to my nasal passages and membranes from a cocaine addiction that I had in my twenties." This claim was never substantiated.

A FORMAL ASSESSMENT OF JULIA'S OUTLANDISH BEHAVIOR

Once they established that this case required skills that were outside their range of expertise, HR referred Julia to the EAP and a series of counseling sessions ensued. The EAP concluded that Julia's case was "extraordinary" and "indicated that there might be serious pathology involved." Based on the recommendations of the EAP, a consensus emerged (including EAP, HR, and the CEO) that external consultants should be called in. The Goldman Consulting Group was contracted. Subsequent coaching and consulting sessions between Josh Julia and Dr. Goldman transpired. Video tapes of Julia's repetitive, obsessive behavior were viewed during sessions. Classified conversations with Julia's colleagues and staff provided additional assessment data. At first Josh Julia was extremely combative and non-compliant with the consultants. Faced with a threat of termination issued by the CEO (via HR), Julia reluctantly agreed to "attempt to participate in good faith." An extensive case history and many hours spent attempting to overcome defensiveness and resistance revealed that Julia was suffering from a rather acute case of a lesser-known mental disorder described in the DSM IV as 300.7 or body dysmorphic disorder (American Psychiatric Association, 2000).

According to the DSM IV, the "essential feature of Body Dysmorphic Disorder (historically known as dysmorphophobia) is a preoccupation with a defect in appearance" (American Psychiatric Association, 2000, p. 466). The DSM IV further states that:

the defect is either imagined, or if a slight physical anomaly is present, the individual's concern is markedly excessive. The preoccupation must cause significant distress or impairment in social, occupational, or other important areas of functioning ...
(American Psychiatric Association, 2000, p. 466)

Moreover, the DSM IV cites that "frequent mirror checking and checking of the 'defect' in other available reflecting surfaces (e.g., store windows, car bumpers, watch faces) can consume many hours a day" (American Psychiatric Association, 2000, p. 466).

Data gathered on Julia revealed that he had been suffering from body dysmorphic disorder since his early teens. His periods of extreme accomplishment and extraordinary, charismatic leadership represented temporary release from his personally imposed cage of restraints. His self-consciousness knew no boundaries. At times he would shun mirrors, banish them from his personal life, eliminate access to them throughout his workplace and otherwise manipulate his environment. Such was the case during Julia's meteoric rise with Elija. His "fall" was simply explained in terms of his *relapsing* back into his more permanent state of body dysmorphic misery.

ESCALATING ORGANIZATIONAL TOXICITY

Somewhat mystified until the later stages of his collapse, the organization around Julia was deeply frustrated, de-motivated and somewhat clueless. They observed only glimpses of the outer surface manifestations of the illness. Julia's success at Elija allowed him to indulge his dreams of "excellence of face" by writing blank checks to a plastic surgeon. Unfortunately, the plastic surgeon did not say "when" and took the surgeries too far. Julia's leadership at Elija became increasingly dysfunctional and his locus of control was belittled to a pathological response to multiple plastic surgeries. Julia's life was reduced to a relentless and twisted pursuit of excellence in his facial features, features he had despised since adolescence. The "ugliness" that he perceived inside could not be offset by the first few "successful" plastic surgeries. He was driven to keep pursuing more and more. He wanted to charm all the mirrors in his life and be able to finally answer the haunting question of "mirror, mirror on the wall, who is the fairest of them all?"

The suffering of interpersonal and workplace relationships is part and parcel of the body dysmorphic victim. Julia dramatically impacted his R&D staff and colleagues, as well as Elija as a whole. *Aerospace engineers were drawn into a systems manifestation of body dysmorphic disorder.* Julia had ordered that overhead and desk lighting be lowered to a minimum. Engineers were surprised by a formal "lighting ultimatum," because there was no accompanying explanation, just an edict in the form of a much publicized email. This order was clearly consistent with characteristic behaviors of a body dysmorphic who controls lighting to either obsessively inspect the perceived defects or disguise them when in public. Employees further reported that Elija would lose his concentration at times when in the midst of a meeting. Oddly, he appeared to be gazing off toward a nearby glass partition and viewing his reflection quite intently. At other interviews the EAP counselors and external consultant learned of consistent reports from four engineers, three males and one female, that they became uncomfortable on several occasions when Julia appeared to be studying their faces and examining their facial features with an intense stare and gaze. These reported discomforts are impossible to quantify but after extensive questioning there was little doubt that the descriptions were accurate. Julia studied the faces of employees in order to gain insight into his own facial preoccupation. Perhaps he was attempting to benchmark a hair line, a nose, or other facial features. Despite the subtlety and peculiarity of this activity (and conjecture), these nonverbal, difficult-to-pinpoint behaviors took a toll on fellow engineers. Rather than participating in a culture of innovation, an atmosphere of repetitive discomforts and idiosyncratic behavior permeated Julia's workplace. Distrust, paranoia and defensiveness took hold throughout the division.

Engineers did not know what to expect of Julia. Would the productive, innovative Julia miraculously reappear or did the engineers have to go through an indefinite menu of bizarre, alogical behavior? Clearly, with a pathology enveloping them it required that the engineers conjure up (with the assistance of HR, EAP, and the external consultant) a brand of emotional intelligence that was outside the box. Despite the fact that the engineers were innovators and made a living outside of the conventions of ordinary analytical, left brain reasoning, there was no interpersonal R&D template for assessing or decoding Julia. It was quite bewildering and deadly. Productivity continued to suffer. The engineers struggled to function in a leaderless organizational world. They sensed that there was no exit, they were in a vortex, an abyss, and the joy of their artistry seemed to be individually and collectively stripped from them. One engineer talked of an "emotional rape," an abandonment by the "real" Julia, and the appearance of a "hideously, self-conscious Zombie" whom nobody recognized. It was no longer a workplace for creativity. Julia was perceived as instrumental in organizational demise and depression.

Lacking sufficient data, it is commonplace for colleagues to wonder what it was that they did to disturb their once charismatic leader and comrade. Such was the case at Elija. Max Elija and a number of the engineers in concert with HR considered numerous scenarios and multiple causality scripts – all in an effort to deconstruct Julia's mental state and destructive behavior. Did the engineering division somehow trigger or fuel Julia's problems?

COUNTERPRODUCTIVE WORKPLACE BEHAVIORS

The soul-searching process revealed that there were in fact what researchers have recently termed counterproductive work behaviors (CWBs; e.g., see Bies & Tripp, 2005; Fox & Spector, 2005; Glomb, 2002; Goh *et al.*, 2003; Keashly & Jagatic, 2000; Lee & Spector, 2004; Penney & Spector, 2002, 2003) present within the engineering division. The CWBs were interrelated to Julia's pathology, as the engineering division found indirect, and at times subconscious responses to Julia through disturbed communication interactions. For example, with the advent of Julia's pathology, there was an accompanying appearance of instances of workplace aggression (e.g., see Baron & Neuman, 1998; Keashly & Rogers, 2001), disturbed inter-actions loosely classified as "desk rage," mild cases of bullying and a variety of reported episodes of incivility between engineers, and between engineers and other divisions at Elija, including HR. Interviews, analysis and data collection revealed that these "milder forms" of workplace disturbance pointed back to the engineers' frus-tration with Julia and inability to find a vehicle for response. The cocoon-like behavior of Julia, where he largely sequestered himself from his staff during the onset of his body dysmorphic disorder, left the engineers with rumors, insufficient data, an absentee leader exhib-iting extremely troublesome behavior, and worst of all, no direct means for communication or exploring what was transpiring. The division was seething within an existential void, dangling in limbo and eventually acting out its frustrations and need for information. Unfortunately, the CEO and HR issued orders that until further notice there was to be no mention of Julia's mental disturbance. All commu-nication between the consultant and Julia's division was to remain at a highly general level, devoid of substantive information. The Elija Ltd. system responded with interpersonal conflict, pain and a network of counterproductive behaviors.

POSTSCRIPT OF A DYSFUNCTIONAL ORGANIZATION
After extensive consultation and organizational therapy (Schein, 2000, 2005) the intervention adapted by Elija was the dismissal of Julia. CEO Max Elija handed down the verdict. Following approximately six months of (Goldman) consultation with Julia and his colleagues, the engineers clearly articulated that they were suffering and that they surmised that something was terribly wrong with Julia. Learning about his termination, there were close to twenty engineers who initially communicated how badly they felt for Julia. Within two weeks of the termination a complex wave of introspection and depression mixed with anger and frustration engulfed the R&D engineers. The collective Elija Inc. mental and emotional state continued to express itself both

internally and externally, most notably over a pending contract with Nippon Airlines that badly faltered and eventually failed. Without Julia at the table, the Japanese were extremely disappointed. The Elija team of engineers responded with a counterproductive negotiation. They were "shell shocked" without their bilingual master negotiator. Particularly noteworthy were the high levels of conflict between members of the Elija negotiating team. Ever since the formal departure of Julia had been announced, the engineers had been laden with interpersonal conflict in the workplace and it had now spread to their global negotiating tables. They proceeded in a bickering, adversarial fashion unable to designate a leader, engage in civilized communication or reach any consensus. Without a united front they were doomed in their partnership with the Japanese. Worst of all, the Nippon negotiators appeared devastated by Julia's absence as the Japanese value consistency, familiarity and strong relationships as building blocks for doing business. They appeared to have little interest in proceeding without Julia on the other side of the table. The Elija team was dumbfounded.

Responding to a request citing "extreme and continuing fallout from the Julia debacle," the Goldman consultants returned to Elija. The consultants addressed the longstanding dysfunctional behavior in the engineering division and vowed to work closely with the engineers to turn things around. The conflict and destructive behavior in the R&D division had become evident within several weeks of Julia's dismissal. In the interpretation of the consulting group, *the individual body dysmorphic disorder suffered by Julia germinated into a larger division-wide pathology in the R&D division of Elija*. During one of many counseling sessions with engineering, one of the engineers blurted out "it's the old rotten apple in the barrel syndrome – Julia was thrown out of Elija but the rot continues." There was no disagreement from Dr. Goldman.

In the case of Elija Inc. the fine line between a disturbed leader and a toxic organizational system is reminiscent of the husband who is suffering from mental illness and unwittingly impacts his entire family system, culminating in abuse, violence and collective pathology (e.g., see Minuchin, 1974). The counterproductive work behavior at Elija continued to escalate for nearly three years following Julia's departure and only subsided after a "revolving door" which saw three leaders come and go in quick succession. The fourth leader, Tyrone Beckman, worked with colleagues, staff, HR, EAP and the external consultants to address the disturbed organizational narratives of the Julia era and successfully provide some healing and new direction. This process was complemented by Elija's growing commitment to relationship management and conflict resolution training. With the assistance of the Goldman group Elija worked with Beckman and the entire R&D division to develop "toxin detectors and healers" (e.g., see Cameron & Lavine, 2006; Frost, 2003).

MORPHING INTO COMPANY-WIDE PATHOLOGY

Highly dysfunctional leadership behavior presents detection, assessment and intervention problems for organizations as depicted in the case study of Josh Julia and Elija Engineering. When the disturbed behavior is deeply rooted, repetitive, self-defeating, irrational and serves as an impetus for a counterproductive workplace, organizations are increasingly discovering that the problem may fall outside of their area of expertise. Highly toxic behavior may require external expertise in the form of management consultants, executive coaches and organizational therapists (e.g., see Schein, 2000, 2005).

Dysfunctional leadership typically escalates and inherently carries with it a capacity for company-wide trauma and toxicity including the prospect for workplace violence. In the case of Elija Engineering *the psychological disturbances experienced by Josh Julia morphed into a division-wide pathology*. In the words of the Goldman consultants, "the R&D division reached a point where the boundaries between Julia and seventy-two engineers and staff were very much blurred. In other words, if Julia suffered from a disorder – this same disorder afflicted all of his colleagues." The Goldman interpretation brings to mind the diagnoses by Kets de Vries of both individual executives and entire companies as neurotic, narcissistic or irrational. Related are Joel Bakan's assessments of "institutional psychopaths" as he names both individual CEOs and Fortune 500s who engage in dysfunctional behavior to the point of warranting DSM-IV-TR diagnoses (Bakan, 2004). Important here is the scope and breadth of the disturbed behavior. It is not a stretch to state that a personality disorder communicated through a negatively charismatic leader may impact many individuals in the workplace as witnessed in the far-reaching behavior of Josh Julia. Conversely, dysfunctional organizational policies and culture may adversely affect individuals and in extreme cases precipitate mental and emotional disturbances. Moreover, disturbances may also be the hybrid, amalgam results of the interface of organizational and individual exigencies. (e.g., see Goldman, 2006a, 2008 a,b; Kets de Vries, 2006).

Of special interest is the fact that Josh Julia's previous employer, a Fortune 100 aeronautics corporation, did not disclose his history of disturbed behavior to Elija Engineering when they were contacted during the interviewing process. In addition, Julia was protected by the Americans with Disabilities Act (ADA) due to the fact that mental health disabilities mandate privileged communication and confidentiality if they do not pose a danger to self (DTS) or danger to others (DTO). Accordingly, in response to the prospect of a disturbed leader, it behooves companies to have their legal staff carefully examine recent case law regarding mental disabilities in the workplace and related interpretations of the ADA.

The Julia case puts management researchers, practitioners and companies on notice. Business is not immune from the heights and depths of human behavior including pathological extremes as evident in Julia's body dysmorphic disorder. Brilliance and pathology can be tightly woven into the personality and behavioral repertoire of a single leader. Great care must be exercised when conducting extremely comprehensive interviews and checks on employees entering into high-level positions within organizations – specifically in those cases when a company is not promoting from within. Within the limits of the law companies must push to unveil pre-existing conditions that may otherwise remain undisclosed, are currently in remission or pose a potential threat to the organization.

THE FARTHER REACHES OF DARK LEADERS

As a final note, *I urge consultants, business leaders and management scholars to extend their repertoire to reach farther and deeper into the dark side of leadership behavior.* Breakthroughs in our understanding of personality disorders and narcissistic traits in leadership are encouraging and may set the stage for further explorations into a broader range of DSM-IV-TR categories present in our everyday workplace. In this chapter I have provided a glimpse into a potentially fruitful and robust area of inquiry via an investigation into the organizational text of an innovative company and leader undermined by somotoform disorder 300.7, body dysmorphic disorder.

10 Destructive leaders and dysfunctional organizations: tearing downs the walls of professional greed, hubris, toxic genius and psychopathology

> We will recognize that our clients do develop ways of operating that are maladaptive; we must have models to help them solve problems and improve their functioning.
>
> (Schein, 2005, p. 138)

LESSONS IN TOXICITY

What are the lessons to be learned from the toxic leaders and dysfunctional companies presented in *Destructive Leaders and Dysfunctional Organizations: A Therapeutic Approach*? Leadership has been alerted to the fact that the study of toxicity is important to the welfare of many employees and potentially can be a troublesome and messy subject to deal with (Jamieson, 2008, p. 225). Despite a growing interest in dysfunctional organizations and toxic leadership it is still a relatively recent subject for scholarly research and consultant reports. The impact of toxicity has in fact been upending. As astutely articulated by Jamieson, toxicity "is a serious – and probably more widespread than is apparent – phenomenon – often with deteriorating affects on individuals and organizations" (Jamieson, 2008, p. 225).

TOXICITY MISMANAGED TAKES ON A LIFE OF ITS OWN

Hopefully the companies and leaders presented in this book serve to open the doors of organizational perception and provide ample reason for early assessment and intervention. In *Destructive Leaders* dimensions of a code alert have been issued.

- Undetected, toxicity spreads.
- Overlooked and avoided, toxicity metastasizes.
- Swept aside and denied, toxicity erodes productivity and motivation.

Toxicity unchecked may in fact be a significant dark force driving organizational misbehavior, counterproductive work practices, grievances and litigation, retention and turnover debacles and the erosion of leadership.

QUESTIONS FOR TOXIC LEADERS AND ORGANIZATIONS

Throughout the book, questions have been posed and responses delivered. In retrospect, some far-reaching questions and concerns provide a framework both for summarizing the book and pointing leaders, companies, consultants and academics in the right direction. In this chapter I ask leadership and companies to consider the following questions:

- Why does toxicity take on a life of its own if undetected or mismanaged?
- How are organizations blindsided by toxic leaders?
- What can be said about organizational denial and resistance to toxicity?
- Who assesses and handles toxic leaders?
- What potential research streams are suggested by *Destructive Leaders*?
- What implications are surfaced for practitioners? (Jamieson, 2008, p. 225)

BLINDSIDED BY TOXIC LEADERS

One of the primary reasons why companies wind up on the couch and in search of treatment is because they find themselves blindsided by toxic leaders who have operated largely undetected. Internally unprepared organizational patients tend to wake up fairly late in the game. It is quite commonplace within the specialized world of treating executive and organizational toxicity to find that the upper echelon is in part mesmerized by the highly productive side of leadership and is caught unprepared by the advent of emotional pain and toxicity. Companies are drawn in by:

- the confidence and certitude of a narcissistic surgeon (see chapter 3);
- the powerful spurts of motivational leadership from an ADHD-propelled turbo-charged engineer (see chapter 2); and
- the extraordinary creativity of a world-class fashion designer and senior manager who is both ignited and tormented by a borderline personality disorder (see chapter 6).

Despite numerous warning signs from followers, colleagues and stakeholders, an upper-echelon response to destructive and undermining leader behaviors can be quite delayed. Why do companies faced with toxicity opt to concentrate on the impressive upside of their leaders' productivity and retreat into patterns of denial, resistance and avoidance when faced with contrary and negative data (Goldman, 2008a,b)? Companies on the couch may have been distracted and drawn away from early internal reports of troubling leadership by contrary indicators. I have personally witnessed misleading metrics on leaders indicating superior performance where toxicity has already taken its grip.

The questioning and monitoring of detrimental and self-destructive practices is critical for organizational health, and the failure to timely do so constitutes a core message in this book. When toxicity is present in leadership and dysfunctional behavior spreads and seeps into the rank and file and operations of companies such as Cornelius, Beach Harbor Heart Institute, Black Valley Enterprises, Sergio Mondo, WinnerWear and Elija Engineering Ltd. who will detect it? Can this be done prior to the widescale penetration of the organizational system?

ORGANIZATIONAL RESISTANCE AND AVOIDANCE

A toxic company is seldom if ever aligned with the steady hand of a stable leader. High highs and low lows are embodied in all of the toxic leaders depicted in this book. Brilliance and extraordinary levels of productivity and innovation are ultimately inseparable from dark, demeaning and unsettling leader behaviors. As an external coach and consultant I have increasingly taken note of and counseled managers who paradoxically perform in *both* the most positive and detrimental manner. *At times it is difficult to fathom that both exemplary and deplorable behaviors coexist within the complex personality of a single leader or organizational system.* This paradox confuses and may serve to unsettle colleagues and subordinates serving under a toxic leader and even shellshocks CEOs and executive boards attempting to make sense out of contradictory messages.

How can a leader such as Josh Julia of Elija Ltd. (see chapter 9) who has generated much excitement, passion, loyal followers and unprecedented corporate profits also have a dark, troubled and poisonous side to his personality and leadership? This study in contrasts was too much of a neurotic rollercoaster ride for the Elija R&D division to handle. The downfall of Julia was subsequently followed by the quick succession of three failed replacements. *Toxicity has a long reach.* After several years of coaching and consulting, Elija Ltd. realized that it had floundered when it came to parting ways with an extraordinarily talented, yet deeply toxic leader plagued by serious psychopathology.

As repeatedly witnessed throughout these pages, the excellence of complex leaders can be quite misleading. Organizations are caught off guard. How can a renowned heart surgeon almost single handedly usher Beach Harbor Heart Institute into an elite category as a center for excellence and months later emerge as the nexus and primary defendant in three medical malpractice suits involving wrongful deaths from routine mitral valve heart repair (chapter 3)? This study in contrasts rivets an organizational system and ultimately wreaks havoc. Was the narcissistic personality disorder diagnosed in an excellent heart surgeon reason for her dismissal or to be seen as an unexpected challenge of dealing with a brilliant leader mired in pathology? As the consultant, I recommended that Dr. Vangella be retained and enter into intensive leadership coaching and psychotherapy. Her extraordinary, world-class skills and performance were ample reason to treat her toxicity.

Of utmost importance is the organizational response to the toxic leader. Is it timely or delayed? Is the toxicity acknowledged or swept into the black box of dark corporate behaviors and secrets? Prolonged avoidance and/or the inability to diagnose toxic leadership were the plight of all of the patients: Cornelius (Javaman); Beach Harbor (Vangella); Black Valley (Blackman and Graystone); Johnstone-Mumford (Dr. Gaston); Sergio Mondo (Burnstein); WinnerWear (Boulder); Cavendish & Bodark (Renee); and Elija Ltd. (Julia). This failure to assess toxicity in leaders proved to be the primary source of escalating organizational dysfunction. Predisposed to view their leaders as innovators and high-level generators of revenue and accelerating stock values, it was a stretch to direct the company gaze toward toxicity. *Once positioned on the consultant's couch as patients, all of the organizations in question were incredulous that their world-class leaders, precedent setters and meal tickets could be also be pivotal in their organization's decline.* It was a difficult pill to swallow.

WHO ASSESSES AND HANDLES TOXICITY?

As described, talk of toxicity typically surfaces when organizations are faced with troublesome levels of intolerance, bullying, burnout, workplace violence, odd or disturbing leadership behaviors and a myriad of people problems (e.g., see Baron & Neuman, 1998). In fact, companies search for explanations and relief from the pain of demoralization, executive abuse, deliberate undermining and toxic behaviors that demean, trivialize, subvert, mislead, ignore and squash constructive criticism or dialogue (Goldman, 2008a).

In viewing the company as a patient, Goldman (2008a,b) has recognized similarities between the spread of toxicity in organizational systems and "attacks on the human immune system ranging from low-level viruses to the highly toxic melanoma cancer that metastasized in Frost's own lymph nodes," ultimately leading to his death (Frost, 2003).

Recognizing that toxicity is widespread in human systems, the question arises as to who is designated to assess and handle this inevitable aspect of organizational life? Supervisors, managers and human resource professionals all emerge as potential front line, in-house toxin detectors. Frost (2003) has made significant inroads en-route to persuading companies that there is an ad hoc phenomenon of self-anointed toxin detectors and helpers, informally operating within the majority of organizational systems. Frost illustrated how organizational members turn to perhaps one or two trusted individuals in their workplace with whom they choose to share privileged workplace and personal issues. Trials, tribulations, workplace stress, conflicts and toxic experiences are communicated. According to Frost, the likelihood of finding a so-called "toxin detector" and "toxin healer" within a given organization is fairly high (Frost, 2003). These supportive personalities and venues offer nurturing, compassion, emotional intelligence, empathic listening, supportive feedback and a place to confide and vent, and have an important role. Frost demonstrates a very high regard for these grass roots toxin detectors and handlers and views them as underground "below-the-radar" figures who occupy strategically important psychological, conflict resolution, and relationship-building roles within companies. Frost's analysis and recommendation reaches into the vulnerability of the toxin detectors as he warns of the possible breakdown and burnout of these organizational helpers.

Although Frost is both instrumental and initially satisfying in addressing everyday toxicity in the workplace, in *Destructive Leaders and Dysfunctional Organizations* I have expanded the conversation and focus to include high-level toxicity in leadership. Whereas lower to mid-range toxicity threats include stress, verbal altercations, disrespect, mental and emotional anguish and a broad array of debilitating behaviors, I have drawn attention to the longer-term, more deeply rooted and potentially far more threatening incidence of psychopathology. Highly toxic leaders and severely dysfunctional organizations require consulting and leadership coaching that incorporates specialized clinical counseling. Assuming that sooner or later an organization will be faced with neurotic workplace behavior perhaps in the form of an ADHD manager (chapter 2) or a leader with a personality disorder (chapters 3, 5 and 6), does this not fall somewhat outside the expertise level of the majority of toxin detectors functioning ad hoc within the workplace? Specifically, the toxin detector as described by Frost and widely acknowledged across Fortune 500s typically lacks formal training as either a consultant or psychologist. The need for more specialized psychological training in detecting, monitoring and interventions with high-level toxicity may raise questions surrounding the viability of counselor training for HR professionals. Moreover, astute companies will scrutinize their current employee assistance program professionals and specifically address whether they are on board for an ongoing incidence of organizational toxicity. An experienced external consultant specializing in high-toxicity leaders and dysfunctional organizational systems can be instrumental in assessing and developing a company's internal preparedness.

THE MOVEMENT TOWARD OUTSIDE EXPERTS

In *Destructive Leaders and Dysfunctional Organizations: A Therapeutic Approach*, the movement toward outside experts is the preferred mode for assessment and intervention. Why? The answer is twofold. First, there are deeply entrenched issues surrounding shame and vulnerability connected to any internal coaching, counseling or consulting disclosures from leaders. Although a host of internal organizational culture variables enter into play I usually encounter leaders who are more comfortable turning to external experts – assuming that trust and willingness to disclose can be established within an initial meeting or two.

Secondly, when dealing with mid-range to higher-level toxicity in leaders and organizations, expertise in psychological and psychopathology is recommended. Although this level of expertise may be available through an employee assistance program, there tends to be a stronger preference among leaders for external rather than internal executive coaching and therapeutic consultation. Leadership is extremely concerned with face issues and places the highest priority on privileged communication and confidentiality. Experience dictates that leadership may question the fidelity of their internal EAP option and feel somewhat threatened by the prospect of highly confidential disclosures being leaked. In contrast, leaders with high-toxicity issues are more comfortable with outside-the-organization disclosures to consultants and coaches who offer off-site venues as well as dual expertise in leadership consultation and counseling psychology. The ability to alternatively talk leadership, productivity, quality, teams and 360 feedback alongside fears, phobias, neuroticism and personality disorders provides a broad spectrum of coverage ranging from surface conflicts to deeply rooted behavioral disturbances.

RESEARCH STREAMS AND CONSULTANT IMPLICATIONS

In positioning the company on the couch the disciplinary lines have been blurred between management and psychology. *Destructive Leaders and Dysfunctional Organizations* points toward the importance of incorporating dimensions of counseling and clinical psychology into the assessment and treatment of toxicity. Consultation narratives have specifically pointed toward the need for a broader diagnostic range extending into what has been identified as high-toxicity leaders. Particularly in the case of successful leaders suffering from personality disorders it is vital that organizations extend their assessment repertoire into the DSM-IV-TR (see American Psychiatric Association, 2000). Kets de Vries & Miller (1984a,b) called attention to the need for both individual and organizational diagnoses. While individual assessments of leader psychopathology have been illustrated throughout *Destructive Leaders*, ranging from narcissistic to borderline to antisocial personality disorder and finally to body dysmorphic disorder, there is the additional frontier of expanding into organizational systems diagnoses. Additional research must continue to address the applications of the DSM-IV-TR in diagnoses of teams, divisions and complex organizational systems.

In the course of reaching DSM diagnoses of leaders I have repeatedly illustrated the systemic implications. Quite simply, researchers may want to investigate how a leader with psychopathology or a personality disorder can instigate a company-wide metastasizing of the toxicity. Along these lines, I urge interdisciplinary research and consultations spanning organizational behavior, leadership, strategy and management with expertise areas ranging from counseling and clinical psychology to industrial and organizational psychology. Organizations are ill prepared to timely and appropriately assess high-toxicity leaders. For example, I have personally observed through the consultations presented in this book how the immediate bosses of the toxic leaders were unable to accurately perceive or diagnose the degree of pathology that was going on. The bosses were capable of appropriately responding to mildly disruptive or "toxic light" behavior but were quite clueless when it came to personality disorders and more seriously destructive leadership. At present the best chance for accurate internal diagnoses of toxic leaders and processes rests with EAPs. The uneven and politically sensitive nature of EAPs in corporate culture does not readily lend itself to reliable assessments and treatments. Surely much can be done to further the functionality of EAPs to tackle toxicity.

If organizations continue to fail to develop appropriate internal skill sets to assess high toxicity then the search for treatment will continue to lie with external consultants, coaches and organizational therapists.

CONCLUSION

As complex human systems, organizations cannot be spared from the dark, troubled and toxic dimensions of behavior. I have hopefully drawn attention to high-toxicity leaders and the widescale effects they have on their companies. Through enhanced monitoring of toxicity in the workplace and expanded efforts of human resource professionals and EAPs, companies can better prepare themselves for the inevitable. In cases of extraordinarily successful leaders plagued by high toxicity in the form of personality disorders and/or psychopathology, early detection and contracting with external leadership coaches, management consultants and organizational therapists is highly recommended.

References

Ackroyd, S. & Thompson, P. 1999. *Organizational Misbehavior*. London: Sage.

American Psychiatric Association (APA). 2000. *DSM-IV-TR: Diagnostic and Statistical Manual of Mental Disorders*. Arlington, VA: American Psychiatric Association.

American Psychological Association 1993. "Guidelines for Providers of Psychological Services to Ethnic, Linguistic, and Culturally Diverse Populations." *American Psychologist*. 48, pp. 45–48.

Argyris, C. 1985. *Strategy, Change, and Defensive Routines*. Boston, MA: Pitman.

Armstrong, D. 2005. *Organization in the Mind: Psychoanalysis, Group Relations, and Organizational Consultancy*. London: Karnac Books Ltd.

Artaud, A. 1958. *The Theatre and Its Double*. New York, NY: Grove Press Inc.

Ashforth, B. 1994. "Petty Tyranny in Organizations." *Human Relations*, 47, pp. 755–778.

     1997. "Petty Tyranny in Organizations: A Preliminary Examination of Anecdotes and Consequences." *Canadian Journal of Administrative Science*. 14, pp. 126–140.

Ashforth, B., Gioia, D., Robinson, S. and Trevino, L. 2008. "Re-Viewing Organizational Corruption." *The Academy of Management Review*. 33, 3, pp. 670–684.

Ashforth, B. & Humphrey, R. 1995. "Emotion in the Workplace: A Reappraisal." *Human Relations*, 48, 2, pp. 97–125.

Babiak, P. & Hare, R.D. 2005. *Snakes in Suits: When Psychopaths Go To Work*. New York, NY: Regan Books/Harper Collins Publishers.

Bakan, J. 2004. *The Corporation: The Pathological Pursuit of Profit and Power*. New York, NY: Free Press.

Balakian, A. 1970. *Surrealism: The Road to the Absolute*. New York, NY: E.P. Dutton & Company.

Baltes, B., Staudinger, U., & Lindenberger, U. 1999. "Lifespan Psychology: Theory and Application to Intellectual Functioning." *Annual Review of Psychology*, 50, pp. 471–507.

Baron, R. & Neuman, J. 1998. "Workplace Aggression – The Iceberg Beneath the Tip of Workplace Violence – Evidence on its Forms, Frequency and Targets." *Public Administration Quarterly*. 21, 446–464.

Barrick, M. & Mount, M. 1991. "The Big Five Personality Dimensions and Job Performance: A Meta-Analysis." *Personality Psychology*. 44, pp. 1–26.

Barsade, S. & Gibson, D. 2007. "Why does Affect Matter in Organizations?" *The Academy of Management Perspectives*. 21, 1, pp. 36–59.

Baudelaire, C. 1965. *Flowers of Evil*. New York, NY: New Directions Books.

Baumeister, R., Smart, L. & Boden, J. 1996. "Relation of Threatened Egotism to Violence and Aggression: The Dark Side of High Self Esteem." *Psychological Review*, 103, 1, pp. 5–33.

Bergan, J. 1977. *Behavioral Consultation*. Columbus, OH: Merrill.

Bernstein, A. 2001. *Emotional Vampires: Dealing with People Who Drain You Dry*. New York, NY: McGraw-Hill.

Bies, R., & Trip, T. 2005. "The Study of Revenge in the Workplace: Conceptual, Ideological and Empirical Issues." In Fox, S. & Spector, P. (eds.) *Counterproductive Work Behavior: Investigations of Actors and Targets*. Washington, DC: American Psychological Association.

Blanton, J. 2000. "Why Consultants Don't Apply Psychological Research." *Consulting Psychology Journal: Practice and Research*. 52, pp. 235–247.

Bowles, M. 1997. "The Myth of Management: Direction and Failure in Contemporary Organizations." *Human Relations*. 50, 7, pp. 779–803.

Bradford, D. & Porras, J. 2005. "An Historic View of the Future of OD: An Interview with Jerry I. Porras." In Bradford, D. & Burke, W. (eds.) *Reinventing Organization Development: Address the Crisis, Achieving the Potential*. San Francisco, CA: Pfeiffer.

Bradford, L., Gibb, J. & Benne, K. 1964. *T-Group Theory and Laboratory Method*. New York, NY: Wiley.

Breton, A. 1972. *Manifestos of Surrealism*. Ann Arbor, MI: University of Michigan Press.

Buber, M. 1965. "Elements of the Interhuman." In Friedman, M. (ed.) *The Knowledge of Man*. New York, NY: Harper & Row.

1970. *I And Thou*. New York, NY: Charles Scribner's Sons.

Cameron, K. & Lavine, M. 2006. *Making the Impossible Possible: Leading Extraordinary Performance – The Rocky Flats Story*. San Francisco, CA: Berrett-Koehler Publishers, Inc.

Cartright, D. & Zander, A. 1968. *Group Dynamics Research and Theory*. New York, NY: Harper-Collins.

Checkland, P. 1981. *Systems Thinking, Systems Practice*. New York, NY: John Wiley.

Conger, J. 1997. "The Dark Side of Leadership." In Vecchio, R. (ed.) *Leadership: Understanding the Dynamics of Power and Influence in Organizations*. Notre Dame, IN: University of Notre Dame Press, pp. 215–232.

Cortina, L., Magley, V., Williams, J. & Langhout, R., 2001. "Incivility in the Workplace: Incidence and Impact." *Journal of Occupational Health Psychology*. 6, pp. 64–80.

Coutu, D. 2004. "Putting Leaders on the Couch: A Conversation with Manfred F.R. Kets de Vries." *Harvard Business Review*. 82, 1, pp. 65–71.

Czander, W. 1993. *The Psychodynamics of Work and Organizations: Theory and Applications*. New York, NY: Guilford Press.

Diamond, M. 1993. *The Unconscious Life of Organizations: Interpreting Organizational Identity*. Westport, CT: Quorum Books.

Duffy, M., Ganster, D. & Pagon, M. 2002. "Social Undermining in the Prediction of Workplace Aggression." *Academy of Management Journal*. 45, pp. 331–351.

Ellis, A. 1993. "Reflections on Rational-Emotive Therapy." *Journal of Consulting and Clinical Psychology*. 61, pp. 199–201.

Ellis, H. 1998. "Auto-Eroticism: A Psychological Study." *Alienist and Neurologist*. 19, pp. 260–299.

Elsbach, K. (ed.) 2005. *Qualitative Organizational Research*. Greenwich, CT: Information Age Publishing.

Fisher, R., Ury, W. & Patton, B. 1991. *Getting to Yes: Negotiating Agreement Without Giving In*. New York, NY: Houghton Mifflin, Harcourt.

Fox, S. & Spector, P. 2005. *Counterproductive Work Behavior: Investigations of Actors and Targets*. Washington, DC: American Psychological Association.

Freud, S. 1931/1950. *Libidinal Types. Collected Papers. Volume 5*. London: Hogarth Press.

Frost, P. 2003. *Toxic Emotions at Work: How Compassionate Managers Handle Pain and Conflict*. Boston, MA: Harvard Business School Press.

Frost, P. & Robinson, S. 1999. "The Toxic Handler: Organizational Hero and Casualty." *Harvard Business Review*. 77, 4, 96–106.

Fuqua, D. & Newman, J. 2002. "The Role of Systems Theory in Consulting Psychology." In Lowman, R. (ed.) *Handbook of Organizational Consulting Psychology*. San Francisco, CA: Jossey-Bass, pp. 76–105.

Gabriel, Y. 1991. "Organizations and Their Discontents: A Psychoanalytic Contribution to the Study of Corporate Culture." *Journal of Applied Behavioral Science*. 27, pp. 318–336.

1999. *Organizations in Depth*. London: Sage Publications.

Gabriel, Y., Hirschhorn, L., McCollom Hampton, M., Schwartz, H. & Swogger, G. 1999. *Organizations in Depth: The Psychoanalysis of Organizations*. London: Sage Publications.

Gallessich, J. 1983. *The Profession and Practice of Consultation*. San Francisco, CA: Jossey-Bass.

Gittell, J. 2003. *The Southwest Airlines Way: Using the Power of Relationships to Achieve High Performance.* New York, NY: McGraw-Hill.

Glad, B. 2002. "Why Tyrants Go Too Far: Malignant Narcissism and Absolute Power." *Political Psychology.* 23, pp. 1–37.

Glomb, T. 2002. "Workplace Aggression: Informing Conceptual Modes with Data from Specific Encounters." *Journal of Occupational Health Psychology.* 7, pp. 20–36.

Goh, A. Bruuresma, K., Fox, S. & Spector, P. 2003. "Comparisons of Self and Coworker Reports of Counterproductive Work Behavior." Paper presented at the meeting of the Society for Industrial and Organizational Psychology, Orlando, FL.

Goldman, A. 1994. *Doing Business with the Japanese: A Guide to Successful Communication, Management and Diplomacy.* Albany, NY: State University of New York Press.

——— 2005. "Leadership Pathology as a Nexus of Dysfunctional Organizations." A paper presented at the *Academy of Management Conference,* Honolulu, HI.

——— 2006a. "Personality Disorders in Leaders: Implications of the DSM IV–TR in Assessing Dysfunctional Organizations." *Journal of Managerial Psychology,* 21, 5, pp. 392–414.

——— 2006b. "High Toxicity Leadership: Borderline Personality Disorder and the Dysfunctional Organization." *Journal of Managerial Psychology.* 21, 8, pp. 733–746.

——— 2007. "Leadership Negligence and Malpractice: Emotional Unintelligence at SkyWaves Aerospace International." A paper delivered at the Academy of Management Conference, Philadelphia, PA. (Winner of a Best Paper Award, Management Consulting Division.)

——— 2008a. "Company on the Couch: Unveiling Toxic Behavior in Dysfunctional Organizations." *Journal of Management Inquiry.* 17, 3, pp. 226–238.

——— 2008b. "Consultant and Critics on the Couch." *Journal of Management Inquiry.* 17, 3, pp. 243–249.

——— 2008c. "Leadership Negligence and Malpractice: Emotional Toxicity at SkyWaves Aerospace International." In Zerbe, W., Hartel, C. & Ashkanasy, N. (eds.) *Research on Emotion in Organizations, Volume 4: Emotions, Ethics, and Decision-Making.* Wagon Lane, Bingley: JAI Press, Emerald Group Publishing Limited.

Goleman, D. 1995. *Emotional Intelligence.* New York, NY: Bantam Books.

——— 1998. *Working with Emotional Intelligence.* New York, NY: Bantam Books.

——— 2006. *Social Intelligence: The New Science of Human Relationships.* New York, NY: Bantam.

Grayson, J. 2003. *Freedom from Obsessive-Compulsive Disorder.* New York, NY: Berkeley Books.

Griffin, R. & O'Leary-Kelly 2004. *The Dark Side of Organizational Behavior.* San Francisco, CA: Jossey-Bass.

Hall, D., Otazo, K. & Hollenbeck, G. 1999. "Behind Closed Doors: What Really Happens to Executive Coaching." *Organizational Dynamics*, 27, pp. 39–53.

Hall, E. & Hall, M. 1994. *Understanding Cultural Differences: Germans, French and Americans.* Yarmouth, ME: The Intercultural Press.

Hallowell, E. & Ratey, J. 1994. *Driven to Distraction: Recognizing and Coping with Attention Deficit Disorder from Childhood through Adulthood.* New York, NY: Touchstone.

Hambrick, D., Finkelstein, S. & Mooney, A. 2005a. "Executive Job Demands. New Insights for Explaining Strategic Decisions and Leader Behaviors." *Academy of Management Review.* 30, 3, pp. 472–491.

2005b. "Executives Sometimes Lose It, Just Like the Rest of Us." *Academy of Management Review.* 30, 3, pp. 503–508.

Hartmann, T., Bowman, J. & Burgess, S. 1996. *Think Fast: The ADD Experience.* Grass Valley, CA: Underwood.

Harvey, S. 1996. "Bosses' Negative Interpersonal Behaviors: A Latent Variable Test of Personal and Organizational Outcomes." Unpublished Doctoral Dissertation. University of Guelph, Ontario, Canada.

Hirschhorn, L. 1988. *The Workplace Within: Psychodynamics of Organizational Life.* Cambridge, MA: MIT Press.

1997. *Reworking Authority: Leading and Following in the Post-Modern Organization.* Cambridge, MA: MIT Press.

Hirschhorn, L. & Barnett, C. (eds.) 1993. *The Psychodynamics of Organizations.* Philadelphia, PA: Temple University Press, pp. xiii–xviii.

Hogan, R., Curphy, G. & Hogan, J. 1994. "What We Know about Leadership: Effectiveness and Personality." *The American Psychologist.* 49, 6, pp. 493–504.

Jamieson, D. 2008. "Editor's Introduction – Reflections on Experience: Company on the Couch." *Journal of Management Inquiry.* 17, 3, p. 225.

Kanfer, R. & Kantrowitz, T. 2002. "Emotion Regulation: Command and Control of Emotions in Work Life." In Lord, R., Klimonski, R. & Kanfer, R. (eds.) *Emotions in the Workplace: Understanding the Structure and Role of Emotions in Organizational Behavior.* San Francisco, CA: Jossey-Bass.

Keashly, L. & Harvey, S. 2005. "Emotional Abuse in the Workplace." In Fox, S. & Spector, P. (eds.) *Counterproductive Work Behavior.* Washington, DC: American Psychology Association.

Keashly, L. & Jagatic, K. 2000. "The Nature, Extent, and Impact of Emotional Abuse in the Workplace: Results of Statewide Survey." Paper presented at the Academy of Management Conference, Toronto, Canada.

& Rogers, K. 2001. "Aggressive Behaviors at Work: The Role of Context in Appraisals of Threat." Unpublished Manuscript, Wayne State University, Detroit, MI.

Kellerman, B. 2004. *Bad Leadership: What It Is, How It Happens, Why It Matters.* Boston, MA: Harvard Business School Press.

2008. *Followership: How Followers are Creating Change and Changing Leaders.* Boston, MA: Harvard Business School Press.

Kelly, K. & Ramundo, P. 1993. *You Mean I'm Not Lazy, Stupid or Crazy!!: A Self-Help Book for Adults with Attention Deficit Disorder.* New York, NY: Scribner.

Kepner, C. & Tregoe, B. 1997. *The New Rational Manager: An Updated Edition for a New World.* New York, NY: Kepner-Tregoe Publishing.

Kernberg, O. 1967. "Borderline Personality Organization." *Journal of the American Psychoanalytic Association.* 15, pp. 641–685.

1978. "Leadership and Organizational Functioning: Organizational Regression." *International Journal of Group Psychotherapy.* 28, pp. 3–25.

1979. "Regression in Organizational Leadership." *Psychiatry.* 42, pp. 24–39.

1989. "Narcissistic Personality Disorder in Childhood." *Psychiatric Clinics of North America.* 12, pp. 671–694.

1998. *Ideology, Conflict and Leadership in Groups and Organizations.* New Haven, CT: Yale University Press.

Kets de Vries, M. 1984. *The Irrational Executive: Psychoanalytic Explorations in Management.* Madison, CT: International Universities Press.

1989. *Prisoners of Leadership.* New York, NY: Wiley.

1993. *Leaders, Fools and Imposters: Essays on the Psychology of Leadership.* San Francisco, CA: Jossey-Bass.

1995. *Life and Death in the Executive Fast Lane.* San Francisco, CA: Jossey-Bass.

2001. *The Leadership Mystique: An Owner's Manual.* London: Pearson.

2006. *The Leader on the Couch: A Clinical Approach to Changing People and Organizations.* San Francisco, CA: Jossey-Bass.

Kets de Vries, M. & Miller, D. 1984a. "Neurotic Style and Organizational Pathology." *Strategic Management Journal*, 5, pp. 35–55.

1984b. *The Neurotic Organization.* San Francisco, CA: Jossey-Bass.

1985. "Narcissism and Leadership: An Objects Relations Perspective." *Human Relations.* 38, pp. 583–601.

1997. "Narcissism and Leadership: An Objects Relations Perspective." In Vecchio (ed.) *Leadership: Understanding the Dynamics of Power and Influence in Organizations.* Notre Dame, ID: University of Notre Dame Press, pp. 194–214.

Kets de Vries & Associates. 1991. *Organization on the Couch*. San Francisco, CA: Jossey-Bass.

Kilburg, R. 2000. *Executive Coaching: Developing Managerial Wisdom in A World of Chaos*. Washington, DC: American Psychological Society.

2002. "Individual Interventions in Consulting Psychology." In Lowman, R. (ed.) *Handbook of Organizational Consulting Psychology*. San Francisco, CA: Jossey-Bass.

Korzybski, A. 1950. *Manhood of Humanity*. Lakeville, CT: International Non-Aristotelian Publishing Company.

Kotter, J. 1990. *A Force for Change: How Leadership Differs from Management*. New York, NY: Free Press.

Kramer, R. 2003. "The Harder They Fall." *Harvard Business Review*. Oct., 81, 10, pp. 58–66.

Lang, D. 2008. "A Multidimensional Conceptualization of Organizational Corruption Control." *The Academy of Management Review*. 33, 3, pp. 710–729.

Lawler, E., Nadler, D. & Cammann, C. 1980. *Organizational Assessment: Perspectives on the Measurement of Organizational Behavior and the Quality of Work Life*. New York, NY: Wiley.

Lawrence, G. 1998. "Unconscious Social Pressure on Leaders." In Klein, B. Gabelnick, F., & Herr, P. (eds.) *The Psychodynamics of Leadership*. Madison, WI: Psychosocial Press, pp. 53–75.

Lee, V. & Spector, P. 2004. "Sources of Conflict at Work and Targets of Counterproductive Behaviors." Paper presented at the meeting of the *Society for Industrial and Organizational Psychology*, Chicago, IL.

Levinson, H. 1972. *Organizational Diagnosis*. Cambridge, MA: Harvard University Press.

1976. *Psychological Man*. Boston, MA: Levinson Institute.

1981. *Executive*. Cambridge, MA: Harvard University Press.

1987. "Psychoanalytic Theory in Organizational Behavior." In Lorsch, J. (ed.) *Handbook of Organizational Behavior*. Englewood Cliffs, NJ: Prentice Hall.

1991. "Consulting with Top Management." *Consulting Psychology Bulletin*, 43, 1, pp. 10–15.

2002. *Organizational Assessment: A Step-by-Step Guide to Effective Consulting*. Washington, DC: American Psychological Association.

Lipman-Blumen, J. 2001. "Why Do We Tolerate Bad Leaders? Magnificent Uncertitude, Anxiety and Meaning." In Bennis, W., Spreitzer, G. & Cummings, T. (eds.) *The Future of Leadership: Today's Top Leadership Thinkers Speak to Tomorrow's Leaders*. San Francisco, CA: Jossey-Bass, pp. 125–138.

2005. *The Allure of Toxic Leaders*. New York, NY: Oxford University Press.

Litzky, B., Eddleston, K. & Kidder, D. 2006. "The Good, the Bad, and the Misguided: How Managers Inadvertently Encourage Deviant Behaviors." *Academy of Management Perspectives*, 20, 1, pp. 91–103.

Livesley, W. (ed.). 2001. *Handbook of Personality Disorders: Theory, Research and Treatment*. New York, NY: The Guilford Press.

Lord, R., Klimoski, R. & Kanfer, R. (eds.) 2002. *Emotions in the Workplace: Understanding the Structure and Role of Emotions in Organizational Behavior*. San Francisco, CA: Jossey-Bass.

Lowman, R. (ed.) 2002. *Handbook of Organizational Consulting Psychology*. San Francisco, CA: Jossey-Bass.

Lubit, R. 2004. *Coping with Toxic Managers, Subordinates and Other Difficult People*. Englewood Cliffs, NJ: Prentice Hall Financial Times.

Luthans, F., Youssef, C., & Avolio, B. 2007. *Psychological Capital: Developing the Human Competitive Edge*. New York, NY: Oxford University Press.

Maccoby, M. 2000. "Narcissistic Leaders: The Incredible Pros; The Inevitable Cons." *Harvard Business Review*. 78, pp. 68–78.

2003. *The Productive Narcissist: The Promise and Peril of Visionary Leadership*. New York, NY: Broadway Books.

2007. *Narcissistic Leaders: Who Succeeds and Who Fails*. Boston, MA: Harvard Business School Press.

Maslow, A. 1971. *The Farther Reaches of Human Nature*. New York, NY: Penguin Books.

Matheny, J. 1998. "Organizational Therapy: Relating a Psychotherapeutic Model of Planned Personal Change to Planned Organizational Change." *Journal of Managerial Psychology*. 13, 5/6, pp. 394–405.

Matheny, J. & Beauvais, L. 1996. "Organizational Culture-Based Identity and Action." A paper presented at the Academy of Management Conference, Cincinnati, Ohio.

McGregor, D. 1985. *The Human Side of Enterprise*. New York, NY: McGraw-Hill/ Irwin.

McLean, B. 2001. "Why Enron Went Bust." *Fortune*. December 24, 2001, pp. 58–68.

Meloy, J. 1992. *The Psychopathic Mind: Origins, Dynamics and Treatment*. Northvale, NJ: Jason Aranson Inc.

Miller, D. 1990. *The Icarus Paradox*. New York, NY: Harper Collins.

Miller, E. 1997. "Effecting Organizational Change in Large Complex Systems: A Collaborative Consultancy Approach." In Neumann, J., Kellner, K. & Dawson-Sheperd, A. (eds.) *Developing Organizational Consultancy*. London: Routledge, pp. 187–212.

Miller, E. & Blum, K. 1996. *Overload: Attention Deficit Disorder and the Addictive Brain.* Kansas City, MI: Andrews and McMeel.

Minuchin, S. 1974. *Families and Family Therapy.* Boston, MA: Harvard University Press.

Misangyi, V., Weaver, G. & Elms, H. 2008. "Ending Corruption: The Interplay Among Institutional Logics, Resources, and Institutional Entrepreneurs." *The Academy of Management Review.* 33, 3, pp. 750–770.

Nelson, D. & Cooper, C. 2007. *Positive Organizational Behavior.* London: Sage.

Paetzold, R., Dipboye, R. & Elsbach, D. 2008. "A New Look at Stigmatization in and out of Organizations." *The Academy of Management Review.* 33, 1, pp. 186–193.

Parker, I. 1997. "Group Identity and Individuality in Times of Crisis: Psychoanalytic Reflections on Social Psychological Knowledge." *Human Relations.* 50, 2, pp. 183–196.

Penny, L. & Spector, P. 2002. "Narcissism and Counterproductive Work Behavior: Do Bigger Egos Mean Bigger Problems?" *International Journal of Selection and Assessment.* 10, pp. 126–134.

2003. "Workplace Incivility and Counterproductive Workplace Behavior." Paper presented at the meeting of the Society for Industrial and Organizational Psychology, Orlando, FL.

Pfarrer, M., DeCelles, K., Smith, K. & Taylor, S. 2008. "After the Fall: Reintegrating the Corrupt Organization." *The Academy of Management Review.* 33, 3, pp. 730–749.

Pinault, L. 2000. *Consulting Demons: Inside the Unscrupulous World of Global Corporate Consulting.* New York, NY: Harper Collins.

Pinto, J., Leanna, C. & Pil, F. 2008. "Corrupt Organizations or Corrupt Individuals? Two Types of Organization-Level Corruption." *The Academy of Management Review.* 33, 3, pp. 685–709.

Pritchard, R., Griffin, R. & O'Leary-Kelly, A. 2004. *The Dark Side of Organizational Behavior.* New York, NY: Pfeiffer.

Quinn, R. 2004. *Building the Bridge As You Walk On It.* San Francisco, CA: Jossey-Bass.

Richman, J., Rospenda, K., Nawyn, S., Fendrich, M. & Drum, M. 1999. "Sexual Harassment and Generalized Workplace Abuse Among University Employees: Prevalence and Mental Health Correlates." *American Journal of Public Health.* 89, pp. 358–363.

Robins, R. & Paulhus, D. 2001. "The Character of Self-Enhancers: Implications for Organizations." In Roberts, B. & Hogan, R. (eds.) *Personality Psychology in the Workplace.* Washington, DC: American Psychological Association, pp. 193–219.

Robinson, S. & Bennett, R. 1995. "A Typology of Deviant Workplace Behaviors: A Multidimensional Scaling Study." *Academy of Management Journal*. 38, 2, pp. 555–572.

Rogers, C. 1989. *Carl Rogers Dialogues: Conversations with Martin Buber, Paul Tillich, B.F. Skinner, Gregory Bateson, Michael Polyani, Rollo May and Others*. Boston, MA: Houghton Mifflin.

Rowley, A. 2007. *Leadership Therapy: Inside the Mind of Microsoft*. New York, NY: Palgrave Macmillan.

Ruesch, J. & Bateson, G. 1968. *Communication: The Social Matrix of Psychiatry*. New York, NY: W.W. Norton & Company, Inc.

Sandowsky, D. 1995. "The Charismatic Leader as Narcissist: Understanding the Abuse of Power." *Organizational Dynamics*. 23, 4, pp. 57–71.

Schaffer, R. 2002. *High Impact Consulting*. San Francisco, CA: Jossey-Bass.

Schaffer, R. & Ashkenas, R. 2005. *Rapid Results: How 100-Day Projects Build the Capacity for Large-Scale Change*. San Francisco, CA: Jossey-Bass.

Schein, E. 1969. *Process Consultation: Its Role in Organizational Development*. Reading, MA: Addison-Wesley.

  1987. *Process Consultation, Volume II: Lessons for Managers and Consultants*. Reading, MA: Addison-Wesley.

  2000. "The Next Frontier: Edgar Schein on Organizational Therapy." *The Academy of Management Executive*. 14, 1, pp. 31–48.

  2005. "Organization Development: A Wedding of Anthropology and Organization Therapy." In Bradford, D. & Burke, W. (eds.) *Reinventing Organization Development – New Approaches to Change in Organizations: Addressing the Crisis, Achieving the Potential*. San Francisco, CA: Pfeiffer.

Schwartz, H. 1990. *Narcissistic Process and Corporate Decay: The Theory of the Organizational Ideal*. New York, NY: New York University Press.

Senge, P. 1990. *The Fifth Discipline: The Art and Practice of the Learning Organization*. New York, NY: Doubleday.

Shaw, J., Duffy, M., Jonson, J. & Lockhart, D. 2005. "Turnover, Social Capital Losses, and Performance." *The Academy of Management Journal*. 48, 4, pp. 594–606.

Spector, P. & Fox, S. 2005. *Counterproductive Work Behavior: An Investigation of Actors and Targets*. Washington, DC: American Psychological Association.

Stacey, R. 1992. *Managing the Unknowable: Strategic Boundaries Between Order and Chaos in Organizations*. San Francisco, CA: Jossey-Bass.

  1996. *Complexity and Creativity in Organizations*. San Francisco, CA: Berrett Koehler.

Strasser, F. & Strasser, A. 1997. *Existential Time Limited Therapy: The Wheel of Existence*. London: John Wiley & Sons.

Taleb, N. 2007. *The Black Swan: The Impact of the Highly Improbable*. New York, NY: Random House.

Tepper, B. 2000. "Consequences of Abusive Supervision." *Academy of Management Journal*, 43, 2, pp. 178–190.

Vaillant, G. & Perry, J. 1980. "Personality Disorders." In Kaplan, H., Freedman, A. & Sadock, B. (eds.) *Comprehensive Textbook of Psychiatry III*. Baltimore, MD: Williams & Wilkins.

Van Fleet, D. & Van Fleet, E. 2006. "Internal Terrorists: The Terrorists Inside Organizations." *Journal of Managerial Psychology*. 21, 8, 763–774.

Vardi, Y. & Weitz, E. 2004. *Misbehavior in Organizations: Theory, Research and Management*. Mahwah, NJ: Lawrence Erlbaum Associates.

Von Bertalanffy, L. 1950. "An Outline of General Systems Theory." *British Journal of Philosophical Science*. 1, pp. 134–163.

1968. *General Systems Theory: Foundations, Development, Applications*. New York, NY: Brazillier.

Walter, J. & Peller, J. 1992. *Becoming Solution-Focused in Brief Therapy*. New York, NY: Brunner/Mazel.

Ward, G. 2007. "Coaching Within and Without." In Kets de Vries, M., Korotov, K. & Forent-Treacy, E. (eds.) *Coach and Couch: The Psychology of Making Better Leaders*. New York, NY: Palgrave Macmillan, pp. 181–199.

Weick, K. 1977. "Enactment Process in Organizations." In Staw, B. & Salancik, G. (eds.) *New Directions in Organizational Behavior*. Chicago, IL: St. Clair Press.

Weiss, L. 1996. *A.D.D. on the Job: Making Your A.D.D. Work for You*. Dallas, TX: Taylor Press.

Wender, P. 1995. *Attention Deficit Hyperactivity Disorder in Adults*. New York, NY: Oxford University Press.

Whetten, D. & Cameron, K. 2007. *Developing Management Skills*. Upper Saddle River, NJ: Prentice Hall.

Whicker, M. 1996. *Toxic Leaders: When Organizations Go Bad*. Westport, CT: Quorum Books.

Index

CPSIA information can be obtained at www.ICGtesting.com
Printed in the USA
LVOW13s1149051113

359793LV00005B/113/P